Life After Graduate School in Psychology

D0023975

LIFE AFTER GRADUATE SCHOOL IN PSYCHOLOGY

Insider's Advice from New Psychologists

EDITED BY

ROBERT D. MORGAN
TARA L. KUTHER
COREY J. HABBEN

Psychology Press
New York and Hove

Published in 2005 by
Psychology Press
Taylor & Francis Group
270 Madison Avenue
New York, NY 10016
www.psypress.com

Published in Great Britain by
Psychology Press
Taylor & Francis Group
27 Church Road
Hove, East Sussex BN3 2FA
www.psypress.com.uk

Copyright © 2005 by Taylor & Francis Group, a Division of T&F Informa.
Psychology Press is an imprint of the Taylor & Francis Group.

Printed in the United States of America on acid-free paper.

10 9 8 7 6 5 4 3 2

Library of Congress Cataloging-in-Publication Data
    Life after graduate school in psychology : insider's advice from new psychologists / edited
    by Robert D. Morgan, Tara L. Kuther, Corey J. Habben.
        p. cm.
    Includes bibliographical references and index.
    ISBN 1-84169-410-X (pbk. : alk. paper)
    1. Psychology--Vocational guidance. I. Morgan, Robert D. II. Kuther, Tara L.
III. Habben, Corey J.

BF76.L56 2005
150.23--dc22

                                                                            2004017284

Dedication

To Rick and Betty Morgan

— R.D.M.

To C.K.

— T.L.K.

To D.B., J.H., K.W., M.P., and C.Z. Eamus Catuli

—C.J.H.

Contents

Preface

Did you know that nearly 4,700 doctoral degrees are conferred in psychology each year? Where do all of these psychologists go? Will there be room for you? Most graduate students and new psychologists (throughout this book, we operationalize the term "new psychologist" as any psychologist who is less than 5 years removed from obtaining the degree) find themselves asking these questions and wondering about their future. *Life After Graduate School in Psychology: Insider's Advice from New Psychologists* is intended to dispel fears and increase your awareness of the many options available to you. Your graduate education has provided you a foundation in psychology and the skills and tools to practice your trade, whether that trade includes research, teaching, clinical services, or applications of psychology to the business world, to list just a few possibilities. Your doctorate in psychology affords you great flexibility and you will most certainly find yourself competitive in today's job market. However, you may be unfamiliar with the flexibility your doctoral degree provides. If you are like us, your graduate education provided minimal guidance on how you can shape your career or how you can use your degree to innovatively develop a professional niche. While you were trained to *apply* psychology to a professional role, you may have learned very little about how to *create* a professional role. This is an important distinction; therefore, our goal in presenting *Life After Graduate School in Psychology: Insider's Advice from New Psychologists* is to offer graduate students, postdoctoral students, interns, and new psychologists the information necessary to make informed decisions about careers in psychology. More specifically, this book will provide you with detailed discussions of innovative career opportunities and professional development and training advice from new professionals who understand your concerns.

We were prompted to edit this book by the realization that all the professional advice books for psychologists seem to be written primarily by senior psychologists. While there is an invaluable perspective that only an experienced psychologist can provide (informed by a wealth of experience and history), there is an equally invaluable perspective and knowledge base that only a new psychologist can provide. A new psychologist can tell you what it is like to find a job and work as a new industrial/organizational psychologist in today's business climate; a senior psychologist can tell you only from the perspective of seeing his or her students do this. A new psychologist can tell you what it is like to try to start a new practice as a new psychologist in today's marketplace; a senior psychologist will more likely tell you what it used to be like to start a new practice and note that "things have changed." The bottom line is that when senior psychologists provide advice on starting and developing a career in psychology, they will draw on two perspectives. These perspectives are (1) their experience when they were new psychologists, which may have happened 15, 20, 30 years ago, and (2) their vicarious experience acquired from watching students and mentees negotiate their way in the profession.

Now that we have completed the first 5 years of our career, essentially ending our tenure as "new psychologists," we have come to realize one thing: new psychologists are the *de facto* experts of the experience of today's new psychologist. It sounds simplistic, and yet it is counterintuitive to the way we are trained: we are trained to believe that senior psychologists are the experts in *all* areas of the profession. We can recall our experience following our departure from graduate school. We not only remember the glaring gaps in our knowledge about the profession; we also remember who helped serve as our new mentors. These were our peers; the ones who had just been down the path we planned to take. Like a future tourist pondering a trip to a new country, we wanted insight and advice from someone who had just made the same voyage. We shared the belief that this profession needed a book providing advice to new psychologists, written *by* new psychologists.

We believe that the most valuable commodity to a new psychologist is information. A well-informed new professional will have a roadmap, while a less-informed new professional will travel blindly. You would not have this book in your hands unless you needed the commodity of information; we hope that this resource delivers. Each chapter is a look into the experience of today's new psychologist, and each author is your personal mentor. Because of this, we deliberately wanted our authors to write in their own unique voice. Each voice reflects a role for a new psychologist. Some of these voices have come from different parts of the world, whether from an office at Microsoft or halfway across the world in a combat zone. Add these voices to those of your senior psychologist mentors; it is our belief that the guidance of both new psychologists and senior psychologists is necessary for any psychologist to truly thrive in a new career. Collectively, the input and mentoring from both perspectives provide the clearest picture of what it's like to be a psychologist in today's world.

This book was inspired by our experiences, as well as those of our colleagues, as students and new professionals in psychology. *Life After Graduate School in Psychology: Insider's Advice from New Psychologists* explores traditional and diverse career opportunities for doctoral-level psychologists. More than 20 young professionals (new psychologists) who share a strong background in the science and practice of psychology have contributed chapters. Their voices of experience and range of perspectives guide readers through the web of professional development and training activities that will prepare readers for psychology careers in the 21st century. The first chapter sets the tone for the volume by exploring the current state of psychology for doctoral recipients. A discussion of statistical data on the employment and job satisfaction of new graduates follows. The chapter ends with a brief overview of career trends for new psychologists and an introduction to the volume.

Subsequent chapters discuss the wide variety of careers that a doctoral-level psychologist may pursue, each written by an emerging leader in the field. The chapters in Parts I and II present careers for psychologists in academia and practice, including teaching-oriented colleges, doctoral degree–granting institutions, university-based research, private practice, group practice, forensic psychology, sports psychology, and more. The chapters within Part III explore business careers, including management consultation, quantitative analysis, software design, and executive management. In Part IV, chapters focus on new and innovative career opportunities for psychologists in the fields of public health, trial consulting, sport psychology, disaster psychology, research consultation, and online psychology.

Each chapter provides an in-depth examination of a position, including an overview of the field, employment settings, professional responsibilities and expectations, typical daily or weekly activities, advantages and disadvantages of the career. Perhaps the most valuable aspect of each chapter is the personal insight each chapter author provides. Each author provides advice on professional development, training needs, tips for how best to prepare for and secure a position, and how to make the transition from graduate student to professional in the field.

It is our hope that *Life After Graduate School in Psychology: Insider's Advice from New Psychologists* will help graduate students, interns, postdocs, and new psychologists evaluate their interest in psychology, appreciate the myriad of career opportunities available, and begin to contemplate how they might tailor their professional careers to meet their interests and professional skills. We believe that psychologists are well prepared with almost unlimited career opportunities, and that with advice from insiders such as the contributors in this book, you will begin to explore the limitless opportunities of your degree. Each chapter is another story of a new psychologist starting a career and exploring opportunities. As you read through this book, we hope you will begin to see that what you do with your career is up to you.

Acknowledgments

We are most appreciative of the constructive comments and helpful suggestions that we received from Michael Platon.

In addition, we thank our editor at Psychology Press, Paul Dukes, for guiding us through the review and revision process and sharing his expertise and insight. Thanks to Jon Mandracchia, Katherine Fitzgerald, and Suzanne Harris for assisting reviewing and commenting on drafts of chapters. Also, many thanks to Jon Mandracchia for formatting the manuscript and Linda Manis for sharing her copyediting expertise and helping us to express our ideas more clearly. Finally, thanks to Erin Buck for coordinating the contributors' revisions during the copyediting process.

I (Robert) thank the graduate students at Texas Tech University for serving as the subjects of my ideological experimentation, and for keeping me grounded regarding the growth and development of our discipline. I offer a special thanks to Robert Ax for broadening my perspective and guiding my thoughts toward the future of psychology, and to Steven Mandracchia for helping me see the limits of formal education and the need to challenge traditional ideologies and standards of psychological applications in any context to move the field forward. I also thank my parents for their consistent support and for teaching me what I didn't want in a career. Last, I thank my family: Stacy for your unwavering support of my career and dedication to taking care of all the things that I cannot, and Taylor, Ryan, and Riley for your joyous existence and for making the future worth changing.

I (Tara) am thankful for the support of many. Several colleagues have shaped my professional development from college, through graduate school, and beyond to my post-tenure years: Norine Jalbert, Mary Nelson, Vinny Prohaska, and Stu Tentoni. Thank you for taking me under your collective wings and helping me to grow and develop. As always, my family has been a rallying force and source of encouragement — thank you.

I (Corey) believe every new psychologist should have a good mentor; every truly fortunate psychologist should have a panel of great mentors. I would like to thank John Robinson, Ben Blom, Stu Tentoni, Neil Massoth, and Larry James for providing me with the most valuable commodities a new psychologist needs: information, insight, encouragement, and support. I would like to give a special thanks to Ron Wuest, who gave me my first job as a psychologist, and Ron Levant, who helped me become professionally active in the American Psychological Association. There are many people to thank, but my career and future would be very different without the guidance of these seven people.

About the Editors

Robert D. Morgan, Ph.D., is Assistant Professor and Codirector of Counseling Psychology Training at Texas Tech University, Lubbock, Texas. In addition, he is Associate Clinical and Forensic Director with Lubbock Regional Mental Health and Mental Retardation. He completed his training in counseling psychology at Oklahoma State University, Stillwater. He completed his predoctoral internship at the Federal Correctional Institution, Petersburg, Virginia and a postdoctoral fellowship in forensic psychology in the Department of Psychiatry at the University of Missouri–Kansas City and the Missouri Department of Mental Health. Dr. Morgan was the recipient of an Early Career Achievement Award presented by Division 18 (Psychologists in Public Service) of the American Psychological Association (APA) in 2003 and is the Secretary-Treasurer of Division 18 of APA. He has published in the area of correctional mental health, forensic psychology, and professional development. Dr. Morgan coauthored (with Tara Kuther) *Careers in Psychology: Opportunities in a Changing World.*

Tara L. Kuther, Ph.D., is Associate Professor of Psychology at Western Connecticut State University. A developmental psychologist by training (Fordham University, New York City), she teaches courses in child, adolescent, and adult development. Dr. Kuther is Chair of the Instructional Resource Award Task Force of the Office of Teaching Resources in Psychology (OTRP) of the Society for Teaching of Psychology, Division 2 of the APA. She is also active in the Council for Undergraduate Research as Psychology Councilor. Dr. Kuther is the author of several books, including *The Psychology Major's Handbook, Careers in Psychology: Opportunities in a Changing World* (with Robert Morgan), and *Graduate Study in Psychology: Your Guide to Success.* Her research examines risky behavior during adolescence and early adulthood, moral development, and ethical issues in research and teaching. To learn more about Dr. Kuther's work, visit her Web site at http://tarakuther.com.

Corey J. Habben, Psy.D., is Staff Clinical Psychologist at Walter Reed Army Medical Center, Behavioral Health Clinic, Department of Psychiatry in Washington, D.C. He completed his doctoral training at Wright State University, School of Professional Psychology in Dayton, Ohio; and the North Chicago VA Medical Center in North Chicago, Illinois. He has previously worked in a group psychiatric/psychological practice in Morris, Illinois. He is former President of Division 51 of the APA; Chair and founding member of the Task Force on New Psychologist Issues of the American Psychological Association of Graduate Students (APAGS), and has been appointed as a representative of several APA task forces including the APA Task Force on Envisioning, Identifying, and Accessing Future Roles in Psychology; the APA Commission on Education and Training Leading to Licensure; and the APA Task Force on Training Issues in the Emerging Marketplace. He has presented and written extensively on issues relevant to new psychologists and students, including new roles for psychologists, career strategies, postdoctoral training, licensure, credentialing, and financial planning.

Contributors

Cindy Kludt Andrews, Ph.D., is Senior Trial Consultant at Trial-Graphix, a national litigation consulting firm in Chicago, Illinois. She offers expertise in the design and implementation of social science research, trial strategy, analysis of group dynamics and persuasion, and juror reactions to general and case-specific facts, trial strategies, and witnesses.

Monica L. Baskin, Ph.D., is Assistant Professor in the Department of Health Behavior at the University of Alabama at Birmingham (UAB) School of Public Health. She recently joined the faculty at UAB from Emory University. Her clinical and research interests primarily focus on minority health and health disparities (e.g., obesity, sickle cell disease, and HIV/AIDS).

Marilu Price Berry, Ph.D., is Assistant Professor in the Department of Anesthesiology at the University of Texas–Houston Health Science Center. She works as a psychologist in the University Center for Pain Medicine and Rehabilitation at Memorial Hermann Hospital. Her clinical practice and research focus on pain and stress.

Shelia M. Brandt, Psy.D., is a forensic and correctional psychologist with the Federal Bureau of Prisons. Her clinical and research interests are in forensic psychology, correctional mental health, and professional development.

Jean-Marie Bruzzese, Ph.D., is Assistant Professor of Psychiatry at the New York University Child Study Center, New York University School of Medicine. Dr. Bruzzese specializes in the development and evaluation of psychoeducational programs for adolescents and their caregivers that focus on asthma self-regulation and childrearing. She also serves on several committees for local, national, and international organizations dedicated to advancing the well-being of children with asthma.

Jennifer E. Carter, Ph.D., is Sport Psychologist for the Ohio State University Athletic Department and Sports Medicine Center. She has led mental skills training for more than 30 college and high school sports teams, and she has presented her research on clinical issues for athletes at several national conferences.

Christopher N. Chapman, Ph.D., is a usability engineer at the Microsoft Corporation. Prior to joining Microsoft, he trained in philosophy and clinical psychology and completed a postdoctoral fellowship in psychophysiology. His work includes papers in the areas of usability theory, philosophy of technology, personality, pain research, and artificial intelligence.

Dionne R. Dobbins, Ph.D., is Senior Project Associate at the Finance Project, a nonprofit policy research and technical assistance organization. She has worked in varied settings and published in the areas of early childhood intervention, family literacy, emergent literacy, Head Start, and adult literacy. During the 2002–2003 year, Dr. Dobbins was a National Head Start Fellow and served as special assistant to senior administrators in the Associate Commissioner's office.

Teri L. Elliott, Ph.D., is a clinical psychologist and International Trauma Consultant and Trainer who specializes in disaster mental health and trauma especially for children. She is also active in research on bullying and works to provide psychological support program training to communities throughout the world. Dr. Elliott's expertise has brought her under contract to write one of the only books on psychological first aid and her articles are in a variety of journals.

Anne Ferrari, Ph.D., is Associate Professor at the College of New Rochelle in New York. She holds a master's in clinical psychology from New York University and a doctorate in applied developmental psychology from Fordham University. Her research interests include adolescent development and parenting styles. Her most recent publication examined the impact of culture on childrearing practices and definitions of maltreatment.

Lisa Y. Flores, Ph.D., is Assistant Professor in Counseling Psychology in the Department of Educational, School, and Counseling Psychology at the University of Missouri–Columbia. Dr. Flores's research and professional interests include Mexican Americans' career and educational career development, multicultural counseling and training, and vocational psychology. She is an editorial board member for *The Counseling Psychologist, Career Development Quarterly,* and *The Journal of Career Development.*

Joshua N. Friedlander, Psy.D., is a clinical psychologist and Captain in the U.S. Army, stationed at Walter Reed Army Medical Center in Washington, D.C. He was deployed for a year to Kuwait and Iraq as part of Operation Iraqi Freedom and completed this chapter during his deployment. Dr. Friedlander currently coordinates psychological care for Operation Iraqi Freedom soldiers at Walter Reed, works in the

Health Psychology Service, which is integrated with primary care, and trains current psychology residents. Previous assignments include the Army hospital in Seoul, Korea.

Richard Gilman, Ph.D., is Assistant Professor in the Department of Educational and Counseling Psychology at the University of Kentucky. His research interests are in professional issues in psychology, positive mental health and resiliency among youth, and perfectionism. He has published more than 30 peer-reviewed papers on these topics and has presented at more than 50 state, national, and international conferences.

Jeanne M. Hinkelman, Ph.D., was Staff Psychologist at Counseling & Psychological Services, and Research Professor in the Department of Psychology at the University of Tulsa. She is currently Assistant Director/Assistant Professor of Counseling and Advising at Monroe Community College. Her clinical and research interests include career development, Hispanic and international issues, musical aptitude and experience, sport psychology, performance enhancement, and stress and coping.

Jane Kasserman, Ph.D., is Senior Consultant at the Philadelphia office of RHR International Company. Her work focuses on executive selection, development, and new role integration; team development; and organizational development. Dr. Kasserman began her professional career as a human factors psychologist, then respecialized in clinical psychology before transitioning into consulting.

Shawn Roberson, Ph.D., is a forensic psychologist and Director of Psychology at the Oklahoma Forensic Center where he conducts pre-trial evaluations, provides expert witness testimony, and participates in training and other professional activities. Dr. Roberson was a coauthor of the *Oklahoma State Forensic Manual* and also has a private practice in trial consulting and forensic psychology.

Julianne M. Smith-Boydston, Ph.D., is a licensed psychologist at the Bert Nash Mental Health Center in Lawrence, Kansas. In addition to supervising a multisystemic treatment team and University of Kansas graduate students, she has conducted workshops and published under a range of topics including disruptive behavior disorders, treatment of juvenile offenders, and empirically validated treatment programs in community mental health centers.

Jodie L. Steele, Ph.D., is Assistant Vice President and Market Researcher at a large financial services company. She is also an adjunct lecturer at a local college and continues to pursue social psychological research with a focus on close relationships and attitude change.

Erika D. Taylor, Ph.D., is a Research Scientist with The MayaTech Corporation in Silver Spring, Maryland. Her work there relates primarily to issues surrounding African Americans and health. She has worked in a variety of environments as a research analyst, program evaluator, and independent consultant. Her primary research interests include issues related to culture and mental health, educational equity, standards-based school reform, and child development.

Terri L. Teague, Ph.D., is a school psychologist practicing in the Prince George's County Public Schools, in the District of Columbia metropolitan area. She currently works with children ranging from toddlers through high-school age, conducting evaluations, providing counseling, and consulting with teachers and parents regarding children's learning and development.

Richard Van Haveren, Ph.D., is a licensed psychologist in the state of Georgia. He currently maintains a private practice in Atlanta, Georgia. In addition, he is an adjunct faculty member with Capella University and Argosy University/Atlanta.

Deborah Vineberg, Psy.D., is a clinical psychologist at the Massachusetts General Hospital and a clinical instructor at Harvard Medical School. She specializes in treating patients with obesity at the Massachusetts General Hospital Weight Center and has a half-time private practice in Boston. Her research interests include depression, binge eating disorder, and bariatric surgery.

Steven Williams, Ph.D., is Director of Research at the Society for Human Resource Management. He was trained as a clinical psychologist and is currently licensed, but has spent most of his professional career conducting research and providing consultation on workplace, personnel, and organizational issues. He has written several publications on these topics, and has conducted workshops for various types of executives.

Darren W. Woodruff, Ph.D., is Principal Research Analyst at the American Institutes for Research in Washington, D.C. He holds a Ph.D. in educational psychology from Howard University, and works in a variety of research and technical assistance capacities on issues of effective school reform, support for at risk youth, and special education.

Today's New Psychologist: Traditional and Emerging Career Paths

TARA L. KUTHER, COREY J. HABBEN, AND ROBERT D. MORGAN

If you're like most students of psychology, you entered graduate school expecting to undergo a transformation, much as a butterfly is transformed from a larva, into a psychologist with a career in private practice or an academic in a college or university setting. Did you know that fewer than 30% of new psychologists fulfill this expectation (Kohout & Wicherski, 2003)? Yet, psychology is a growth field (U.S. Bureau of Labor, 2003). For example, in the two decades between 1975 and 1995, the number of Ph.D. psychologists grew more than 180% (from 28,389 to 80,713; American Psychological Association Research Office, 2003). There are more psychologists today than ever before, with no signs of slowing. As a whole, psychology is one of the most popular fields in which to earn a doctoral degree, with 4,700 doctoral degrees conferred in 2000–2001, just behind education and engineering (National Center for Education Statistics, 2003).

The face of psychology is changing, too. More women are choosing graduate study in psychology (comprising 47% of psychology graduate school enrollments in 1977 and 73% in 2000) and earning doctorates in psychology (comprising 33% of psychology doctorates conferred in 1976 and 71% in 2001) (American Psychological Association Research Office, 2003). Increasingly, people of color are studying psychology, representing 12% of graduate school enrollments in 1980 and 22% in 2000, and earning doctorates in psychology (8% of new doctorates in 1977 and 16% in 2001; American Psychological Association Research Office, 2003).

Not only has the demographic face of psychology changed, but so too has the financing of graduate degrees. Whereas full funding for graduate study was once a given, less than one third (29%) of graduate students in psychology were funded by assistantships, fellowships, or traineeships in 1999; the remainder relied on self-support and a variety of loans (National Science Foundation, 2002). It's not surprising, then, that most new psychologists (69%) begin their careers in debt. Specifically, 74% of psychologists in the health service provider subfields graduate in debt, with a median debt level of $42,000 (mean = $51,084; Kohout & Wicherski, 2003). Of psychologists in research-oriented subfields, 57% begin their careers in debt, with a median debt level of $23,500 (mean = $31,053; Kohout & Wicherski, 2003). Clearly, employment prospects are important to new graduates for professional and financial reasons; however, traditional career paths in psychology have muddied — choosing a path and finding a job after graduate school are no longer straightforward tasks.

Changing Opportunities in Practice and Academia

Psychology remains a growth field and the greatest number of psychologists flock to the health service provider subfields of clinical, counseling, and school psychology (with a 300% rise from 10,027 psychologists in 1975 to 40,835 in 1995; American Psychological Association Research Office, 2003). Questions about the supply–demand ratio of psychologists abound as the absolute number of psychologists relative to the population has grown substantially. Between 1988 and 1995, the number of licensed psychologists grew by more than 40% (Robiner & Crew, 2000), and there is little reason to believe that it has slowed since. Instead, some argue that the number of psychologists exceeds both societal needs and capacities to remunerate (Robiner et al., 2002). As evidence of market saturation, consider that (1) each year more internship applicants apply for limited slots (with 15% of applicants left unmatched in 2002); (2) new psychologists in the health provider subfields report declines in employment opportunities and satisfaction; and (3) new psychologists experience a drop in earnings and a surge in defaulted loans relative to prior generations of psychologists (Pion, Kohout, & Wicherski, 2000; Robiner et al., 2002).

Although some argue that these warnings about market saturation are overly grim (Peterson & Rodolfa, 2000), the continuing growth in the number of psychologists, coupled with larger social policy shifts, is changing the nature of psychological practice. The days of receiving your diploma and immediately hanging a shingle to start your own private practice are generally long gone. Traditional independent psychological practice is becoming economically unfeasible and group psychological practices are on the rise (Cummings, 1995; Hersch, 1995). Discourse on the dire state of psychological practice largely focuses on the culpability of managed care and the underutilization of psychologists as well as the increasing use of master's level professionals within provider networks (Cummings, 1995; Humphreys, 1996; Robiner et al., 2002). New doctorates in the service areas of psychology generally are less positive about job opportunities; their declining optimism is approaching that of the traditionally pessimistic academic psychologists (Pion et al., 2000).

Although the changing nature of psychological practice has received the lion's share of attention, academic paths for psychologists are also changing. Fewer psychologists enter academia each year; the overall proportion of psychologists working in academia dropped from 55% in 1973 to 33% in 1999 (Ballie, 2001). The past three decades have witnessed a rise in part-time and nontenure-track positions such that 43% of faculty are part-time appointments (National Science Foundation, 2002) and nontenure-track positions of all types account for more than half of all faculty appointments in American higher education today (American Association of University Professors, 2003).

Tenure, itself, is under attack as business-oriented administrators lament its inefficiency and as academic women lament its inequity. Most states are considering or implementing policies to introduce or intensify performance reviews of tenured faculty (Austin, 2001; Siciliano, 1997). More colleges are offering renewable contracts rather than tenure (Wilson, 1998) under the rationale that hiring faculty members on annual or multiyear contracts enables institutions to save money and maintain flexibility. Professors criticize the practice of contract hiring as exploitative, aimed at diminishing the faculty's role in institutional governance by eliminating tenure, and as a threat to academic freedom. In the two decades between 1975 and 1995, the proportion of full-time faculty working on contract rose from 19 to 28% (Leatherman, 1999). Overall, women are more likely to be victims of the shift away from the tenure track, as about 30% of all female full-time faculty work in such posts, as compared to 14% of all male full-time faculty (Leatherman, 1999).

The feminization of psychology has not been accompanied by a shift in the status of female psychologists in academia. Women earn more than two thirds of the doctorates in psychology but comprise 39% of the full-time psychology faculty in 4-year institutions (American Psychological Association, 2000). This figure is comparable to national estimates of faculty across disciplines, which indicate that women represent 36% of full-time and 45% of part-time faculty overall (National Science Foundation, 2000). In addition, the prevalence of women in academia varies by Carnegie institutional classification. Women comprise about a quarter of full-time faculty at research institutions, baccalaureate institutions, and comprehensive colleges, and 17% at doctoral institutions. In 4-year colleges and universities, women faculty hold fewer high-ranking posts than men, are less likely to be full professors, and are more likely to be assistant professors (National Science Foundation, 2000). These patterns are mirrored among psychology faculty as women are less likely to have tenure (30%) than men (52%) (American Psychological Association, 2000).

Full-time tenure-track faculty positions are becoming scarcer, overall. Many higher education budgets have been slashed during dire fiscal times; public institutions have cut programs, frozen hiring, and raised tuition, but still fall victim to the financial squeeze (Selingo, 2002). Despite college enrollments reaching record heights, with the coming of age of Baby Boomers' children and the rise in the number of students returning to college to escape a poor economy, many institutions have continued to reduce tenure-track faculty lines. For psychologists who are fortunate enough to obtain a tenure-track position, requirements for tenure are increasingly stringent. The pressure to publish and obtain grant funding is greater than ever and teaching and research records that would have earned faculty tenure at prestigious institutions years ago are no longer enough (Trower, 2001).

Clearly, traditional expectations to complete a doctorate in psychology and hang a shingle or scale the ivory tower are not in line with current realities of psychological practice and higher education. Difficult as it may be, do not let these dire warnings be a source of discouragement. Despite the influx of new psychologists, only 2% were unemployed and seeking employment in 2001 (American Psychological Association Research Office, 2003). Psychologists are highly marketable because their skills in interpersonal communication, research methodology and statistics, and information synthesis and analysis generalize to a wide variety of settings.

Where Is the New Psychologist Employed?

Employment settings for psychologists vary among the health service provider and research-oriented subfields (Kohout & Wicherski, 2003). Psychologists in the health service provider subfields are found primarily in health-care settings including hospitals, managed care organizations, and other human service settings (52%), followed by higher education (15%), business and government settings (12%), school and educational settings (19%), and independent practice (8%). Psychologists in research-oriented fields tend to be employed in higher education settings (54%), business and government settings (34%), health-care settings (6%), and school and educational settings (5%).

These findings indicate a wide range of employment settings for new psychologists, but leave us with many questions. There is a surprising paucity of data available on the quality of new psychologists' experience in the workforce. Regularly conducted surveys of doctoral-level psychologists' employment collect information about work settings, salaries, and perceptions of the job market (e.g., American Psychological Association Doctoral Employment Survey), but there are few qualitative sources of information about new psychologists' career experiences. What are the various work settings like? More importantly, what other careers do new psychologists enter? The pages of this book offer early answers to these questions and elucidate the many paths a psychologist may take.

The Silent Conversation:
Alternative Career Paths for Psychologists

A substantial proportion of early-career psychologists work in business and government settings, as well as many other unorthodox places; however, most psychology students feel uninformed about such "alternative careers" — careers outside of the traditional areas of practice and academia. Our heads remain in the sand and our unawareness of the wide range of career possibilities persists because alternative careers are taboo topics in most departments. It's not that graduate faculty aren't generative toward their students; rather, many are simply constrained by the educational requirements of a comprehensive doctoral program. Others, unfortunately, are just uninformed. Most of today's senior faculty entered the ivory tower in a very different time. As psychologists, we are well aware of the influence of the sociohistorical context in which we are embedded, but sometimes fail to apply that understanding to our own lives. Hence, we fail to recognize that the views of senior faculty regarding career paths are shaped by their experiences, which are very different from our own. Also at fault is the culture of academic institutions that rewards faculty who seek to clone themselves and penalizes faculty whose students do not go onto careers in research or practice.

An implicit theme of this book is that you must determine your values to find your career path. Your values may not mirror those of your professors. Graduate study is a socialization process whereby we come to internalize knowledge and a professional identity; however, you must choose your career and your career does not have to be one sanctioned by your mentor or graduate school professors. This statement is deceptive in the sense that it is easy to grasp but a challenge to employ.

For example, I (T.K.) was reared in a graduate department that expected me to pursue a research career at a prestigious institution as a research associate or professor. Although I loved conducting research and welcomed an academic position, I also hoped for balance in my life. Specifically, I placed formidable geographic limitations on my job search. Time and again throughout this book you will encounter admonitions that it is inadvisable to place geographic limits on your job search. I foolishly ignored this piece of advice in the interest of seeking personal happiness and was extraordinarily fortunate to win a position as an assistant professor at a comprehensive state institution with more teaching than I expected *or* my graduate school professors respected. At first, I internalized the criticism and looked for a position at a more research oriented institution. It took several years for me to begin to let go of these expectations, realize that they were my professors' wishes and not my own, and accept that the path I chose is different from that my professors would have chosen for me. I have come to enjoy the flexibility of my position and the overall balance of research and teaching — and realize that I have made the decision that is right for me. It is our hope that the chapters in this book will help you assess your interests, aspirations, and values and determine what career path is right for you. We encourage you to move beyond others' expectations, determine what you truly wish, and take steps to achieve your career goals.

Overview

Life After Graduate School in Psychology: Insider's Advice from New Psychologists is organized into four parts, reflecting four collections of roles for psychologists: academic and research roles, practice and clinical roles, business roles, and applied roles, many of which you may not have considered. Each of the four parts of this book is composed of chapters that represent multiple paths within a given career context. While we do not assume that the chapter authors are representative of all new psychologists, they offer a number of diverse views and singular voices about the many career paths that psychologists take. Each chapter explores a career option, providing information about the field, typical responsibilities and activities entailed in the career option, what a typical day or week is like, advantages and disadvantages to pursuing the career option, and advice for graduate students and early career psychologists who are considering that career path.

Part I explores research and academic career paths. All academic careers hold some activities and roles in common, which are collectively known as the Big Three: research, teaching, and service. However, you'll find that each academic path entails different ratios of the Big Three, which leads to very different climates and experiences. For example, institutions of higher education vary in terms of the balance between research and teaching. Two of our chapters provide insight into the varying nature of professor positions. In Chapter 2, Anne Ferrari describes her career as a professor within a teaching-oriented liberal arts college and the associated opportunities to touch students' lives, as well as the personal, professional, and ethical dilemmas that accompany faculty–student relationships. In Chapter 3, Lisa Flores and Robert Morgan convey their experiences as professors at doctoral-granting institutions in which the balance tips more heavily toward research than service. They provide advice on how to balance the multiple roles of researcher, teacher, mentor, and colleague, and how to transition beyond the imposter syndrome to establish your professional identity.

Some academic positions combine research with clinical activities. For example, Marilu Berry (Chapter 4) discusses her work as a health psychologist in an interdisciplinary pain center and medical school, in which she engages in clinical work with patients suffering pain, conducts research on pain management, and teaches medical students about communication skills, the psychological aspects of pain management and coping, and referral strategies. Not all psychologists employed by medical schools work directly with patients, however. In Chapter 5, Jean-Marie Bruzzese explains her role as an applied developmental psychologist in a medical center where she develops educational programs for parents and children and evaluates the efficacy of those programs. Although these chapters do not provide the definitive last word on career paths in academia, they offer insight into the diversity of environments and experiences that academic psychologists face.

In Part II, we explore practice and clinical roles of psychologists. Jeanne Hinkelman (Chapter 6) describes her work in a university counseling center, and discusses how readers can seek such positions, find ways to integrate research into their work, and thrive in university counseling settings. By now you're aware of the challenges facing psychologists who choose career paths in independent practice. Deborah Vineberg (Chapter 7) chronicles her journey in carving out her own practice and the advantages and disadvantages of striking out on one's own. Given the financial, management, and marketing challenges, group practice is an option for new psychologists who wish to work in private practice settings. Corey Habben (Chapter 8) discusses the variety of forms that group practices take and dispels common myths about group practice that may prevent new psychologists from considering this viable alternative.

Many new psychologists engage in practice and clinical roles within nontraditional service settings. For example, in Chapter 9, Julianne Smith-Boydston provides an overview of her work in a community mental health clinic, in which she engages in practice, administration, supervision, program evaluation, and grant writing. Given the diverse needs of such centers and the opportunities they provide for creative thinking, she advises that new psychologists not write them off as "microcosms of obscurity." Shawn Roberson (Chapter 10) explains his work as a criminal forensic examiner, conducting clinical evaluations of criminal defendants to answer specific legal questions, writing reports based on his assessments, and providing expert testimony.

Psychological practice in nontraditional settings presents unique opportunities and challenges in the professional, ethical, and personal realms. For example, Joshua Friedlander (Chapter 11) describes his work as a clinical psychologist in the U.S. Army. He shares his initiation to the Army in graduate school, residency training, his tours in Korea and at Walter Reed Army Medical Center, and finally his wartime deployment as part of Operation Iraqi Freedom (a deployment that occurred during the writing of his chapter). A similar set of challenges is faced by psychologists who work in correctional settings. In Chapter 12, Shelia Brandt describes the culture shock that many psychologists encounter when they begin practice in correctional settings, as well as the range of duties in which psychologists in correctional settings engage, including crisis intervention, psychotherapy, personnel selection, and the supervision of paraprofessionals. She explores the unique ethical questions and tensions psychologists experience between their duties to provide treatment and promote security.

Richard Gilman and Terri Teague (Chapter 13) round out our discussion of practice and clinical roles of psychologists by examining alternative settings for school psychologists, including residential treatment, neuropsychology, early intervention, and pediatric settings. School psychologists have greater flexibility in the roles they choose and the clientele they serve than most new psychologists realize.

Many new psychologists choose to apply their skills to the business world. Part III explores these roles. In Chapter 14, Jane Kasserman explains her work as a management consultant in which she provides individual-, group-, and organizational-level interventions to enhance communication and functioning at all levels. Jodie Steele (Chapter 15), a social psychologist, describes her experiences as a quantitative analyst conducting consumer behavior and attitude research in both advertising and banking settings. Christopher Chapman (Chapter 16) explains how a strong set of methodological and statistical skills can carry you far, regardless of the area of psychology in which you specialize. Although trained as a clinical psychologist, he conducts usability research at Microsoft Corporation. He studies how people understand computer systems and software and how to improve customers' interactive experiences with computer interfaces. Steven Williams (Chapter 17) discusses opportunities in management consulting in which psychologists help executives and managers improve the functioning of all or part of an organization by applying industry and market research to the workplace.

Part IV examines applied roles for psychologists. Monica Baskin (Chapter 18) explores a setting that many psychologists are unfamiliar with: public health. She explains the scope of public health and where psychologists with such interests find employment. Baskin describes her own work in academia, conducting research and teaching within in a school of public health, as well as her applied work, designing and evaluating public health interventions with community organizations and nonprofit public health agencies.

A number of unique consulting opportunities are available to psychologists. In Chapter 19, Cindy Kludt Andrews, a trial consultant, discusses her work in conducting research and providing consultative services to evaluate how a judge or jury will perceive and react to case theories, themes, issues, arguments, witnesses, evidence, and exhibits, and to enhance attorneys' persuasive impact. Jennifer Carter (Chapter 20) describes the field of sport psychology and her work in consultation with athletes and sports teams. Teri Elliott (Chapter 21) describes her consultative work in the emerging field of disaster psychology. She defines the field, discusses the varied roles that psychologists take in preparedness, planning, and response to natural and human-made disasters, and describes the physical, emotional, and personal challenges of providing direct support to responders, victims, and community in coping with catastrophic events. Erika Taylor, Dionne

Dobbins, and Darren Woodruff (Chapter 22) discuss their work as research consultants in educational and policy contexts. Finally, the Internet is an emerging area of opportunity for psychologists. Chapter 23 provides an overview of this new and relatively undefined career context for psychologists.

As we've seen, and the chapters in this book illustrate, the proliferation of psychologists, as well as their changing demographic profile, is changing the nature of careers in psychology — encouraging and sometimes forcing new professionals to seek innovative career opportunities. Our hope in developing this book is to increase awareness and provide a broad overview of traditional and emerging paths that a psychologist may pursue. We hope the voices within this book will serve as the impetus to help you realize that you hold the reins on your career. *The psychologists who will be most successful in the coming years are those who are adaptable, open-minded, and not afraid to explore new and nontraditional career avenues.* Whether you opt for a traditional role, an emerging role, or create your own niche in professional psychology, the choice is yours.

References

American Association of University Professors (2003). *Part-time and non-tenure-track faculty appointments.* Retrieved on October 31, 2003. Available: http://www.aaup.org/Issues/parttime/index.htm.

American Psychological Association (2000). *Women in academe: Two steps forward, one step back.* Retrieved on October 31, 2003. Available: http://www.apa.org/pi/wpo/academe/summary.html.

American Psychological Association Research Office. (2003). *Where are new psychologists going? Employment, debt, and salary data.* Retrieved on October 31, 2003. Available: http://research.apa.org/WPA2003.pdf.

Austin, J. (2001). Tenure: Under fire, but hunkered down. *Science's Next Wave.* Retrieved on October 31, 2003. Available: http://nextwave.sciencemag.org/cgi/content/full/2001/06/20/6.

Ballie, R. (2001). Where are new psychologists going? *Monitor on Psychology.* Retrieved on October 31, 2003. Available: http://www.apa.org/monitor/dec01/wheregoing.html.

Cummings, N. A. (1995). Impact of managed care on employment and training: A primer for survival. *Professional Psychology: Research and Practice, 26,* 10–15.

Hersch, L. (1995). Adapting to health care reform and managed care: Three strategies for survival and growth. *Professional Psychology: Research and Practice, 26,* 16–26.

Humphreys, K. (1996). Clinical psychologists as psychotherapists: History, future, and alternatives. *American Psychologist, 51,* 190–197.

Kohout, J., & Wicherski, M. (2003). *1999 doctorate employment survey.* Retrieved on October 31, 2003. Available: http://research.apa.org/des99report.html.

Leatherman, C. (1999). Growth in positions off the tenure track is a trend that's here to stay, study finds. *Science's Next Wave.* Retrieved on October 31, 2003. Available: http://nextwave.sciencemag.org/cgi/content/full/1999/09/01/28?

National Center for Education Statistics (2003). *Digest of education statistics, 2002.* Retrieved on September 21, 2003. Available: http://nces.ed.gov/pubs2003/digest02/index.asp.

National Science Foundation (2000). *Land of plenty: Diversity as America's competitive edge in science, engineering and technology.* Retrieved on October 31, 2003. Available: http://www.nsf.gov/od/cawmset/report/cawmset_brochure.pdf.

National Science Foundation (2002). *Science and engineering indicators, 2002.* Retrieved on September 21, 2003. Available: http://www.nsf.gov/sbe/srs/seind02/start.htm.

Peterson, R. L., & Rodolfa, E. R. (2000). Too many psychologists? Worrying about Robiner and Crew (2000) and worrying with them. *Professional Psychology: Research and Practice, 31*(3), 272–275.

Pion, G., Kohout, J., & Wicherski, M. (2000). "Rightsizing" the workforce through training reductions: A good idea? *Professional Psychology: Research and Practice, 31*(3), 266–271.

Robiner, W. N., Ax, R. K., Stamm, B. H., & Harowski, K. (2002). Addressing the supply of psychologists in the workforce: Is focusing principally on demand sound economics? *Journal of Clinical Psychology in Medical Settings, 9*(4), 273–285.

Robiner, W. N., & Crew, D. P. (2000). Rightsizing the workforce of psychologists in health care: Trends from licensing boards, training programs, and managed care. *Professional Psychology: Research and Practice, 31,* 245–263.

Selingo, J. (2002). States with the biggest deficits take aim at higher education. *Chronicle of Higher Education.* Retrieved on October 31, 2003. Available: http://chronicle.com/prm/weekly/v48/i32/32a02401.htm.

Siciliano, M. (1997). Tenure: Post tenure review in Texas — The faculty view. *Science's Next Wave.* Retrieved on October 31, 2003. Available: http://nextwave.sciencemag.org/cgi/content/full/1998/03/29/182?

Trower, C. (2001). Alleviating tenure torture. *Science's Next Wave.* Retrieved on October 31, 2003. Available: http://nextwave.sciencemag.org/cgi/content/full/2001/08/08/9?

U.S. Bureau of Labor (2001). *Occupational outlook handbook.* Retrieved on June 19, 2004. http://www.bls.gov/oco.

Wilson, R. (1998). Contracts replace the tenure track for a growing number of professors. *Science's Next Wave.* Retrieved on October 31, 2003 at http://nextwave.sciencemag.org/cgi/content/full/1999/09/02/1?

11

Academic and Research Careers for New Psychologists

2

Teaching-Oriented Institutions: "And Those Who Can't"

ANNE FERRARI

In my role as an assistant professor at a liberal arts college, I've encountered many conservative statements such as: "I can't write this paper, pretending that I'm gay because it could never happen!" "I'm sorry but a paper about the pros and cons of legalized drugs would be against my religion." "OK, we know, we know, men are pigs ... could we please talk about something else?" These comments have inspired me in my work to challenge students' thinking and have taught me that learning is a lifelong and reciprocal process. Education is the one entity that can serve to level the playing field in a world that unfortunately is still struggling with issues such as sexism, racism, and ageism. College professors are in positions of enormous power to open minds, expand horizons, and to change and improve lives. If I can help students become less racist, homophobic, judgmental, or teach them to seek answers, ask questions, or to be curious, then I've done some good and this brings me great joy. And much to my surprise, I find that I've learned quite a bit from my students along the way.

Why Be a Psychology Instructor?

As a first-generation college student and single mother, I knew first-hand the impact education could have on a life. Growing up in a small conservative community where racism and sexism abounded, my psychology courses helped me to understand my world and to rise above it. I could think of no better occupation than one that would allow me to give back to others what psychology professors gave to me.

Finding part-time teaching positions in the popular major of psychology is relatively easy to do, so I, like many of my colleagues, taught as an adjunct as a way to earn money during my graduate school years. Adjunct professors are part-time instructors; they usually receive no fringe benefits although some city and state schools have begun to offer health benefits to adjuncts who have taught for at least two consecutive semesters. Because many liberal arts institutions require only a master's degree for adjunct teaching, most graduate students can begin teaching after their first or second year of graduate school, when a master's degree is usually completed. The pay varies considerably, with some institutions paying as little as $1,500 a course and others as much as $4,000.

As I busily taught as an adjunct during my graduate years and gained the approval of various psychology departments in New York, I foolishly thought that my hard work would be rewarded with a full-time position. However, the chairs of these departments apologetically told me that although they would love to hire a full-timer, this just wasn't in the budget. Positions within departments became available only when a full-time member retired or relocated, and once this occurred, competition was already great.

As my oral defense of my dissertation grew nearer, I became more jaded and desperate about finding a full-time position. I was teaching five classes a semester, all at different institutions. Some of the classes paid top salary; some paid lower, but even still, my yearly salary amounted to only about $20,000. Many institutions would not even consider a candidate who was ABD (All but Dissertation); some would consider a candidate, but only if the oral defense date were set. I also worried about my publication record. Although I participated in much research that was presented at various conventions, I was yet to be published.

Fortunately, after applying to four local colleges, I received an offer from the College of New Rochelle, a small teaching, liberal arts college with a population of about 500 female undergraduates. My doctorate, ample teaching experience, and familiarity with diverse groups qualified me. I would be required to teach a full load, four classes, as well as serve on college-wide committees. However, publication of research was not required.

What It's Like at a Teaching Institution

The small teaching college is typically more concerned about superb teaching than about a publication record. As an example of this, my college does four classroom observations of untenured faculty each year: one each by the dean, the chair, a colleague of the assistant professor's choice, and a colleague of the administration's choosing. A formal written report is submitted for each, describing the observation based on class content, organization, quality of instruction, classroom climate, teacher–student interaction, and the teacher's strengths and weaknesses. In addition, student evaluations are collected for each course, each semester.

Student evaluations are also taken very seriously by small teaching colleges. As an adjunct, I remember listening in on the conversations of untenured faculty in various schools who complained that the "nice" professors received the good student evaluations leaving the "real" professors who "actually taught" with undue criticism. I didn't believe them then, nor do I now. It is more probable that the "good" professor who "actually teaches" will be the well-liked one because (surprise!) most students really want to learn. Although there is some truth in what these disgruntled employees were mumbling, it is not the whole story. The "easy A" professor may get some good student evaluations, but such a professor will also receive criticism from the hardworking students that the course was too easy, not challenging, not stimulating, and that they learned nothing. Yes, we all want to be liked by our students at first, but we can be liked by being good, fair teachers who really want our students to learn. It should be difficult to receive an A in your class; it should be attainable, but a challenge (not like one of my college professors who said only God gets an A). When students do receive an A, they can feel very proud. Such a standard gives more meaning to B and C grades, as well.

Unlike the large, research-based institution, which demands publication for the attainment of tenure, the small teaching college values service to the college. Instructors are expected to join committees, attend meetings, perform student advisement, attend student ceremonies, such as graduation and convocations, create new courses, and to be involved with the college community. Some of my involvement in the college includes advising about 35 students, serving as advisor to a school's honors literary magazine, to the psychology club, to Psi Chi, to the straight and gay campus alliance, and serving as a member

Table 2.1 Activities of an Assistant Professor in a Small Teaching College

Teaching Duties

Preparing class lectures
Designing new courses
Updating old courses
Grading tests, papers
Working with students on independent research projects
Meeting with students for remedial support
Maintaining course management intranet site

Service Duties

Attending faculty meetings
Attending college committee meetings (i.e., college senate, search committee, etc.)
Serving as advisor to student-run clubs and publications
Assisting with recruitment by attending open houses, freshman orientations, etc.
Advising individual students
Writing student letters of recommendation

Research Duties

Attending or presenting at professional conferences
Seeking research opportunities outside of college for own intellectual advancement

Miscellaneous Duties

Designing and updating departmental Web site
Answering voicemail, e-mail
Filing and maintaining student records

of the college Appeals Committee, the Council of the Faculty, the College Senate, and a subbranch of the senate, Student Services. I have also created a new honors course and served as the chair for the hiring of a new honors director. Although I have recently been published, many of my colleagues have not and this has in no way prevented them from securing tenure. More important to the college are their teaching and service. As a professor wishes to advance in rank, however, from associate professor to full professor, publications and professional activities become more important. Of utmost concern to the college for tenure, however, is that the professor be an excellent teacher who motivates students to achieve. For a complete list of duties performed in a small, teaching college, see Table 2.1.

A Day in My Professional Life

It's Tuesday morning and I've arrived at my office at 8:35, which gives me exactly 1 hour before class. Although this seems like enough time to review my notes, after checking my voicemail and e-mail and responding to my messages, I still feel rushed before class. Prior to class, a student pokes her head in my door and asks if her son can sit in on class. She tells me that she is having problems with her ex-husband and the child was kept home from school. Although my college does have a formal policy that prohibits children in the classroom for insurance reasons, it is generally not enforced. As a woman's college, it is hard for most professors to refuse a child's temporary admittance to a class, and I am no different. In fact, I keep a secret stash of small toys and books that my own children have outgrown in my desk drawer just for occasions like this. I make sure I ask my student if her son is receiving counseling services, especially since there is much conflict in their home at this time. She assures me that both she and her son attend family counseling. Because this is an experimental psychology course and I will not be discussing sex or any other topics inappropriate for a ten-year-old, I allow her son to sit in, and similar to other children I've had in the classroom, he is well behaved and not disruptive.

I have another class directly after this one with only 10 minutes to get to a different building. I am giving a test next period and realize that I forgot to drop a copy of the test off at our Learning Center, where one of my students who is learning disabled will take her exam. I rush off to the Learning Center, drop off the test, and rush over to class. Because I am 5 minutes late, I tell the class that they will have 5 minutes beyond the normal class time to finish their exams.

After the test, I return to my office. It's 12:30 and I have 30 minutes to myself before office hours begin. I usually like to go over to the faculty room for lunch. It's nice to get together with faculty from other departments whom I rarely get to talk with otherwise. My institution provides a lovely faculty/staff area for lunch, with free tea, coffee, and ice water available all day. Although this may sound like a small offering, it is a greatly appreciated one that I never had available to me in other institutions. However, lately I rarely have time to share a joke and a bite to eat with my colleagues, as I seem to become busier each semester. Instead, I wolf down a quick lunch at my desk.

I'm actually glad that I did not go to the faculty lounge because a previous student of mine, who graduated last year, has stopped by. It is lovely to see her and I hug her in my greeting. She is doing well but is upset because she cannot find work in the field of psychology. She is currently working as a billing clerk. She has gone on some interviews at residential facilities, but has not accepted job offers because they were either too low paying or seemed to be more babysitting duties than psychology. I remind her that she may have to accept such a job and then work her way up through the institution. Perhaps she could volunteer there on weekends to see how she feels about such work. I also encourage her to apply to graduate school. Because I regularly clip help wanted ads in the field of psychology from local newspapers, I am able to offer her some other possible job opportunities in her field before she leaves. She promises to keep in touch and jots down my e-mail address.

It's 1:00 and my office hours have begun. I have an appointment with a student who had plagiarism issues in her last paper. Perhaps taking my advice regarding citations literally, she directly quoted three pages worth of information in the methods section of her lab report placing quotation marks on the entire section. She argues that there was no way to reword this information and she had to quote it. Because other parts of her paper were correctly done, she did not fail this assignment, but her grade was very poor. I want to be sure that she understands what she did wrong so that she will not repeat her mistake on her next lab report. I give her an extra assignment for practice, in which she must read a certain section from a psychology text and put it into her own words.

It's 1:30 and I need to prepare for the lab portion of my experimental psychology course. We are learning how to perform a statistical analysis called a t-test using SPSS computer software having just done one by hand in class earlier this week. I have prepared a worksheet that will walk the student through the necessary steps. Because the copier has run out of toner, I print the copies from my computer.

At 2:00, lab starts. Students enjoy lab because of its applied emphasis. Because we are a small college and cannot afford a site license for SPSS, I have only loaded it on my own personal computer. Students work in pairs and, as there are only eight students in the class, it doesn't take very long. While students are waiting for the computer, they are occupied with other work. In addition to our SPSS assignment, the class must decide the topic of their final experiment. The students will be responsible for researching this topic area, devising or choosing an instrument to measure this phenomenon, distributing the instrument among the college population, entering the data and analyzing the data using SPSS, and writing a complete research report. They decided to examine whether women on an all-female campus spend significantly less time on looks and/or dieting as a result of lack of competition for males, compared to women on a coed campus.

It's 3:55 and class was officially over 5 minutes ago. There is a class waiting to get in. I quickly shutdown the computer and leave. Teaching three classes on Tuesdays always tires me out so I head on home.

Foci in a Liberal Arts College

Influencing World Views

Many topics will arise in class that may not be part of your lecture, but that need to be addressed, nonetheless. It is important to be flexible and to include what is relevant to the students. It is also extremely important to address areas of intolerance, such as racism and sexism. Assignments such as Gay for a Day, the brainchild of my mentor Reesa Vaughter, asks students to put themselves in the shoes of a gay individual. They are asked to imagine, for one day, that they are gay (understanding that the student may actually be gay, students may also write the perspective as in the closet or out of the closet). They must pay attention to the little activities that they take for granted, for example, calling their significant other on the phone at work, and record how these activities would be different. Although such an assignment is not expected to change strong religious convictions, which many students have about gay life, it is expected to assuage any anger and increase tolerance.

Protecting Students

Being an ethical professor also necessitates protecting your students. Because psychology lends itself to the sharing of personal experiences in the classroom, many students disclose information without realizing its effect on their peers. A few years ago in another institution, in a class titled Psychology of Sex Roles, a foreign exchange student laughingly reminisced how a 92-year-old woman from his country had been raped. "Why would they rape a 92-year-old," he wondered. For a few moments, there was a silence. Then the trouble began. The women of the class (who were the majority) angrily attacked the exchange student; a few even rose from their seats and began to approach him. Anticipating a riot, I quickly pointed out to the class that, although we may not like what he said, his words represented the opinions of many. While others are savvy enough to not share such thoughts due to fear of reprisals, he chose to speak his mind. I encouraged the class to be the instructor for the rest of the period. How could we reach this young man and others like him? The class began to problem-solve rather than blame and I sighed in relief.

As professors, every student in our class must feel safe. Similar to the elementary school teacher, who must protect her students from teasing, a professor must protect freedom of expression. Students such as the above-mentioned foreign exchange student actually provide us with a wonderful opportunity to teach tolerance and restraint. And like the elementary school teacher who is a role model and sometimes the idol of young children, so too is the professor in many ways. A derogatory statement on my part regarding the foreign exchange student may have intensified the class's feelings and perhaps ostracized him for the rest of the semester or longer. On a small campus with limited socializing opportunities, this could be especially damaging.

Helping Students/Boundaries

Students are eager to share their own and their families' psychological disturbances with their professors. Because small classes are considered to be more beneficial to economically and academically disadvantaged students than those who are not (Dillon & Kokkelenberg, 2002), the small college may be more likely to attract such at-risk students, and the professor at this institution may be privy to a variety of student personal information. Over the years I've heard about students' child custody battles, financial crises, eating disorders, anxiety disorders, learning disabilities, and sexual abuse. Although as professors we cannot counsel our students as this would create a dual relationship, this does not mean that we cannot be empathetic and understanding when a student blurts out this information. As my colleague, Lisa Paler, states, "We cannot do therapy, but we can be therapeutic." Some professors, afraid of appearing unethical, quickly dismiss the comment or make a hasty recommendation for a referral. When a student shares personal information with me, I generally provide some general empirical information on the topic, offer my encouragement, and then make a referral to our counseling center.

Understanding and Appreciation for Diversity

The proportion of American students who are minorities has grown. In 1976, minorities represented 16% of college populations; in 2000 this figure grew to 28% (*Digest of Education Statistics*, 2002). My own small college changed from a predominately white, upper-middle-class student body to a currently more diverse mix. Teaching ethnic minorities requires that we be cognizant that certain groups may feel apprehensive and distrustful of institutions as a result of possible discriminatory treatment in the past. Also, most of our students are first-generation college students and do not have experts at home to seek advice from. Our role as advisors becomes even more important for these students. For example, some students believe that a bachelor's in psychology will allow them to be a wealthy psychologist when they graduate. We owe it to all of our students to be as honest as possible so that they have an understanding of the major that they are undertaking, because they may not receive this advice from home. Although I feel strongly that education should be appreciated for its intrinsic value, I also believe that the first-generation minority student may represent a separate and distinct case. To this student, jobs are a very real and pragmatic concern, especially if the family is currently living in or near poverty. The idea that education should be valued in and of itself, without ties to the practical nature of employment, may be more a mind-set for those who never had to worry about getting a job, apartment, or feeding a child. I do not believe that discussing jobs and their salaries takes anything away from the educational experience and may be necessary in the case of the minority student.

Advantages and Challenges

Getting to Know Students

I believe that psychology courses are empowering courses. Since the small teaching college allows for more dialogue in the classroom, a professor learns a great deal about students' lives. Although many students suffer from medical students' syndrome, thinking they have every disturbance in the *Diagnostic and Statistical Manual of Mental Disorders (DSM)*, they also learn which behaviors are normal. Once during a lecture on human sexuality about children and masturbation, a young mother raised her hand and asked, "To get them to stop, you should beat them, right [she did not mean abuse]?" As awful as this sounds, I was really glad that she asked this question. Here was an opportunity to learn about normal child behavior and discipline. We were able to discuss the various studies done on physical punishment, effective discipline, and sexual behavior as well as the various societal, cultural, and familial pressures that influence our parenting. I would like to think that education empowered this young mother to reconsider the way that she was raised for a healthier upbringing for her son and would prompt her to research answers to parenting problems she might have in the future.

Staying With It

Teaching should reflect contemporary concerns. I've always thought that professors, in general, age well. Perhaps that is because our students help us to stay young by keeping us up to date with the current slang, music, and dances. However, they also let us know when our class material is outdated. As conscientious educators, we must make it our business to keep abreast of the changes in our field and how these changes relate to the cultural niche of our students. For example, a lecture of psychoactive drugs and their impact on human behavior would not be complete without mention of Ecstasy, Special K, and Ritalin. However, a professor using notes from 10 years ago may not realize such an omission. Professors owe it to their students to be aware of the changes in society that affect their students so that their lectures might be relevant to students' lives.

Grading

An area that all professors must struggle with is the grading of papers and exams. My small teaching college assigns numerous writing assignments across disciplines in an effort to improve writing, which tends to be a problem for our population. A new psychology professor may not realize that students have enormous writing difficulties. Students make many errors with homophones, run-on sentences, lack of paragraph structure, and lack of organization. Consider for example this excerpt taken from a psychology and law exam, "He touched her in a sexual manor" (to which the professor replied, "Where is this sexual manor?"). Although it takes time and energy to correct such errors, more writing practice is necessary to help students combat these problems. The area of psychology necessitates writing assignments, and although the psychology professor may choose to not penalize the student for writing errors, corrections still need to be made and practice needs to be given. I assign numerous short writing assignments in class, which are not formally graded, but which are corrected and counted as homework assignments.

It is often very difficult to grade a typical research paper. Problematic issues that arise include plagiarism and favoritism. To combat the plagiarism problem, the chair of one community college advised me to assign no research papers for introductory-level courses. The chair stated that students invariably plagiarize, therefore the professor must spend time and energy finding the plagiarized source, and the student learns nothing in the process. Instead, he advised me to offer short, critical-thinking papers. In some respects, I still follow his advice. I will often assign an interesting article or story for students to read, and then ask them to write a two to three page paper answering a predetermined question. For example, my students read Lois Gould's "X: A Fabulous Child's Story," which describes a fictional child who was raised with a gender-neutral identity. The class then wrote a paper discussing the pros and cons of such socialization and whether such a gender-neutral identity is possible. Such an assignment fosters critical thought, a component that many industries say is lacking in their newly graduated hires. Interestingly, many students have difficulty writing such a paper. I always get a least one paper that is a review of the theories of gender identity and does not answer the questions posed.

Objectivity is also an important issue when grading papers. This is especially a concern when a research paper is assigned. Students will often complain about their grade and point out that they did everything that was required of them, so why is their grade lower than their friends? Sometimes it is difficult for a professor to articulate exactly why one paper is better than another; sometimes one paper will just flow better than another. However, it is extremely important that students understand where they could have improved. My own lowest grade in graduate school was from a professor who admitted to grading "interpersonally." Realizing that subjective methods of grading were problematic for both my students and myself, I currently use a rubric for grading. I establish a number of objective standards prior to beginning grading, which will be associated with a certain number of points off. Because I use the same rubric for each student, assignments can be compared among classmates. I recommend using objective standards for the grading of all papers, whenever possible, as it enhances student learning and the feeling of being treated fairly.

Ethical Challenges

In teaching psychology, the topic of ethics comprises at least one class lecture for every psychology course taught. Therefore, one would think that psychology professors would be well versed in ethical behavior and treatment of students, and therefore there should be no need for an ethics section of this chapter. Unfortunately this is not the case. Perhaps it's not unlike the shoemaker's son whose soles have worn thin, or the barber's child who sports an unruly hairdo, but psychologists need to heed the words they preach. In my own limited history as a psychology student and professor, I have witnessed numerous occasions of unethical behavior by professors who should have known better. Problematic areas include sexual relationships and socializing with students. At the small teaching college, where the gossip circuit is strong, relationships with students may irreparably damage both the student's and the professor's reputations.

Some professors, especially younger ones, may feel that they have more in common with students than they do with the aging faculty who are their colleagues. This is especially problematic for the relocated faculty member who recently took a position miles from family and friends. Although we can sympathize with this lonely individual, we cannot condone this behavior. Any relationships with students must wait until after that student has graduated. I remember a relationship that existed between a graduate student colleague of mine and a much senior member of the faculty. Although the class was sickened to witness their flirting back and forth during class, everything seemed fine until they broke up. At that point, the tension in the class was so thick that you could cut it with a knife. I don't remember learning anything that semester, but I did lose respect for my professor, who instead of being a wise elder became a dirty old man.

So many subtle biases already exist in the professor–student relationship, and professors may often be unaware of them. We are humans and as human we will always favor some students over others for inexplicable reasons. Students may remind us of ourselves, our family members, or of someone we dislike. With so many subtle biases present, it makes no sense to add a larger, more blatant bias by socializing with students. Rather, we should be concerned with maintaining as much objectivity as possible. One way to do this is by creating objective standards for grading papers, as already mentioned, but another may be to grade papers blind by having students identify themselves by a code number only. This tactic is greatly appreciated by students.

Transference

College students look up to their professors and often try to emulate them. There is more psychological transference in these relationships than we realize. An example of transference arose in an adolescent psychology class, where we were discussing rites of passage of other cultures, scarification, and how tattoos perhaps represent our society's version of scarification. I mentioned that my daughter got a tattoo while away at college and how I was not emotionally prepared for this event. Then, 2 weeks later, a young woman came up to me after class and showed me her new tattoo. Although tattoos are extremely popular among the college-aged population, I could not help but think that the idea somehow came from me. Professors have great power to sway students' thoughts and opinions, and therefore we must be careful in expressing our own personal biases. We do not want our students to agree with us or do what we say just because we are the professor; we would rather they use the information that they have obtained in class to form their own opinions.

Preparation for an Academic Career in a Liberal Arts College

To be competitive in a very competitive job market, possessing a variety of teaching experiences is optimal. Prior to actually securing employment as an adjunct professor, I guest-lectured for my mentor to gain classroom experience. Many of my classmates obtained teaching assistantships. If a college was desperate to find an instructor for a course that I had never taught before, I would agree to teach it even though it would demand a great deal of preparation. In this way, my experience in teaching grew more diversified, thereby making me more marketable. Colleges also appreciate a professor who is willing to create novel experiences for students. This can include creating new courses, but also teaching old courses in new ways. Ideas to lend novelty to courses can be obtained from organizations such as the Society for the Teaching of Psychology located online at http://teachpsych.lemoyne.edu/teachpsych/faces/script/index.html.

Because the small teaching college cares most about teaching, a candidate should be prepared to offer a model class. Sometimes the institution will allow candidates to choose the topic that they will be lecturing on; others will assign a topic. If the candidate chooses the topic, it should be a topic area that the candidate would possibly teach for that department. If you choose the area of your dissertation, be sure to teach that area as it would apply to a psychology class, and not just summarize your research and findings. Teaching colleges need to know that candidates can teach new material on relatively short notice in an insightful and relevant manner. The model class is the candidate's opportunity to demonstrate this ability.

The type of lecture that would be given at the small teaching college varies greatly from that of a larger institution. Classes tend to not exceed 25 students and can sometimes be as small as 10. Classroom discussion is therefore expected, and a potential candidate needs to know how to elicit class discussion in a meaningful way, to prevent students from veering off on a tangent, and to demonstrate respect and interest in students' comments.

Interestingly, at a recent search at my institution for a tenure-track position, much attention was paid to the candidates' cover letters. Candidates should use the cover letter to show their fit with the institution. Specific mention should be made of experience with students similar to the population of the college, whether it's females, diverse groups, or first-generation college students. A cold, brief cover letter is equated with a cold, disinterested professor. The cover letter offers candidates an opportunity to show why they are a good fit for the institution.

Most importantly, the best preparation, training, or advice that I can offer to potential professors is to truly love working with young adults. This is not an age group for everyone. Young adults tend to be needy, impressionable, and insecure. According to Benton, Robertson, Tseng, Newton, and Benton (2003), American college students have, over the past 13 years, increasingly needed help with anxiety/stress disorders, depression, suicidal ideation, and personality disorders. Your interactions with them will not end in the classroom because being a professor in a small institution demands a more holistic approach. You will also advise, refer, recommend, and tutor your students. They, in turn, will challenge, exhaust, amuse, invigorate, and teach you.

References

Benton, S. A., Robertson, J. M., Tseng, W. C., Newton, F. B., & Benton, S. L. (2003). Changes in counseling center client problems across 13 years. *Professional Psychology: Research and Practice, 34*(1), 66–72. Retrieved May 20, 2003, from American Psychological Association Web site: http://www.apa.org/journals/pro/press_releases/february_2003/pro34166.html.

Digest of Education Statistics. (2002). Retrieved October 15, 2003, from the National Center for Education Statistics Web site: http://nces.ed.gov/pubs2002/digest/chs.html.

Dillon, M., & Kokkelenberg, E. C. (2002). The effects of class size on student achievement in higher education: Applying and earnings function. Retrieved July 21, 2003, from Office of Institutional Research, Binghamton University Web site: http://buoir/binghamton.edu/papers/parers.htm.

3

Doctoral Institutions: On the Other Side of the Fence

LISA Y. FLORES AND ROBERT D. MORGAN

At some point, most graduate students think about an academic career in a doctoral degree-granting institution. However, even for those who seriously consider an academic career, what one witnesses as a graduate student is not necessarily indicative of the actual professional roles and responsibilities of psychologists in doctoral degree-granting institutions. Thus, the purpose of this chapter is to provide an overview of this career choice including professional responsibilities and expectations, typical activities, as well as advantages and disadvantages to an academic career in an institution that grants doctoral degrees.

Our Career Development

Before describing the duties of academic faculty, it might be useful to provide some background on how we ended up in our positions. We were initially attracted to the study of psychology because of its focus on understanding human behavior and our desire to help people. We also learned as undergraduate students that graduate study in this field

LIFE AFTER GRADUATE SCHOOL IN PSYCHOLOGY

was necessary to obtain good jobs. The first author entered graduate school unsure of what she would do with the degree, but expected to be involved in practice-related activities. This changed after gaining skills and confidence in research and teaching and with the guidance of her mentors in graduate school. Her decision to pursue an academic position did not crystallize until the 4th year of her graduate studies, when she realized that she wanted to continue much of the activities she was engaged in as a doctoral student within a university setting. Similarly, the second author did not decide until his predoctoral internship that his heart was with academia. Although he continues to enjoy his applied work with offenders, the stimulation of the academic environment, the opportunity to mentor bright students, and the freedom to pursue questions of interest were all that was needed to persuade the pursuit of an academic career.

Professional Roles

In Table 3.1, we list the typical job duties required of assistant professors working in large, doctoral degree-granting departments. Below, we provide more description of the professional roles and responsibilities of assistant professors in these settings.

Researcher

Research requirements will vary from institution to institution. For example, the number of publications, the journals in which you publish, the number of first-authored or sole-authored articles, and with whom you publish are all research standards that vary depending on the institution for which you work. Although it is rare to find an institution that will tell you the exact number of research publications required for tenure, all institutions have a written policy pertaining to tenure requirements. We suggest that you obtain a copy of this policy manual so that you will have an idea of what is expected of junior faculty. Moreover, we have found it valuable to consult with our tenured colleagues for advice on how to progress toward tenure. We also believe it is wise to meet with your department chair and, in some instances, your college dean on an annual basis to receive feedback regarding your progress toward tenure.

In doctoral degree-granting universities, research occupies approximately 40% of your work week and is the role that typically makes new faculty the most nervous. However, we recommend that you keep in mind that being a productive researcher is not all about numbers of publications but about enjoying the process of scientific inquiry. You

Table 3.1 Common Duties for Assistant Professors in Large, Doctoral Degree-Granting Departments

Research Duties

Writing, writing, writing (manuscripts, chapters, research grants)
Developing new research projects
Analyzing data
Facilitating research team/lab meetings
Reading articles in research area
Preparing presentations/invited talks
Reviewing manuscripts for professional journals
Presenting at professional conferences

Teaching Duties

Developing class lectures
Teaching graduate and/or undergraduate courses
Designing new courses
Grading, evaluating students

Service Duties

Advising students
Attending faculty meetings
Attending student committee meetings (thesis or dissertation defenses, oral comprehensive exams)
Attending department/college/university committee meetings (search committees, advisory board meetings, program area meetings, etc.)

Miscellaneous Duties

Meeting with students, colleagues
Responding to e-mail, phone calls

---

probably enjoyed research as a graduate student or you would not be pursuing an academic career in a doctoral degree-granting institution. Thus, maintaining this passion will serve you well as you navigate the grind of the tenure process. As you spend the first couple of years building your lab and developing a research pipeline, remember those things about research that you had enjoyed as a graduate student and continue those activities in your career. Pursuing research opportunities with colleagues and graduate students can ease your research load and provide you with a rich source of enjoyment.

Teacher

As a member of a graduate faculty, approximately 40% of your time is devoted to teaching activities. You will be responsible primarily for graduate teaching and training; however, you also will likely teach undergraduate courses. The courses you teach will depend on the needs of the program and department as well as your areas of interest. New faculty typically spend a significant amount of time in their first few years preparing courses and updating the courses in subsequent years with the constantly expanding literature, so it is a good idea to try to teach the same classes for as long as possible, especially if they fall in your area of expertise and complement your research.

Although you are in a doctoral program with primary responsibilities to the graduate program(s), you also may have some undergraduate teaching responsibilities. These may range from broad-based courses (e.g., abnormal psychology, sensation and perception, history and systems of psychology), but also may be specialized to your interests (e.g., forensic psychology, health psychology). You should consider negotiating your undergraduate teaching responsibilities during your interview before you accept a job; however, if you have no preferences for what undergraduate classes you teach, you may be perceived as a good team player willing to teach a variety of undergraduate courses.

Service

Service activities typically consume a significant amount (approximately 20%) of your responsibilities as a faculty member, although this should not be where you spend most of your work time. Service pertains to any activities you engage in that contribute to the operation of the department, college, university, or professional community. Service typically includes serving on a committee, but can also consist of serving as a faculty sponsor for a student organization, counseling students at the university counseling center, or serving as an *ad hoc* reviewer for a professional journal.

Most programs will protect junior faculty from high service demands in their first couple of years, however, faculty who are members of underrepresented groups in higher education often report finding themselves spending more time on service activities than their faculty counterparts (Fouad & Carter, 1992). You may want to avoid doing more service than what is expected from junior faculty, and actively think about how to prevent service activities from eating away at your research time. For example, one of us requested a teaching reduction when asked to chair a standing department committee because junior faculty were not expected to chair committees.

Mentor

Perhaps one of the most meaningful roles you may play as a faculty member will be to serve as a mentor for students. Students will look to you to learn how to become a professional, much like you did with your mentor. All faculty serve as role models; however, we believe it takes additional effort to be a mentor. Mentoring entails developing an ongoing relationship with a student in which you share your own professional developmental process, providing training opportunities for the student to explore career options, assisting the student in developing a professional network and identity, and guiding and advising the student throughout his or her career decision making. Although becoming an effective mentor will not weigh heavily in your tenure and promotion process, it is one way that faculty find that that they can have a significant and lasting influence in the lives of their students and, in turn, the profession.

Types of Academic Appointments

Generally, there are three different routes to obtaining a faculty academic appointment: tenured (or tenure-track) faculty, term faculty, or adjunct faculty. *Tenured (tenure-track) faculty* comprise the core faculty within a department and are involved in research, teaching, and service activities as part of their job responsibilities. Tenure-track faculty begin at the assistant professor rank and are evaluated for tenure and promotion after approximately 5 to 7 years. *Term faculty* are non-tenure-track faculty at the university who are hired to teach courses on a temporary basis and can include contract faculty or visiting faculty. Contract faculty are appointed to faculty status on an annual or multi-year basis and must continuously renew their contracts. They are hired to teach courses that the department is unable to cover as a result of temporary faculty shortages. Visiting faculty, on the other hand, are brought in temporarily to teach courses in their area of expertise or to fill temporary faculty shortages. Another type of academic appointment is the adjunct status. An *adjunct faculty* member is a part-time position held by a professional from the community or sometimes an administrator at the university or a faculty member from another department who offers course instruction or clinical supervision. Most doctoral degree-granting institutions limit adjunct faculty status to undergraduate teaching; however, psychologists who maintain scientific activities are sometimes permitted to teach graduate-level classes.

To Be or Not to Be (in Academia): Advantages and Disadvantages

There are several aspects about obtaining an academic position at a research-oriented university that are especially attractive. The diversity of tasks in your workload translates into work schedules that can vary day-to-day and week-to-week; thus, boredom is rarely an issue. Working in a stimulating scholarly environment with intelligent and motivated colleagues and students is also a benefit to this job. Moreover, the independence to manage your work schedule and "be your own boss" is a facet of this job that is especially rewarding. Faculty appointments are typically for 9 months, and faculty can often choose to teach during the summer to supplement their income or use the time to focus on research and writing. In addition, private practice and consultation are roles that some faculty engage in outside of their professorial duties. There are obvious benefits to providing professional services (e.g., additional income, professional recognition); however, you should recognize and consider the potential pitfalls, such as lack of support within your academic department for pursuing applied interests and taking time away from research and writing activities, as highlighted by Cohen, Morgan, DeLillo, and Flores (2003). Finally, the job security that is provided by tenure can also be a comfort if you decide to pursue a career in academia.

As with all jobs, there are also some downsides to being a faculty member at a doctoral degree-granting university. You can talk to any faculty member, and few will tell you that they entered this career because of the money. To put it simply, academics do not earn a lot of money compared to psychologists in other settings. Annual merit raises are usually small and dependent on the state's budget allocation for higher education. An additional drawback is the stress associated with the position; many assistant professors find themselves constantly worrying and may experience significant amounts of stress over tenure and promotion. Moreover, by the very nature of the job, there is always work to be done and some faculty may spend a lot of time working to meet the rigorous demands of the job. Rarely do you feel that work is completed at the end of the day, semester, or academic year. Faculty members have to learn to feel comfortable taking time away from the office knowing that there is work to do.

Preparing for a Career in Academia

As previously discussed, an academic career in doctoral degree-granting institutions offers many benefits, but also presents many stressors that other careers in psychology do not entail. Preparing for a career in academia during your graduate studies is critical to your success.

This is your opportunity to learn the norms of the academic community, to engage in many of the same activities that you will as an assistant professor, to assess your interest and skill levels in these activities, and to determine whether you want to continue these activities in your professional career. To be competitive for an academic position after graduation, you should take advantage of training opportunities above and beyond the requirements to graduate, as most graduates are entering academic positions with considerable experience. Astute graduate students will seek professional experiences and skills that will enable them to obtain a job and succeed in academia. Many students enter graduate school with no intentions of pursuing an academic career (this was the case for both of us) only to find that their interests and skills are well suited to an academic career. But what type of skills and experiences do you need, and where and when do you obtain them?

Independent Research Skills

If you plan on pursuing a career in academia, it is especially important to become involved in additional research projects beyond your thesis and dissertation. To succeed in a doctoral degree-granting institution, you must become an independent researcher and your success in academia is dependent on your research productivity. Thus, as a graduate student you should begin to develop the knowledge and skills to facilitate your own lab, to conceptualize and complete your own research projects, and, most importantly, to identify a specific area of research you would want to develop into your "research program." Programmatic research involves research projects that naturally build off one another and lead to a specific direction of inquiry. Thus, as you progress in graduate school you should seek opportunities to obtain more independence in the lab as well as accept tasks with increasing responsibilities. In other words, you want to demonstrate the skills of becoming increasingly independent and less reliant on your mentor to develop ideas, design and implement research methodology, analyze and interpret data, and resolve research dilemmas as they occur.

Teaching Experience

Although teaching is not mandatory to graduate, students planning on an academic career will need some teaching experience. In a study of the graduate training experiences of recently hired counseling psychology faculty, Gore, Murdock, and Haley (1998) reported that new assistant professors taught an average of 9 undergraduate- and 1.5 graduate-level classes. Most graduate programs offer teaching assistantships; ideally serving as sole instructor for a class where you are responsible for creating a syllabus, selecting readings, and planning lectures is good preparation for an academic career. However, if teaching assistantships in your graduate program do not include independent instructor responsibilities, you can ask to guest-lecture in courses that are in your specialty area. The emphasis in doctoral degree-granting institutions is on research and, thus, you may find that you are still competitive with minimal teaching experience; however, any teaching experience you can acquire will enhance your marketability.

Diverse Training

You may also improve your academic marketability by pursuing diverse training and coursework. The broader your training, the more you may offer to prospective programs. Take advantage of opportunities for nontraditional coursework or experiences. For example, if you are interested in business-related matters, take a class in the business department. Pursuing nontraditional experiences as a graduate student may allow you to bring a fresh perspective to your job and may subsequently increase your marketability.

Postdoctoral Training: Is It Really a Trap?

The goal of postdoctoral training is to provide an opportunity for the development of specialized knowledge and skills (e.g., neuropsychology, health psychology) or advanced research skills. Postdoctoral training is generally a 1- or 2-year advanced training opportunity that occurs after the completion of the Ph.D. or Psy.D. Although many students, particularly those interested in private practice, may view a postdoctoral program as simply delaying their entry into the profession, a research postdoc can benefit those interested in academic positions because it allows them to teach, conduct research, and perform other academic-related responsibilities. The postdoc can significantly increase your marketability in academia. If you are interested in an academic career, you should seek postdocs that are "academic" in nature with at least some emphasis on research development. For example, one of us (R.D.M.) completed a forensic psychology postdoc. Fellows not only learned specialized knowledge and skills in forensic psychology, but traditional academic duties such as research, presenting in grand rounds, and coursework/readings were emphasized.

Of course, research-oriented postdocs are even more productive for your academic marketability. In addition to specialized research skills, the completion of a postdoc provides you with extra time to complete and submit current projects for publication. It is no secret that, when it comes to academic jobs in doctoral degree-granting institutions, your odds of landing a desirable job become progressively greater when you have more publications. Thus, an extra year or two of research experience should enhance your application.

Mentoring

In our opinion, nothing is more critical to your academic success than developing a positive mentoring relationship with a faculty member during graduate school and the early years of your academic job. A good mentor can assist you in the development of the requisite skills to gain entry and progress in your profession and can help you become aware of the politics and expectations of the academic community. Some advantages of a mentoring relationship include career advancement, professional development, building a professional network, and increasing a sense of one's professional identity (Wright & Wright, 1987). You will develop the knowledge and skills required for an academic career from your mentors, but more importantly, you will learn how to behave as a professional.

Mentoring should not end when you complete your degree. In fact, many doctoral degree-granting departments are adopting mentoring models whereby new faculty are assigned to an advanced faculty member for mentoring. The goal of this mentoring is to orient new faculty to the department and university, as well as guide new faculty during the initial stages of their academic career. As a new academician you will have many questions and experience multiple hurdles, dilemmas, and doubts (e.g., Cohen et al., 2003) and a mentor will help you navigate these obstacles. We received excellent mentoring during graduate school, but were both surprised by the amount of mentoring we required once we began our academic careers.

Securing an Academic Position: The Hiring Process

Learning of Job Opportunities

Traditionally, most psychology jobs in doctoral degree-granting institutions are identified through newsprint searches in the *Monitor on Psychology* published by the American Psychological Association (APA) or the *Chronicle of Higher Education*. However, with technological advances, more people are checking online for faculty postings via the APA Web site (http://www.apa.org/ads/) and through the *Chronicle of Higher Education* Web site (http://chronicle.com/jobs/). Also, it is common practice for job openings to be posted on professional listservs in the same fashion that they are submitted to the professional publications and Web sites. These position announcements are typically forwarded from listserv to listserv so that they are eventually forwarded to all relevant electronic groups. Thus, the Internet and word of mouth appear to be equally important for learning of jobs as the traditional published method.

Developing Your Application

One of the most important materials in your application packet is your cover letter. The academic cover letter is unlike cover letters for other job applications. Cover letters for most professional jobs are one to two paragraphs; the academic cover letter tends to be much more detailed and between one to three pages in length. In an academic cover letter you will want to discuss your research interests and accomplishments, your teaching experiences, other applicable skills and expertise, and your fit for the position. In addition to a cover letter, many colleges and universities will ask for a teaching and/or research statement. The teaching statement will be your opportunity to share your teaching philosophy, the courses you would like to teach, and your credentials as an instructor. On the other hand, the research statement describes your research interests, the plan and goals you have for your research program, and your research potential. Although your vitae describes all of these domains, the cover letter and professional statements are your opportunity to present your case for why you should be hired, so think carefully about these aspects of your application.

The remainder of your application to doctoral degree-granting institutions consists of your academic vitae and letters of reference. Academic vitae come in different styles; however, the content for presenting your accomplishments is generally the same. You should consider formatting your vitae according to the expectations for the position. For example, list research experiences before teaching and clinical experiences. Be thorough when reviewing your vitae to ensure that you have included all relevant experience, but also to ensure that you have not misrepresented yourself or accidentally included any erroneous information.

Typically, you should solicit three letters of recommendation in support of your academic application. The purpose of these letters is to provide additional information regarding your qualifications and abilities, as well as your interpersonal style. Universities are not only interested in hiring the best candidate, but they also strive to hire good people who will interact well within the department. Thus, letters of recommendation typically inform the hiring institution of the type of person you are and how well you will "fit in." Collegiality carries much weight in academia.

Last, you may be asked to include reprints or preprints of your research. Work samples provide hiring committees further data about your scholarly skills and abilities. Consider submitting empirically based studies or papers. Doctoral degree-granting institutions are recognized based on their research accomplishments, and thus committees want to review your work to ensure that it is of high quality and that you will contribute to high-caliber science.

The Interview

After reviewing all applications, academic programs will typically develop a short list of three persons to invite to the campus for an interview. During this interview, you will meet with the departmental students and faculty, department chair, and college dean, visit the campus and city or town, and give a job talk. By far, the most stressful, yet most crucial aspect of the interview is the job talk. The other time you spend meeting with people (individual or small group meetings, meals) may be perceived as more comfortable, less stressful interactions, but don't lose sight that you are still on an interview and that you are being evaluated during these times. It is important to remember that once you are invited for a campus interview, you are on a very short list and they are invested in your having a positive and productive visit. Nevertheless, you want to make a positive impression, so do your homework.

What homework? Remember, you have submitted an application packet to the institution you are visiting, so the faculty know your professional qualifications very well. You will need also to be familiar with them. You will not be expected to recite all of the faculty's professional accomplishments, but being aware of research interests, seminal works, and honors or awards will provide you information to discuss during your visit and also demonstrate your interest in them and the program. Thus, use the Internet and colleagues to learn as much as possible about the department and faculty.

Most academicians consider the job talk the most important aspect of the interview process. The job talk is a 60 to 90 minute presentation (including time for questions) about your research program. The goal of this presentation is for the faculty to learn more about your research interests and skills as well as your teaching and presentation skills. This talk can make or break your interview. Your objective during this job talk should be to demonstrate the programmatic nature of your research, and your goal is for those who attend your job talk to leave with no questions regarding your ability to conduct and explain your research.

Last, this is an interview so you will be asked questions; however, you are also expected to ask questions. You should identify the type of information that is important to your decision on which job to accept, and then develop a list of questions to illicit this information. If you are unsure what types of questions to ask, consult with your mentors, faculty, and peer colleagues.

Getting the Offer

The department chair is usually the person who will extend the formal job offer. If you are in this position, congratulations! You should be very proud of yourself for this accomplishment because academic positions are quite competitive. When you receive this call, listen to the details of the offer and ask how much time you have to consider the offer. Never accept the position at this point, even if you know that you want to go there. As uncomfortable as it is for some of us, it is critical that you attempt to negotiate the offer. This is one of the few times in your career that you will have the power to change the conditions of your contract. Some (or even all) of your requests may be turned down, but you will never know if you could have acquired additional resources to help you perform your job better unless you attempt to negotiate. Negotiating is part of the process and there are several areas that you may want to consider negotiating such as: salary, start-up monies, lab space, teaching load for your first year, courses you will be expected to teach, summer salary, funding for a return trip to the town or city to secure housing, or a research or teaching assistant. We suggest that you talk to others in academia (e.g., mentors, other new faculty) to brainstorm what may be reasonable requests during your negotiation process. Keep in mind that once you accept the offer, it is difficult to ask for additional things not listed in your contract, so be sure that you try to negotiate for everything you will need to begin your academic career successfully.

Now That You Have the Job: How to Succeed in Your First Years

Surprisingly for some, your first couple of years as a faculty member will exceed the stress levels you experienced during your most hectic semesters in graduate school. Few things are guaranteed in life, but as a beginning faculty member you can be assured that at some point in the first few years you will feel overwhelmed, overworked, anxious, stressed, lost, bewildered, and, above all, incompetent. These feelings are par for the course for most new assistant professors. One of us (LYF) was warned of this as a graduate student and advised never to make a career decision (that is, decide whether or not you are cut out for this job) until she had been in the position for at least 2 years. There is simply too much going on during your transition to make a major career decision. Moreover, after you have made it through your first few years, you will realize that the first years are qualitatively different from other stages of your career.

It is not unusual for new psychologists in academia to set high, and sometimes unrealistic, expectations for their first year. For example, a new academician might expect to publish two empirical studies in the first year, to obtain stellar teaching evaluations from students, to provide insightful and outstanding reviews of manuscripts, to automatically understand the politics of the program or department, to have students who are hard working and motivated, to perform job duties so that everyone is happy with the work, and to have some time to welcome a new puppy into her or his home. It is important that you set high standards and goals for your performance in the first years on the job and make every attempt to reach these goals, and we also want to stress that you may not be able to do everything while you are in the middle of transitioning into a new job and living in a new area. You will exert a lot of energy in your first year as you work to adjust to your new environment while trying to hit the ground running. Keep in mind that it will take some time before you feel that you (and your research program) have hit your stride and that you are performing at your peak level.

Developing Your Professional Identity

Developing a professional identity is a process. It is common for new faculty members to begin their careers feeling incompetent and fearing that they will be exposed as a fraud in the world of academia. Although not everyone will admit it, the "imposter syndrome" is something that many of us experience at some point during our first year (and often beyond our first year). These feelings may be particularly heightened if you are a member of an underrepresented group in academia, such as women and racial and ethnic minorities. For more information regarding the special concerns that women and persons from diverse racial and ethnic groups may encounter, refer to the following

APA publications: *Surviving and Thriving in Academia: A Guide for Women and Ethnic Minorities* and *Women in Academe: Two Steps Forward, One Step Back.*

It is natural that concerns about one's competencies surface because this is a time when new faculty members assume more responsibilities and start to perform their job duties with more independence than they had as graduate students. Remember that it will take some time before you feel a confident professional identity emerging, but if you stick with it, you will begin to feel more secure and self-assured in your role. Indeed, it took both of us at least 2 years in this position before the competency concerns diminished and we felt more at ease in our professional roles. At the same time, it is important to own your role as a professor. You spent many years training for this position and proved that you have the skills and potential to succeed at the job.

Networking

As new faculty members, we found it especially helpful to network with other junior faculty in our departments, in other departments across the university, and from other universities across the country. Getting to know other faculty who are at the same stage of their own career development as you are helps to normalize your experience. In addition to serving as a support network, this can be a group that can also provide some social outlets as you build your friendship network in your new area.

Finding Mentorship

As previously noted, we strongly believe mentoring is essential to your success in your academic career; thus, we recommend you seek mentoring from more-advanced junior and senior colleagues. You will also likely rely on your mentors from graduate school. Try to learn from your mentors' experiences and avoid encountering some of the same challenges they experienced. If a formal mentoring program is not already established in your department, take advantage of programs at your university or professional organizations. For example, most universities have an office for faculty development to help faculty advance their skills. These offices may provide mentoring programs for junior faculty or brown-bag seminars focusing on issues pertinent to new faculty members.

Time Management and Making Wise Commitments

Learning how to manage your time and knowing when to say "no" are two skills that, if you do not already possess, you will need to develop as a new faculty member. Because research productivity is so important to your success, you should carve out time during your week that is devoted to writing and other research tasks. Some new faculty find it useful to block out a whole day of the week for research, while others may carve out 2 to 3 hours daily during their most productive time of the day. Regardless of what you decide to do, it is crucial that you set aside a significant amount of time during your work week to focus solely on research and writing.

Another pitfall among new faculty members is spending too much time preparing for classes. As mentioned earlier, teaching will consume a lot of your time in your first years; however, be careful not to let this cut into your research productivity. To help manage the time you spend developing your lectures and planning classes, you may want to consider asking mentors and senior faculty who have taught the same class if they would share their lecture notes so that you can have a foundation to work from instead of starting from scratch. Additionally, you can find another junior colleague at another university who is teaching the same course and split the work. Finally, a senior faculty member once advised one of us (LYF) to start planning for class the day before the class meets so that you have an imposed deadline, otherwise, he indicated that you will always find something to add to your lecture if you had the time.

Maintaining Balance in Your Life

If we have painted an accurate picture of the first few years working at a large, research-oriented university, you may be questioning whether you have time to pursue your interests outside of work. The answer is yes and no. We are strong advocates for maintaining a sense of balance between your work and your personal life. You will be effective and efficient in your professional role only if you take the time to do the things outside of work that you enjoy. Moreover, a personal life helps to keep your work in perspective, particularly at times when a manuscript you have submitted is rejected from a journal or a lecture you have worked so hard on is not well received by your students. You should be aware, however, that finding the time to pursue outside interests will take work and good time management on your part and there are times during the academic year that you may find the balance tipping more toward work. As you learn to effectively juggle the multiple demands of your job, you will find more time for your personal life than you initially envisioned. Give yourself permission to enjoy those activities outside of work that are meaningful for you and that you find relaxing and rejuvenating.

Summary

In this chapter, we have described the different aspects of working as a faculty member in a large, doctoral degree-granting institution. We have identified some of the pros and cons of these positions and provided advice on how best to prepare for this job as a graduate student. Based on our experiences on the academic job market and early transition period, we have illustrated the roles and responsibilities of junior faculty and what you can realistically expect to encounter in your first years. Finally, we have provided advice throughout on how to navigate these processes. If you choose to pursue a career as a faculty member in a large, doctoral degree-granting institution, we are certain that you will find it to be a challenging career, yet one that is filled with many rewards and opportunities for personal and professional growth.

References

American Psychological Association. (1998). *Surviving and thriving in academia: A guide for women and ethnic minorities.* Washington, D.C.: Author.

American Psychological Association Task Force on Women in Academe. (2000). *Women in academe: Two steps forward, one step back.* Washington, D.C.: Author.

Cohen, L., Morgan, R., DeLillo, D., & Flores, L. Y. (2003). Why was my major professor so busy? Establishing an academic career while pursuing applied work. *Professional Psychology: Research and Practice, 34,* 88–94.

Fouad, N. A., & Carter, R. T. (1992). Gender and racial issues for new counseling psychologists in academia. *The Counseling Psychologist, 20,* 123–140.

Gore, P. A., Murdock, N. L., & Haley, S. J. (1998). Entering the ivory tower: Characteristics of successful counseling psychology faculty applicants. *The Counseling Psychologist, 26,* 240–257.

Wright, C. A., & Wright, S. D. (1987). The role of mentors in the career development of young professionals. *Family Relations: Journal of Applied Family & Child Studies, 36*(2), 204–208.

4

Interdisciplinary Medical Setting: The Multiple Roles of a Health Psychologist

MARILU PRICE BERRY

Health psychology is an exciting field that is attracting more interest since psychologists were formally recognized as health service providers. There is a growing recognition of the mind–body connection as research illuminates psychosocial influences on the onset and course of illness. Research has shown that factors such as stress affect the immune system as well as general health. Health psychologists utilize the biopsychosocial approach in evaluating and treating a variety of physical and mental health issues, and the rehabilitation model is substituted for the more traditional biomedical model in treating these conditions. Primary prevention (i.e., health promotion and disease prevention) is part of the health psychologist's role in health-care settings, and this focus is seen in programs promoting healthy diet and exercise. Other roles are secondary care (e.g., smoking cessation and weight management programs) and care in tertiary settings (e.g., pain centers, palliative care). The focus with individuals with chronic health problems is on quality of life and improvement of function. In addition to their clinical work, health psychologists help to develop empirically based treatments in health care and contribute to research and evaluation.

Employment Settings: Where Do Health Psychologists Work?

Health-care and medical facilities comprise some of the fastest-growing employment settings for psychologists. In these settings, they work as clinicians, consultants, teachers, administrators, and researchers. Health psychologists are employed by hospitals, medical schools, outpatient medical clinics, and research laboratories. Some health psychologists work in private practices with the majority of their referrals coming from physicians. Others work on a multidisciplinary team within a physician group practice. Collaborative work between psychology and medicine has helped to address the lifestyle and behavioral factors that comprise many of the top health risk factors in the United States. Specialty areas within health psychology include pain, cardiovascular disorders, neuropsychology, HIV/AIDS, eating disorders, oncology, sexual dysfunction, geriatrics, palliative care, primary care, and women's reproductive issues.

Activities and Responsibilities: What Do Health Psychologists Do?

One of the appealing aspects about being a health psychologist is the variety of roles that you can serve (Table 4.1). As examples, you can provide psychotherapy to someone adjusting to having a chronic illness (such as cancer), teach biofeedback to someone with headaches, and provide consultation to a physician about how to recognize depression in the elderly. Much of the work involves psychoeducation in which patients are taught what to expect from their illness, how to communicate with their physician, and how to increase health-promoting self-care practices and coping techniques. Teaching is also done in the context of training medical and psychology students, lecturing to nursing and medical staff, and providing consultation and liaison services to physicians. In the context of a medical setting, the health psychologist can write grants for training and research, develop treatment protocols, run research studies, and perform outcome research.

Health psychologists assess and evaluate individuals prior to many different types of procedures and surgeries. A range of health factors are assessed, including psychological symptoms and history, mental

Table 4.1 Common Work Duties of a Health Psychologist

Clinical Activities

Providing individual, couple, and group psychotherapy to patients and their families
Providing skills training (biofeedback, relaxation techniques, communication)
Consulting/liaising with physicians
Providing presurgical screening and preparation
Assessing prior to placing someone in specialized treatment or on a medication
Promoting health behaviors

Teaching Duties

Developing lectures on health psychology topics
Teaching medical students, residents, and psychology trainees via lectures/classes
Teaching via modeling (trainees observe clinical activities)
Evaluating trainees

Research Duties

Writing grants
Developing treatment protocols
Performing outcome research
Writing manuscripts, book chapters
Preparing presentations (professional conferences, grand rounds)
Presenting professional talks

Other Duties

Paperwork/writing progress notes and reports
Dictating patient notes and letters to referring doctors
Attending departmental faculty meetings
Attending medical school committee meetings

status, substance abuse, coping strategies utilized, level of social support, use of medication, and adaptation to the illness or injury. Results of the evaluation may be used by transplant teams to assess suitability for an organ transplant, by surgeons prior to a back surgery or gastric bypass, by pain specialists prior to implanting a spinal cord stimulator or morphine pump, and by physicians placing a patient on opioid medications. During these screenings, the psychologist evaluates how realistic the person's goals are for treatment, their level of preparedness for the procedure, how willing and able they are to comply with the treatment protocol, and their emotional stability and ability to cope with possible negative outcomes. An individual may be deemed appropriate and ready for surgery, appropriate pending further preparation, or inappropriate. Psychological screening and preparation by a health psychologist greatly improve outcomes and are becoming the standard of care prior to many surgeries and procedures.

In addition to assessment and evaluations, clinical practice as a health psychologist entails short-term treatment, primarily with a cognitive behavioral approach. Psychotherapy addresses the individual's adjustment to the illness or injury and teaches skills for coping more adaptively with the medical problem. The psychologist may provide support and encouragement as the individual copes with loss and grief over a loss of function, potential disfigurement, shortened life expectancy, or inability to live the same type of life they were leading before the health problem. Treatment may address depression, anxiety, anger, grief, trauma, or substance abuse. These problems may have existed prior to the health problem and may either cause or exacerbate the health problem. Alternatively, the medical problem may have caused the psychological distress. Treatment may also cover work problems, relationship and family stress, sexual difficulties, problems with their physician, and frustration with the health-care system itself.

Cognitive behavioral interventions are typically brief and directive. These include biofeedback and relaxation training for a variety of medical conditions, pain, anxiety, and stress. Other interventions include cognitive restructuring and challenging negative self-talk, communications skills training, promoting healthy behaviors, and anger management.

Case Example: Working in an Interdisciplinary Clinic and as a Faculty Member for a Medical School

As an example of the variety of roles a health psychologist can fulfill, I will describe my job as a clinical assistant professor for a university-based medical school and health science center. I am employed by the Department of Anesthesiology at the medical school, and my primary work setting is an interdisciplinary pain center located inside the associated hospital.

The majority of my clinical work is with individuals who have chronic pain and are referred by the pain specialist anesthesiologists with whom I work in the clinic. These patients have a variety of pain conditions (e.g., back and neck pain, arthritis, headaches, pancreatitis, complex regional pain syndrome, phantom or stump pain, fibromyalgia) and are sent to me as part of interdisciplinary treatment.

These individuals see the physicians for medication and/or procedures such as nerve blocks, and they see me for help adjusting to life changes such as being unable to work, inability to do many things they used to be able to do, and chronic pain. The pain and illness have affected their lives in many ways, and some individuals have difficulty coping with these changes. Many are depressed, anxious, or angry about their illness, injury, and subsequent pain and disability. Others engage in behaviors that have a negative impact on their condition, and I work with them on making lifestyle changes and improving their motivation for self-care. Some of these negative behaviors include smoking, overeating, inactivity, use of alcohol and illicit drugs, misuse of medication, and not complying with treatment recommendations.

Treatment may include individual, group, or couple psychotherapy. My approach is cognitive behavioral and includes education about chronic pain, training in relaxation and biofeedback techniques, challenging negative thought patterns, and improving self-care. Therapy usually includes elements of supportive psychotherapy and motivation enhancement interviewing.

I am also called on to evaluate and treat inpatients on the hospital floors. I get calls from rehabilitation specialists, orthopedic surgeons, rheumatologists, internists, burn unit staff, and many others. Again, there is great variety in presenting problems and medical diagnoses. It helps to have some familiarity with medical terms including diagnoses, anatomy, and medications. These patients may be having trouble coping with a new injury, complications from surgery, or the chronicity of the condition that has brought them back into the hospital. Some of these inpatients have a history of depression, anxiety, or other mental health issues that exacerbate their medical problem and influence their recovery. Others are seen as drug seeking or are causing problems with the nursing staff. Because my specialty is pain, much of the work is teaching skills for coping with pain, whether it be acute, postoperative, or chronic pain.

As faculty for the medical school, one of my roles is teaching. Although I do not teach a formal structured course on health psychology, I do train medical students, residents, and fellows who rotate through our clinic. These trainees come from the department of anesthesiology, and my job is to make sure that they understand the role of a psychologist in the medical setting, know when and how to refer patients to a psychologist, and know how to handle problematic behavior. Much of the training is on basic communications skills such as empathic listening and conveying complicated information to patients. Teaching is done in formal lectures to the trainees and informal teaching as we discuss cases as a team. Residents and fellows sit in on psychological evaluations and group sessions and are provided with relevant readings.

Another role is research. I have developed and run research protocols on pain-related topics in our clinic as well as at neighboring hospitals. Undergraduate and graduate students from a university research program have worked with me on these projects, and this has provided another opportunity for teaching as well as collaborative research with a variety of colleagues in the medical center. As faculty for a medical school, I have access to a wonderful library and solid computer support.

One dynamic part of working in a large medical center is the many opportunities for continuing education. Through the medical school departments there are weekly grand rounds with guest speakers and experts in their fields. These are free and usually occur during lunchtime. Conferences, in-services, dinner lectures (sponsored by pharmaceutical companies), and related events abound. I have never had a problem fulfilling my continuing education requirements for the year, and the lectures provide more familiarity with medical terms. I have also presented at grand rounds for other hospitals in the area.

As part of my administrative duties, I provide educational lectures about pain and interdisciplinary treatment to managed care providers. This helps them understand the role of a health psychologist in a medical setting and thus assists with getting these services authorized by the insurance company. Despite the growing recognition of psychology as a health-care profession, insurers still appear reluctant to pay for psychological services for physical health problems.

Preparation: How to Become a Health Psychologist

There are many routes to take if you are interested in becoming a health psychologist. Health psychologists typically hold a Ph.D. or Psy.D. in clinical or counseling psychology. Graduate programs offer different levels of training: coursework, subspecialty tracks or certificates, preceptorships, and programs specifically for health psychology. During graduate school, you can sign up for clinical practica in medical settings and typically work 1 day a week in this area. A list of doctoral programs offering training in health psychology is available through the Web site for the American Psychological Association (APA) Division 38 (Health Psychology) at www.health-psych.org. Guidelines recommend exposure to health-care settings, multidisciplinary faculty, and experienced mentors in health psychology. You can also complete a 1-year predoctoral internship in a medical setting such as a local hospital, veteran's hospital, or primary care practice. This supervised experience enables you to learn whether the medical setting suits you and provides you with experience working alongside physicians. Lists of internships with major and minor rotations in health psychology are available through the APA Division 38 Web site and on the Web site for the Association of Psychology Postdoctoral and Internship Centers (APPIC; www.appic. org).

Before deciding to specialize in health psychology, it is important to note that it is recommended to first obtain a solid generalist training in psychology. Basic psychology skills are needed as a foundation for this work. Some recommend starting to specialize during graduate school, while others recommend waiting until postdoctoral training to specialize. There are 1- and 2-year postdoctoral fellowships available across the country that specialize in health psychology or behavioral medicine. A directory of postdoctoral opportunities is available on the Division 38 and the APPIC Web site. These fellowships may be general health psychology or may be subspecialized into areas such as pain management, substance abuse, eating disorders, oncology, cardiac rehabilitation, HIV/AIDS, and primary care.

Many professional organizations provide information relevant to health psychologists. I recommend joining Division 38 of the APA to begin receiving its bimonthly journal *Health Psychology* and the quarterly newsletter *The Health Psychologist*. Its Web site (www.health-psych.org) has information about training programs, student awards, listservs, meetings, and current research. The Society of Behavioral Medicine (www.sbm.org) is another organization that supports health psychologists and provides relevant clinical and research information. The Association for Applied Psychophysiology and Biofeedback (www.aapb.org) focuses on biofeedback and other self-regulatory methods. Networking with other students and professionals through these organizations, over the Internet, and through supervised experience is an important way to develop your knowledge base and familiarity with health psychology concepts.

Look into registering as a health service provider at both the local and national levels. When working with the licensing board in your state, check to see if it offers a certificate as a health service provider. It would also be helpful to become registered with the National Register of Health Service Providers in Psychology. As an added bonus, the National Register helps to document your training and hours of supervision for the future. These certificates can help to clarify that psychologists do function as providers of health care and that this function is legitimate. Specialty board certification in clinical health psychology is available through the American Board of Professional Psychology (ABPP) after completing the required training and 4 years of postdoctoral experience as well as passing the examination process (www.abpp.org). Table 4.2 summarizes the typical steps to becoming a health psychologist.

Table 4.2 Typical Steps in Becoming a Health Psychologist

Ph.D. or Psy.D. in counseling or clinical psychology
Graduate coursework, specialty track or certificate, or full program in health
 psychology (HP)
Predoctoral internship with major or minor rotations in HP
Postdoctoral fellowship (1 or 2 years)
Membership in professional organizations in HP and related areas
Registration as a health service provider
ABPP Board Certification in Clinical Health Psychology

Securing a Position: How to Find a Job as a Health Psychologist

Begin thinking about your career options while you are still in graduate school. Whether you choose to specialize your training in health psychology earlier or later, it is important to have both general skills and specialized experience and training in this area. Choosing to complete a formal postdoc is likely to help both by the contacts you make that year as well as by providing you with advanced training in this special area. Professional networking at many levels is a must. Attend professional meetings relevant to the field and get your name out there by presenting papers and networking at the meeting (e.g., lunch roundtables, talking to presenters after their papers). During practica, internship, and fellowship, make contacts with professionals who might be helpful in recommending you for a position later.

Many position announcements stem from membership in professional organizations related to health psychology. Membership provides opportunities to network, present papers, stay up on the research, and communicate with colleagues (and potential colleagues) on listservs. Most importantly, position announcements are listed in newsletters and on Web sites as well as e-mailed to members of various listservs. I receive several health psychology-related position announcements each week via e-mail. These e-mails come to members of the Division 38 listserv and to members of the APA New Psychologists listserv. These positions are both postdocs and faculty openings. Many of these are not listed in the *APA Monitor*, but the *Monitor* is still a good place to look for openings in your area.

It is important to find a niche. Some psychologists market themselves to existing physician practices and either join the practice or set up a relationship with these physicians for frequent referrals. For example, a psychologist with expertise in smoking cessation and stress management may market their practice to cardiologists; a psychologist with experience in reproductive issues could join a group of ob/gyns to help women with fertility problems, marital stress, and many other women's issues. Start by contacting the physicians with a brief letter explaining how you could help them and ultimately save them time and hassles with what they may see as difficult patients. Again, with physicians, be brief. Follow up with a phone call or an appointment to meet with them at their office.

Provide talks in the community. When looking for work you may need to give talks for free. Topics could include general stress management, conflict resolution, communication, or even how to handle holiday stress. The key is to get out there in the community so that you can connect with potential employers or referral bases. Start by calling community or religious groups, hospitals, and clinics, and let them know you are available to give talks. Be sure to bring business cards to hand out and use the opportunity to put your foot in the door.

Another way to find and secure a position is to collaborate on research. In graduate school or during your professional training, work with other students, professors, supervisors, or other health-care professionals on research projects. This exposes you to more people and provides you with name recognition as papers are published and presented with your name on them.

Advancement and Promotion: How to Get Ahead

Getting ahead means finding out what is expected of you and then surpassing those goals, but the specifics depend on your work setting. If you are in an academic setting like a medical school, talk to the chair of your department on a regular basis to discuss your progress and goals. Read the promotion and tenure guidelines for your school; they are probably published on the school's Web site or are available by calling faculty affairs. If you are on the tenure track, you will be expected to bring in funding to support your salary, publish extensively, provide exemplary clinical work, and teach effectively. Funding means writing and being awarded grants, and this begins by getting on other colleagues' grants to establish a research record. Publishing and presenting your research at the local, national, and international level is expected. Bringing in funding from your clinical work is important, as is being respected by your peers and known for good clinical work. Teaching is also important, and providing data such as evaluation forms from your classes or lectures can document your teaching effectiveness.

If you are on the clinical track at a medical school, it is important to document the above issues but with less emphasis on grant writing and publishing. It is vital to talk to your chair to ensure that the chair's expectations are in line with yours. Ask your chair what you need to do to be promoted. My chair advised me to document my clinical work by writing up case reports and developing a course program in behavioral medicine for the residents. Depending on expectations, you may emphasize clinical work, teaching, or research.

In an academic setting it is important to join committees affiliated with the institution and hold positions on them to show your community involvement. Also, work on greater name recognition for yourself and your clinic so that your referrals increase, thus bringing in more clinical dollars to support your salary. Offer to give presentations at grand rounds and other lecture opportunities.

If you are in a non-academic setting, it is important to find out how you can best meet the needs of your referring sources. Make yourself available to them by phone and by physical office location. The closer and more accessible your office is, the easier it will be for them to send you their patients. Provide them with brief written reports after you initially evaluate their patients and be clear about the treatment plan. Learn their language and beware of too much "psychobabble" in your own. Help them clarify their initial request for treatment. Keep them up to date so they can see how helpful you are in treating their patients. Keeping referring doctors happy translates into becoming indispensable and appreciated for your role in treating their patients, and this means advancement and increased referrals for you.

While developing your career as a health psychologist, stay current on research in this field so that you are providing research-validated treatment. Read journals and attend workshops on relevant topics. Attend conferences to meet with your psychologist colleagues as well as professionals from other disciplines. Psychologists in a health-care setting are expected to be knowledgeable about psychopharmacology, so take continuing education on this topic regularly. Note that prescription privileges have been approved in New Mexico for psychologists who complete the required training, and this specialized training will be closely examined as other states consider the practice for themselves.

Advantages and Disadvantages: Why Choose Health Psychology

Health psychology is an exciting, dynamic field that continues to grow as psychologists are recognized as health-care providers. The variety of patients and presenting problems as well as the interaction with professionals from other disciplines keeps it from becoming boring. I have found that I am constantly learning new medical terms and having to stay on my toes about new medications and treatments, and this is challenging and fun. Health psychologists have flexibility in their work settings and can work in private practice, as part of an interdisciplinary group practice, in outpatient clinics or hospitals, in a research lab, or as faculty for a medical school. They may change roles and settings several times within the same day, going from consultant to biofeedback trainer, from group therapist to teacher, from hospital bedside to lecture hall. The focus on quality of life and health-promoting behaviors is very positive and rewarding. Also, the pay for health psychologists appears to be quite good in the medical setting, perhaps due to the large salaries your physician colleagues are receiving.

The possible downsides to health psychology are related to being in a medical setting. Frequently, your clients are very ill and may have a terminal illness or disabling or disfiguring medical problems. The hospital setting is depressing or distasteful for some people who don't like the smell, the lack of windows, and the sterile atmosphere. You may be in patients' rooms when their dressing is changed, they give a blood sample, or they are given a physical exam. You may be interrupted frequently by people coming in and out of the room and may have to do therapy while another person is there if the patient is in a shared room. Many times your patients are hostile and angry, and they may be confused, insulted, and anxious about having to see a psychologist.

Systems issues are prevalent in the medical setting. Some physicians may not understand or value your services or input. Other physicians may come across as demanding, patronizing, and insensitive to you and to your patient. Part of your job is to develop better communication across these lines to better serve the patient. Confidentiality in hospitals or other multidisciplinary settings is limited due to the number of providers involved and the existence of a common medical chart. This is handled by being upfront with the patient at the outset of treatment.

Another frustration in health psychology is the lack of mental health parity in managed health care. There are problems with reimbursement for psychological services related to medical problems: insurance companies may not pay for or authorize psychological treatment (e.g., smoking cessation, education for compliance with diabetic protocol) if the patient has no psychiatric diagnosis. The patient may not have mental health benefits, in which case the medical insurance company will not be willing to authorize psychological services even if they are directly related to the medical problem. When the patient does have mental health benefits, they are typically "carved out" to another insurance company, and this separation of mind and body leads to more confusion and division in service. The patient (and you) can get caught in the middle. Much of the provider's time can be spent writing letters of necessity to insurance companies and educating them regarding the role of health psychology services.

Recently, six new health and behavior current procedural terminology (CPT) codes were developed by APA to recognize interventions related to managing medical illness in patients who do not carry a primary mental health diagnosis. For example, these billing codes will cover teaching patients with diabetes the importance of self-care practices such as diet, exercise, and frequent monitoring of their blood sugar levels. They will also cover teaching relaxation skills and cognitive restructuring to an inpatient with acute pain such as a sickle cell crisis, even when the individual is psychologically stable. Unfortunately, reimbursement for these codes outside of Medicare can be difficult.

Another disadvantage is the unwritten hierarchy in medical settings. Some of the lessons I have learned along the way have been difficult ones. When working with physicians, don't use too much psychological jargon in your reports or in person. If you sound like some "shrink" or "New Age oddball," you may be immediately written off by physicians, and your knowledge and work will be discounted. To justify your position and importance on the team, show physicians how you can help them with difficult patients. If you need approval and praise from your co-workers, this may not be the field for you. When working in a medical setting, the M.D. will always be on the top of the hierarchy (they even have their own hierarchy, with surgeons at the top), and a Ph.D. psychologist will likely be viewed with some skepticism at least initially. Most important, be flexible. Other words of advice are to balance your time between self-promotion and clinic promotion, look for mentors in the field, and stay current through teaching and research.

Health psychology is a growing, exciting field with many diverse opportunities. If you think it may be a good fit for you, read up on the training and education requirements and attain a solid generalist training as your foundation. Get experience in health-care and medical settings and immerse yourself in the medical culture and environment so that you can start to speak the same language as your colleagues from more medically oriented disciplines. Remember that the health-care system demands the use of empirically supported treatments. You can be involved in developing these studies as a clinician and researcher, and you also need to make informed decisions to utilize appropriately validated treatments. To be a health psychologist takes not only a certain level of training and experience but also a certain personality style of being flexible, tolerant, direct, assertive, and willing to persevere despite a lack of external support. When you find your niche, it can be a rewarding experience as you develop rapport with and the respect of colleagues from a variety of disciplines, colleagues who may never have had a positive experience with someone from a mental health field. Working with people with chronic pain and chronic illnesses has been challenging, exciting, and rewarding for me, and I have never been bored in this setting.

Suggested Reading

Belar, C. D., & Deardorff, W. W. (1995). *Clinical health psychology in medical settings: A practitioner's handbook* (rev. ed.). Washington, D.C.: American Psychological Association.

Gatchel, R. J., & Oordt, M. S. (2003). *Clinical health psychology and primary care: Practical advice and clinical guidance for successful collaboration.* Washington, D.C.: American Psychological Association.

Marks, D. F., Murray, M., Evans, B., & Willig, C. (2000). *Health psychology: Theory, research and practice.* London: Sage.

Resnick, R. J., & Rozensky, R. H. (Eds.). (1996). *Health psychology through the life span: Practice and research opportunities.* Washington, D.C.: American Psychological Association.

Suggested Web Sites

American Board of Professional Psychology: www.abpp.org.
APA Division 38 (Health Psychology): www.health-psych.org.
Association for Applied Psychophysiology and Biofeedback: www.aapb.org.
Association of Psychology Postdoctoral and Internship Centers (APPIC): www.appic.org.
National Register for Health Service Providers in Psychology: www.nationalregister.com.
Society of Behavioral Medicine: www.sbmweb.org.
U.S. Department of Health and Human Services: www.healthfinder.gov.

5

Medical Schools and Centers: The Merger of Developmental Psychology and Pediatric Asthma Education

JEAN-MARIE BRUZZESE

Psychologists come in many shapes and sizes, although the popular stereotype is that of the clinician. Because of this stereotype, people are often surprised to learn that I am a developmental psychologist with a specialty in applied developmental psychology and that I am employed as Assistant Professor of Psychiatry at the New York University Child Study Center (NYU CSC), which is part of the Department of Psychiatry at the New York University School of Medicine (NYU SOM). In this role I develop educational programs for parents and children and evaluate the efficacy of these programs. I am also licensed in the State of New York. If you're like the many people I encounter, you may be wondering: What is an applied developmental psychologist? What types of programs are developed in psychiatry departments? What do you do on a daily basis? How did you get involved in a medical school? In this chapter I hope to answer these questions and more by describing a research position in a medical center, which I consider a nontraditional career in academia.

An Overview of Applied Developmental Psychology

I was drawn to psychology because I enjoy science while simultaneously having a desire to help children. However, I knew that I did not want to work as a clinician "fixing" problems. Instead, I was interested in preventing them from occurring and in fostering healthy development. Once I learned about applied developmental psychology, I knew I found a field that offered the best of all my interests. Applied developmental psychologists promote the health and well-being of individuals by using developmental theory and knowledge as the foundation of their work (Goldstein, Wilson, & Gerstein, 1983). We use scientific methods to formulate a knowledge base of biological, social, emotional, and cognitive growth from conception to death, or as we said in graduate school "from the womb to the tomb." This foundation is applied to the natural settings of individuals in a variety of context.

My Employment Setting: A Medical Center

When deciding to work at a medical center versus a traditional academic setting, consider some of the important differences that make medical centers unique. Unlike colleges and universities, medical centers are in the business of treating patients. Treatment is a key function that drives research, which in turn affects the financial stability and reputation of the institution.

This focus on treatment means faculty and staff at medical centers interact with patients, their families, and at times representatives from pharmaceutical companies. These interactions in turn lead to a work climate that is more formal and conservative than that of traditional academic settings. For example, guests at medical centers tend to be greeted by a receptionist who announces their arrival to faculty. This formal environment is also exhibited in the dress — business casual is often not acceptable in many medical centers; faculty members are expected to wear suits. Often jeans and sneakers are not permitted in medical centers, even for entry-level positions such as bachelor's-level research assistants and data entry clerks because they are not considered professional attire.

Related to this is the physical setting of medical centers versus colleges and universities. The former are housed in hospitals and office buildings, while the latter are traditionally housed on college campuses, which have a more relaxed environment.

Given the focus on treatment, faculty members of medical centers primarily include medical doctors. There is in an unwritten hierarchy with Ph.D. faculty members lower on the ladder of importance, with the result that Ph.D. faculty often struggle to gain acceptance. Moreover, senior administrative positions, such as directors of clinical services, often are limited to M.D. faculty.

Another difference between medical centers and traditional academic institutions that might be of importance to you is size: Departments in medical centers tend to be larger. The larger departments in traditional academic institutions tend to be the size of departments in smaller medical centers. For example, the Pediatric Pulmonary Division of Columbia University, College of Physicians and Surgeons (a specialized unit within a larger department) has approximately 25 staff members, including faculty and support staff and the NYU CSC has more than 200 faculty members and support staff.

To me the most important distinction between medical centers and traditional academic institutions is that medical centers tend to be more collaborative. This is evidenced by the multidisciplinary teams within departments as well as by collaborations with other departments within the medical center and outside agencies. For example, the NYU CSC is comprised of developmental psychologists, clinical psychologists, psychiatrists, research sociologists, a statistician/epidemiologist, and database analysts. At my prior position at the Pediatric Pulmonary Division of Columbia University, I worked with pulmonologists, nurse practitioners, exercise physiologists, a sociologist, and an experimental psychologist. As is common among professionals who study the psychosocial aspects of illnesses, my work in asthma requires successful collaborations among the psychiatry department (i.e., the NYU CSC) and departments that treat patients for the illnesses (i.e., the Pediatrics and Pulmonary Departments at the NYU SOM and Columbia University). Often collaborations with the city and state agencies, such as schools and health departments, are imperative to successful completion of research that is conducted through medical centers.

Psychological Research in Medical Centers

Psychiatric departments in medical centers often are dedicated to understanding, preventing, and treating mental health problems in children, adolescents, and adults. To this end, much of the research consists of clinical trials testing the efficacy of psychotherapeutic or pharmacological interventions in both clinic-based and real-life settings (e.g., schools, day care centers, community-based organizations). The following are examples of such studies from pediatric psychiatry:

- Evaluating the effectiveness of cognitive behavioral therapy and medication in the treatment of adolescent depression.
- Assessing the efficacy of an educational program to teach high school students with asthma self-regulatory skills to manage their disease effectively.
- Evaluating the efficacy of a school-based intervention program to treat social anxiety disorders in adolescents.
- Testing the efficacy of treatment specifically designed to help children with attention deficit hyperactivity disorder (ADHD) improve their ability to organize their materials, their time, and their school and home activities.

Another important area of research in psychiatry departments is prevention research. Here, researchers use their skills to avert problem behavior. Examples of such studies include the following:

- Testing the efficacy of an intervention aimed to improve parenting skills in caregivers of 11- to 14-year-olds to prevent substance use in the adolescents.
- Promoting child social and academic competence and preventing mental health problems, school failure, and juvenile delinquency by strengthening families of preschoolers from socioeconomically disadvantaged communities through parent-to-parent networks.
- Preventing post-traumatic stress disorder through immediate intervention following trauma.
- Reducing adolescent pregnancy by exposing teenagers to an infant simulator for 2 weeks to modify unrealistic and romanticized teen views of adolescent pregnancy and parenting.

Last, descriptive research is an important factor in psychiatry departments. Because of the focus on treatment, the goal of descriptive research is often to identify risk factors for the development of psychopathology. Examples are as follows:

- Psychosocial profiles of children in foster care.
- Studies to understand family functioning, morbidity due to diabetes, and diabetes management skills.

- Brain imaging to determine risk factors for development of psychopathology.
- Family studies comparing depressed, anxious, and normal mothers to identify risk factors for the development of disorders.

My Responsibilities

Despite a faculty title, I really consider myself a scientist in a medical center. As such, my responsibilities fall into three categories: (1) implementing current research projects; (2) developing new research projects; and (3) teaching. I spend approximately 80%, 15%, and 5% of my time on each of these tasks, respectively. See Table 5.1 for a summary of the specific tasks within each of these categories.

Implementing current research projects is my primary responsibility. At present, I have two such major efforts under way: (1) a program to teach high school students with asthma how to self-regulate their disease so that their asthma symptoms are minimized leading to a higher quality of life and less psychological distress; and (2) a program for caregivers of 11- to 14-year-olds designed to teach them parenting skills that are associated with less substance use in youth. On both of these projects I supervise staff members with very different responsibilities. On a daily basis this ranges from supervising

Table 5.1   Common Work Duties for Assistant Professors Working in Medical Schools

---

Current Prevention and Treatment Studies

Supervising research team on:
    Recruiting research participants
    Data collection and data entry
    Program implementation
Revising current treatment/program manuals for future studies
Analyzing data
Disseminating research results (e.g., peer-reviewed articles, abstracts for
  presentations at conferences, and book chapters)
Performing administrative duties (e.g., Institutional Review Board applications,
  reports to funders)

Developing Future Research Studies

Developing a new intervention based on a comprehensive review of the literature or
  improving existing interventions
Choosing and writing measures to evaluate the intervention
Pilot-testing the new intervention to determine the feasibility of implementing the
  program and providing preliminary data
Writing a grant to acquire funding to run a full evaluation of the intervention

Teaching and Other Duties

Teaching a class to medical students, residents, or fellows every year or so
Mentoring students one-on-one research projects
Attending research meetings

---

bachelor's-level research assistants on recruiting and enrolling participants, survey implementation, and data entry to supervising master's-
level researchers who are coordinating the day-to-day activities. I
employ weekly team meetings to supervise the master's-level health
educators in the asthma program and master's- and Ph.D.-level group
facilitators who implement the parenting program. During these meetings we discuss the prior week's groups, focusing on how participants
responded to the curricula and problems they may have encountered
implementing the programs. I provide feedback and we problem-
solve on ways to overcome these challenges. This information is used
to revise the curriculum as needed. Additionally, I work closely with
the database analyst to ensure we develop a comprehensive database
that is easy to use.

As data are entered, I also begin to analyze the data and dissemi-
nate results at professional meetings. Because these two projects are
currently in the early stages, both are only in year 2 of 5 years, I am
not preparing papers for peer-reviewed journals at this time. However,
I have data sets from prior projects, and I try to spend a half day a
week analyzing these data and writing articles for peer-reviewed journals. This strategy of having multiple projects at different stages is
important; it allows a continuous flow of data and, thus, the potential
for an uninterrupted stream of peer-reviewed publications.

My role on these projects also includes administrative duties.
These duties vary weekly, but generally include the following:

- Addressing human resource issues such as hiring staff and
  scheduling time off.
- Monitoring budgets to ensure money is spent as proposed.
- Writing yearly reports to the funding agents summarizing the
  progress made during the year and what the plans for the next
  year entail.
- Addressing Institutional Review Board (IRB) issues, which
  include writing the initial proposal for approval to conduct our
  research, submitting yearly renewals, informing the IRB of any
  potential ethical issues that may have occurred when conducting
  the research, staying apprised of ethical requirements (e.g.,
  changes to our consent forms resulting from the new Health
  Insurance Portability and Accountability Act (HIPPA) regulations), and ensuring my staff have taken the appropriate IRB
  courses and are conducting themselves in ways that are consistent with the ethical guidelines for research.

In addition to implementing current research projects, I also spend
part of my time developing new projects. Much like your graduate

research, this aspect of my job begins by reading any and all articles and book chapters on the topic to develop the theoretical foundation of the intervention and to begin choosing constructs important to evaluate. Developing new interventions also entails meeting with a multidisciplinary team on a weekly or bi-weekly basis to discuss what we have read and how we would use it in an applied setting; our goal is to begin translating the research findings into an intervention. Once we begin writing the curriculum, we focus on our evaluation measures, ideally choosing valid and reliable measures or, if need be, writing questions to assess our program's efficacy. We also begin to think about the population we will be implementing the program with and how to secure a sample of participants. And, of course, there is always the search for funding! We constantly look for sources of funding to ensure we can begin pilot testing a project, which is the next step once the curriculum and evaluation measures are written. We try to begin this process 2 years before we "need" a grant, or before our current funding runs out. I have learned that it takes at least 2 years to pilot-test a project, write the grant, submit it for review, and, as is almost always required, revise the grant based on feedback from the reviewers and resubmit.

The last of my responsibilities, teaching, is very limited. Teaching at a medical center is very different from that of faculty members in psychology departments at colleges and universities. For example, some faculty members with backgrounds in human development teach a class once a year in child development to medical students and/or pediatric psychiatry residents. Others with a clinical background might teach, for example, a course in cognitive-behavioral therapy or in family therapy. Teaching also comes in the form of supervision of advanced graduate students (e.g., interns, fellows, postdocs). Currently, my only teaching responsibilities are mentoring an undergraduate student in the NYU Department of Psychology who is completing a senior thesis and serving on the dissertation committee of a doctoral student in public health at another university.

Advantages and Drawbacks to Working in a Medical Center

There are several major advantages to conducting research in a medical center as opposed to a traditional university setting. One is that my primary responsibility is research, not teaching. Teaching responsibilities may not occur every semester. For someone like me who is much more passionate about research than teaching, but still enjoys some teaching, this is a good balance.

Another important advantage to working in a medical center is the salary, which, like other predominately research-focused institutions, is typically higher than that at traditional academic settings. For example, in New York City someone just out of graduate school with a few publications might expect a starting salary of approximately $62,000 to $65,000 a year. This might increase to $70,000 if the person has completed a postdoc or has a young investigator grant. With good scholarly activity (e.g., publications and securing grants), within 7 to 9 years, this salary could be in the $85,000 to $95,000 range. Based on surveys of its members, the American Psychological Association Research Office (Singleton, Tate, & Randall, 2003) reports that for many regions in the United States the median salary in 2001 for research exceeded that of faculty in universities with fewer years of postdoctoral degree experience. For example, in the South Atlantic region researchers with 6 years experience reported a median income of $68,500 versus $61,500 for faculty in universities with 18 years postdoctoral degree experience. In the Pacific region median salaries were reported to be $66,000 after 7 years experience and $61,500 after 15 years experience for research positions and faculty positions in universities, respectively.

Another advantage to working in a clinical setting such as a medical center is the availability of clinical populations for applied researchers. Because the focus is on treatment, many individuals and families turn to medical centers for help. For example, recruiting research participants into a study evaluating the efficacy of an art therapy program for patients with Alzheimer's is easier when you are affiliated with a center that treats people with Alzheimer's.

Related to this is another advantage — because you have access to clinical populations, you may be able to begin a clinical practice. For example, many faculty members at the NYU CSC, in addition to their research positions, see patients. You can develop this as part of your role in research (e.g., teaching youth with attention deficit disorder organization skills), or it can be done in addition to your research responsibilities, as a second-job if you will.

For me, at this point in my career, the most important advantage to working in a medical center is the opportunity for mentorship and continuing education. Faculty members often participate in scholarly meetings such as grand rounds where experts from both within and outside the medical center present their work. Many departments also offer regularly scheduled research meetings where faculty present their work for constructive feedback, which is particularly helpful when designing a study or applying for a grant. Also offered in many centers are case presentations and journal clubs, where a current research article is presented and discussed. These meetings, which are often not available in traditional academic settings, provide an experience where the excitement of learning and scholarly dialogue often experienced in graduate school is continued. In addition, new projects and collaborations are often generated from these meetings, and I value the opportunity to discuss projects with colleagues who come to the table with different experiences and specialties. Constructive feedback/criticism serves to strengthen projects, which is particularly helpful at early stages of your career.

Paradoxically, some of the advantages of medical centers are also drawbacks. For example, because of the limited teaching responsibilities, fewer students are available to help conduct research. Graduate students are not searching for projects for their master's theses, so there are fewer "hands" to work on your projects. You have to be creative and find ways to bring in staff when your budget is low. These include forming a relationship with the undergraduate colleges to develop internships or volunteer opportunities for students who wish to gain research experience.

Perhaps the greatest drawback to a research position in a medical center is the lack of job security. Your salary is driven by grant dollars, or "soft money," so when the grants end, so does your job. While there is great joy in being awarded a grant, knowing, for example, that in 2 years if you do not secure another grant you and/or your staff are out of work, can be very stressful.

Another drawback to a research position at a medical center is the amount of time spent in your office. Unlike faculty positions in psychology departments at colleges and universities, my position is a 12-month position where I'm expected to be in the office 5 days a week. This translates into limited time to write, limited time off to recharge my battery, and less flexibility with respect to family.

Licensure: To Be or Not to Be

Yes! Yes! Yes! You might be thinking how can you do that with your training — you don't have a clinical background? Why — as a developmental psychologist you don't treat patients? Developmental psychologists who complete their training from an APA-accredited program and obtain the supervision are eligible for licensing. Clinical experience is not required; research and teaching experiences that are supervised appropriately also count toward licensure. Check with the states where you may want to be licensed for the specific details regarding appropriate supervision.

Licensure may also be important depending on your career choices. The bottom line is that you never know when you may need it, and it opens the door for more opportunities. For example, based on your skills in program development, implementation, and evaluation you may be eligible to direct an intervention that is billable (i.e., eligible for third-party reimbursements). However, without a license you might be overlooked for the job. Also, depending on where you work you may have the opportunity to develop a faculty practice (i.e., private practice) as I do at the NYU CSC. While I have yet to take advantage of this, I might develop a practice that includes conducting developmental assessments or treating parents and their children with asthma who may be having difficulty adjusting to the disease. The latter will stem from my research in asthma. Although this sounds like an exciting way to make additional money, a word of caution is warranted: Private practice, even in the university setting, is a second job. You will still need to carry out your research responsibilities effectively, especially if you want to secure grants. See the section in this chapter on recommended readings for additional information regarding licensure.

Tips for Securing a Medical-Center Faculty Position

I believe the greatest thing you can do to secure a research position in a medical center is to gain both good research and applied experience beyond what you may have received in your classes in graduate school. Because the focus in medical centers is empirically based treatment, it is important to have a good balance of both applied and research experiences. Clinical skills do not necessarily translate into good research skills. Therefore, if your graduate school training provided you with comprehensive applied opportunities, such as clinical internships, counseling experiences, program implementation in a practicum, or testing experiences, then your next step should be to secure experience where you can further advance your research skills. Some suggestions are to complete a research-based postdoctoral fellowship, which are typically offered at medical centers, to work as a project coordinator on a study that is treatment or prevention focused, or to volunteer, if need be, on such a research study. When looking for these experiences, the research topic is important but not the most important factor you should consider. Of course, if you really like the topic, you will enjoy your work even more, or if the topic complements your applied experience, then the experience will be even better. However, what is more important is that you refine your research skills as well as develop new skills because proficiency in research can be translated to any research topic. Personally, I would hire someone who has virtually no experience with asthma but has great research skills before hiring someone with limited research skills but an excellent knowledge of asthma. Simply stated, I can teach about asthma more easily than I can develop research skills in an individual.

Alternatively, your graduate experiences may have prepared you well in research. Perhaps you designed and conducted a master's-level study in preparation for your dissertation, or you may have had a fellowship where you assisted a faculty member on her or his research. Because research experiences do not always teach skills needed to provide treatment successfully in a real-world setting, you would need to augment a sound research foundation with applied work. You may want to consider completing a clinical fellowship, gaining counseling experience, or implementing a treatment or prevention program, which would ideally be grounded in scientific theory.

When looking for either research or applied positions, do not just rely on advertisements; many positions may not be widely advertised. Let people know you are looking and begin to ask mentors, supervisors, and colleagues to keep you in mind if they hear of position openings — many of the jobs in our field are best advertised by those we know. Additionally, as you may have done when applying to graduate school, do your homework and find settings where you would be interested in working. Learn about some of the researchers and clinicians by reading their publications. Then take the initiative and send your resume to a few of those with whom you would be most interested in working, asking them to forward your curriculum vitae (CV) to colleagues if they do not have a position. And don't forget to follow up the CV with a phone call and interviews with a thank you letter!

Things to Look for in Jobs/Training Opportunities

When you begin your quest for that perfect position or training opportunity, remember no position is perfect. But I can suggest a few things that you should bear in mind when considering job offerings as these will allow you to further enhance your career.

On-the-Job Supervision. Be certain that your supervisor is available to meet with you on a regular basis to provide you feedback regarding the work you are doing and to teach you enough for you to reach the next level in your career.

Opportunity to Secure Grants for Young Investigator. When considering different job/training opportunities, be certain to determine the amount of support you will have in applying for a young investigator grant. Ask about the track record of the department in helping young investigators secure these grants, how much support and training you will receive in preparing the application, and how active their grants office is in informing staff of grant opportunities in a timely fashion.

Scholarly Meetings. Will you have the opportunity to participate in different scholarly meetings so you can continue to learn?

Supervision for Licensure. Because I earned my graduate degree from a department that had an APA-accredited clinical program I was eligible to sit for the licensing exam. Unlike APA-accredited clinical, counseling, and school psychology programs, which require internships and fellowships and as such provide an opportunity for supervision, the developmental program did not offer this. Because of this, I had to be certain that my jobs counted toward my supervision. Ask if there is anyone qualified on staff who would be willing and able to supervise you.

Salary. Of course, something to always consider. Negotiate as high as possible and obtain in writing any future offers or promises. Keep in mind that salaries are often dictated by what is already written in a grant. If the salary is lower than you would like, ask about other ways the institution might be able to provide you financial assistance. Will it pay for your daily parking? Will it pay for your cell phone? Does the institution assist with child care expenses? If your goal is to secure a grant soon, discuss what this would specifically mean for your salary should you be awarded the grant.

Conclusion

I hope that I have provided you with helpful tips and insights into the world of research in a medical center. If you enjoy research much more than teaching, then a faculty position in a medical school may be right for you. It is a great place where you can focus primarily on research, while still dabbling in teaching.

References

Goldstein, D., Wilson, R. J., & Gerstein, A. I. (1983). Applied developmental psychology: Problems and prospects for an emerging discipline. *Journal of Applied Developmental Psychology, 4*, 341–348.
Singleton, D., Tate, A., & Randall, G. (2003). *Salaries in psychology: 2001*. Washington, D.C.: American Psychological Association. Retrieved October 6, 2003, from http://research.apa.org/01salary/index.html.

Suggested Reading

Bolster, R. (1995). An interesting career in psychology: A research psychologist in a medical school. Retrieved from www.apa.org/science/ic-balster.html.
Fisher, C. B., & Koocher, G. (1990). To be or not to be? Accreditation and credentialing in applied developmental psychology. *Journal Applied Developmental Psychology, 11*, 381–394.
Fisher, C. B., Rau, J.-M., & Colapietro, E. (1993). The Fordham University doctoral specialization in applied developmental psychology. *Journal of Applied Developmental Psychology, 14*, 289–302.

Practice and Clinical Roles
for New Psychologists

6

University Counseling Center: Bridging the Gap between University Counseling Centers and Academia

JEANNE M. HINKELMAN

For many, variety is "the spice of life." If you're like me, you seek diversity in your day and look for opportunities to involve yourself in varied activities. For psychologists who enjoy an array of professional activities (e.g., clinical practice, teaching, research, consultation, training, clinical supervision), many options exist. When I graduated with my Ph.D., I was interested in pursuing a career that would offer me flexibility with how I spent my time and allow me to be creative in my job. I was fortunate to find such opportunities in positions in a university counseling center (UCC) and an academic appointment.

The purpose of this chapter is to introduce graduate students and new professionals in psychology to the possibility of combining positions (in my case a staff psychologist position in a UCC with an academic appointment) in a university. This chapter includes an overview of (1) the UCC setting, (2) activities and responsibilities of psychologists in UCCs, (3) the challenge of combining UCC positions with research activities, (4) how to prepare for a career in a UCC, as well as secure a position and make the transition to professional life, and (5) advantages and disadvantages of a career in a UCC. This chapter gives a brief overview of the author's personal experiences, salient issues, advantages and disadvantages of the two job settings, and tips on how to survive and thrive.

University Counseling Center: The Setting

The mission of UCCs is to assist students in achieving effective personal, social, educational, and vocational development and adjustment. A staff psychologist in a UCC will generally provide assessment, individual and group therapy, and psychoeducational outreach and consultation to members of the university community. Activities are mostly clinical and administrative, and involvement in clinical training and supervision is usually required.

Our office, for example, is staffed by two full-time, licensed psychologists (including the director and myself), and anywhere from two to five psychology trainees (students completing practica or predoctoral internships). The clientele of the UCC includes students, faculty, staff, prospective students, and alumni and their significant others. The vast majority of clients who use our services are undergraduate, graduate, and professional students who are seen at no charge. Clients are seen for an average of two sessions.

UCC clients present a wide range of concerns, such as vocational indecision, anxiety, depression, substance abuse, interpersonal conflicts, suicidal and psychotic thoughts and behaviors. Our office is usually contacted in most emergencies that are labeled as "psychological." UCCs at small institutions like ours tend to see a higher percentage of their student body and see students with primarily social/emotional problems (Tryon, 1980).

Responsibilities and Activities of a Psychologist in a University Counseling Center

The UCC has the dual missions of education of student counselors and service to clients (Scanlon & Gold, 1996). Staff psychologists in a UCC provide psychoeducational and clinical interventions for concerns related to career decision making, impaired academic or interpersonal functioning, anxiety, depression, and crisis management. Specific duties include counseling to help clients develop and implement plans for coping more adaptively with personal problems, goal setting, providing information to enable individuals to formulate realistic personal, educational, and vocational plans, and following up with results of counseling to determine reliability and validity of treatments used.

In my position, for example, I typically work approximately 45 to 55 or more hours per week in the counseling center during my 9-month contract. Approximately 50% of my time is spent doing individual counseling, another 20 to 30% is spent doing outreach presentations, and the remaining time is spent doing administrative tasks, attending staff and committee meetings, consulting with faculty and staff or particular departments and programs on campus, and providing clinical supervision and training. I supervise psychology trainees, including the entire range from beginning trainees who are seeing their first clients through advanced practicum and predoctoral interns. The UCC is both a training site for the University of Tulsa (TU) American Psychological Association (APA)-accredited graduate programs in clinical and industrial-organizational psychology, as well as a site in the APA-accredited Northeastern Oklahoma Psychology Internship Program (NOPIP). I have been actively involved as an individual and group clinical supervisor, sit on the NOPIP consortium committee, and provide training programs for NOPIP interns. See Table 6.1 for a summary of responsibilities and activities of a psychologist in a UCC.

Table 6.1 Responsibilities and Activities of a Psychologist in a University Counseling Center

Psychoeducational and Clinical Interventions
Crisis management
Psychological assessment
Individual, couples, and group counseling
Outreach presentations/workshops
Consultation with faculty, staff, particular departments, and programs on campus

Administrative Tasks
Attending staff meetings
Attending committee meetings
Attending predoctoral internship committee meetings

Clinical Supervision and Training
Training for APA-accredited graduate programs
Training for APA-accredited predoctoral internship program
Individual and group clinical supervision for practicum students, predoctoral interns, and postdocs

Combining Practice and Research in a Joint Appointment

Combining positions is one method for an individual to address the challenge of having multiple interests and skill sets. In my case, I was looking for an opportunity to engage in diverse activities such as those found in the two positions in which I work. More specifically, I was looking for opportunities to counsel, train/teach, and conduct applied research, and I was able to find them by combining UCC and academic positions.

I currently hold a 9-month full-time position as Staff Psychologist in Counseling and Psychological Services, as well as a research associate (faculty) appointment in the Department of Psychology at the University of Tulsa. Under my staff psychologist hat, I report to the director of Counseling and Psychological Services, which is administratively a part of the Division of Enrollment and Student Services. In my research associate role, I report to the chair of the Department of Psychology, which is in the College of Arts and Sciences. My counseling job is a regular administrative senior staff position and pays all of my salary. My research associate position is in title only; it does not provide any other compensation or benefits except indirectly by making me eligible to apply for external funding. I also have graduate faculty status, which allows me to supervise graduate research assistants who are working on research with me for academic credit. This is just one example of how dual positions may operate. There are many options for similar combined careers both for the practitioner and nonpractitioner.

For my research associate position (see Table 6.2 for a summary of responsibilities and activities of a psychologist in a research associate position), I spend 1 to 20 hours per week outside of my counseling

Table 6.2 Responsibilities and Activities of a Psychologist in a Research Associate Position

Research Duties
Scholarly writing (manuscripts, chapters, books, research grants)
Developing new research projects
Analyzing data
Supervising undergraduate and graduate research assistants
Meeting with research assistants
Reading articles in research areas
Preparing conference presentation submissions/papers
Reviewing colleagues' manuscripts
Presenting at professional conferences

center job doing research, scholarly writing, and supervising under-graduate and graduate research assistants. During any particular semester I may have 1 to 10 students working with me on various research projects. I meet with my research assistants in my office in the counseling center. Before my appointment as a research associate, I taught a research methods course as an adjunct instructor. There are specific advantages and disadvantages to a joint appointment, as dis-cussed later in this chapter.

Preparation for a Career at a University Counseling Center

It is important for one to be well versed in multiple areas. Training for a UCC position might include coursework or supervised experience in required skill areas (e.g., clinical, research, supervision, consultation, training). A combined position will generally require a Ph.D. in an applied field (e.g., counseling, clinical, industrial-organizational) of psychology. Experience that would enhance your curriculum vitae (CV) would include completing supervised experience in a variety of settings that are appropriate for your degree (e.g., clinical practica for counseling and clinical students, practica in a business for industrial-organizational or human factors students). Some areas are easier to obtain experience in than in a course, but academic credit may be pos-sible and is worth checking into. It never hurts to have more experi-ence "officially" documented on your transcript. If you can obtain experience and have it count as an independent study, that will at least get the experience on your transcript.

In terms of preparation for UCC positions, it is important to receive high-quality, diverse clinical training in areas such as counseling theo-ries, approaches, interventions, and techniques. In addition, courses in group therapy and consultation can add to your clinical training. It is important to complete at least one practicum in a UCC setting, and additional practica in assessment and hospital clinical work can add to your clinical experience and make you a more attractive candidate for a UCC position. Some doctoral programs and predoctoral internships in clinical and counseling psychology also offer supervision training and experience, which can make you more marketable to UCCs.

Securing a Position at a University Counseling Center

Overall, be as clear as possible about your career goals and what you want from your job and job environment. This is necessary so that you do not end up in a position that you do not really want. For exam-ple, you will want to be clear about the size and type of UCC where you want to work. UCCs are located at small to large private and public colleges and universities. Many UCCs are located in administrative buildings that house other student affairs and services offices. Some UCCs are located in student health centers where psychiatric services may be available. Other UCCs are stand-alone operations.

You might consider obtaining some career counseling to help you clarify what it is you desire and steps that may be required to achieve your goals. Chances are you have been so immersed in graduate study and completing degree or licensure requirements that you have not taken as much time as you might need to work on your own personal career development. Before you apply for any jobs, prepare a job description that you believe represents the type of position you are looking for and a cover letter and resume/CV with the knowledge, skill, and experience you have that will contribute to such a position, as well as your specific career goals.

Network, network, network! I cannot say it emphatically enough. Advisors, faculty, supervisors, colleagues, relatives, and friends are the best sources for finding jobs. A large proportion of open jobs are never advertised publicly. Let people know what you are looking for so that they can inform you if they become aware of openings. Conferences, conventions, and workshops are also good places to do networking. There are often job announcements posted, resumes collected, and interviews conducted at these events. You may also want to target a particular institution or location. Directories, phone books, and the Internet are additional resources for finding agencies or institutions that might fulfill your job and career needs.

More networking never hurts. Your friends might tease you about the stack of business cards you have collected and given out, but trust me, networking works. You can also make direct contact with institutions of interest. Most institutions have Web sites where you can obtain contact information from departmental/office pages or via a searchable directory. You can then contact a specific person working in the area of interest via phone (i.e., cold calling) or e-mail. E-mail lists related to the type of position of interest or your professional interests may be another way of accessing job announcements or letting people know you are looking. Let them come to you! Your own personal Web site is another method of letting people know that you are on the job market. You can post your CV as well as a description of the type of position you are looking for. And don't forget about using listservs. They not only can provide you with insight into what is happening in your field, but also can give you another way to network.

In making application for specific positions, begin by looking and applying early. For example, I started applying for jobs early — my first application for a UCC position was sent in November of my predoctoral internship year. I sent out approximately 40 applications in a national search. I applied for postdocs, faculty, UCC, and research positions.

Factors affecting the job search may include geography, licensure, flexibility, salary, benefits, and required activities. Searches are typically restricted by geographical location. The fewer commitments or restrictions that you have, the easier it will be for you to find employment.

It usually takes at least a month or two to hear anything from employers once your application is sent, at which time you may receive an acknowledgment of receipt of your application, an affirmative action card to complete and return, an invitation for an interview, or a rejection letter. Job interviews can vary in length from one-half to two days long and involve meetings with agency staff, directors, deans, or vice presidents of relevant divisions or schools, and other constituents you may be working with, as well as a job talk.

Professional organization publications including newsletters, journals, and special interest group publications often contain job announcements or solicitations for resumes from potential job candidates. Some publications you might look at include trade journals, professional association newsletters (e.g., *APA Monitor*), *The Chronicle of Higher Education,* magazines, and newspapers. However, keep in mind that newspaper advertisements are one of the resources that have the lowest potential for helping you find and secure a position. Technology also allows for easy access to job information. You can look at Web sites of specific institutions (check personnel or human resources pages) and professional organizations that post job announcements.

Special Considerations for Securing Joint Appointments

Securing a combined position generally takes some research and assertive creativity. You first need to explore the options by asking the proper questions of the appropriate administrators. To do this requires that you have a clear idea about the types of activities in which you want to engage. It also requires that you inquire about matters that may not automatically be raised (e.g., asking to interview with the academic department chair when you are on an interview for a counseling center position).

When discussing combining multiple positions, there are at least two different perspectives regarding which type of position makes the most sense to acquire first. Some have often heard the argument that it is better to get a certain type of position first, then branch out into your other areas of interest as the first type of job may be harder to get. For example, some people can do private practice or consultation anywhere, but if they do not live where there is a college or a university, they could not branch out and obtain an academic position. Likewise, others have heard the argument that it is better to work a few years in a clinical setting and become licensed before seeking an academic position. This provides focused time to meet licensure requirements and opportunity to gain applied experience that may enhance your ability to teach and do clinically relevant research.

If you want a combined position that includes an academic appointment, look for multidisciplinary agencies and positions with multiple activities (e.g., teaching or research) listed as the job activities or responsibilities. Look also for an agency that is tied to an academic department, or that lists training and supervision of psychology trainees as part of the agency's mission and staff responsibilities. Look at the Web pages of agencies and departments of interest. In addition, it might be in your best interest to do some background investigation of the particular agency and departments of interest by researching back issues of various professional periodicals (such as *The Chronicle of Higher Education*).

Wherever you look, remember that looks can be deceiving — for example, just because a UCC position is listed as a "faculty" or "tenure-track" position does not necessarily mean there are teaching or research responsibilities involved. Some institutions designate staff psychologist positions as "staff," others as "faculty," some "administrative," and others as "administrative/faculty" or "faculty/staff," or any other permutation of these that you can come up with. These designations are often given by human resources staff who typically do not have much knowledge of what a position as staff psychologist entails, except for the limited information that may be provided in a job description. Because they are not informed, they may not understand all of the roles and activities in which UCC or psychologists in general may engage.

Making the Transition: Surviving and Thriving

Be sure you know what is expected of you in your professional positions. Sometimes expectations across agencies or departments may not coincide, or may even clash. Be sure to keep in touch with those who are evaluating your work and let them know what you are doing in order to meet the expectations laid forth. Remember that expectations and your responsibilities may change over time, as you settle into your new position. For example, if you were not licensed upon hire, you may be licensed during your first couple of years out of graduate school in your new job. Licensure brings with it potential additional responsibility, as you are now declared eligible to provide independent psychological services, although you are still expected to consult where appropriate. Upon licensure you may be given new responsibilities, including supervision of predoctoral interns, additional training responsibilities, or other responsibilities as your boss sees fit to assign.

When in doubt, consult! If you aren't sure what exactly you are supposed to be doing in your new job, ask for some guidance from your boss or colleagues. Psychologists have a responsibility and duty to consult on issues they are not clear on; consultation with colleagues is expected by those in the field. Don't be afraid to contact a former advisor or supervisor and say, "Would you mind if I ask you a question about X ... or could you tell me who I might ask for such information?" In certain situations, you may also want to consult your state psychology board of examiners, professional organization resources, or colleagues at other institutions as new experiences and questions arise. It is also possible to consult with the Ethics Office of the APA. Keep a notebook to document your questions and the answers you receive from different sources. Be sure you note the names and numbers of the people you speak with about the issue, as well as what they had to say about it and any other resources they may cite.

During the first year or two, there is a shift from role as student to new professional, which can bring with it many new stressors. At this time, adjusting to your new responsibility level can be a challenge. Chances are that if you are in a clinical position you will have a heavier client load than you were used to in graduate school practica. You may have to adjust to changes in administration in one of your departments or in the university as a whole. Many academic institutions can be quite volatile in terms of faculty, staff, and administration turnover, and you may find that some of your new colleagues are leaving when you are just getting to know them.

Taking care of yourself is important! Combined roles and transitioning between positions creates stress in addition to that of each position alone. To function effectively, you will need to make sure you are doing the basics — eat right, get enough sleep, exercise, engage in pleasant activities you enjoy outside of work. Try to be choosy about what activities you become involved with at work, as well. If you can, delegate tasks that do not interest or energize you. Of course, there will be some undesirable tasks that cannot be avoided, but management of these and redistributing the rest can make the difference between minor irritation and major stress. Be sure to take breaks as needed — get away, take a vacation, travel to places of interest near or far away. Make sure you have a life outside of the university or institution. If you find you are spending the vast majority of your waking hours at the office (e.g., including evenings and weekends), something probably could stand to change. Try to set goals and priorities for yourself and your career. Focus on what is important, and delegate or discard what you ethically can of the rest. One of my colleagues makes it his goal to try to "only do things that are fun." Choose your battles wisely. It is helpful to find supportive colleagues inside and outside of the institution. You will have to work effectively with a wide variety of people. Be sure to obtain social support from someone you trust and who cares about your well-being.

Advantages and Disadvantages of a Career in a UCC

UCC positions are typically very diverse, requiring a range of activities and responsibilities. For some people this may be a plus; others may wish to be more specialized in their work. In larger UCCs, there is usually more opportunity to specialize, whereas in smaller centers, like the one in which I work, you really need to be a generalist. Another advantage of working in a UCC, versus working in a private practice, is that you usually automatically have a group of colleagues (other psychologists) with whom you can readily consult on a regular basis.

The work hours at a UCC are usually Monday through Friday from 8:00 A.M. to 5:00 P.M. or thereabouts, plus some evening and weekend hours for crisis on-call and outreach activities. So, if you are looking for flexibility of work hours, there is not usually much in a UCC job. Hours can also be long at times, especially during busy parts of the academic year (particularly midterm through final exams) or if you are dealing with a crisis situation in which someone needs to be hospitalized.

Advantages and Disadvantages to a Combined Appointment

There can be a number of challenges inherent in balancing multiple responsibilities in a variety of settings. These challenges include understanding the function of the various professionals (faculty instructors, center director, department chair, other college and university administration) with regard to client service needs and counselor training needs (Scanlon & Gold, 1996). In general, there is little interaction between faculty advisors in academic departments and counselors in the UCC. Relationships between faculty and counseling staffs are good, but are typically limited to contacts essential to the counseling and related work of the UCC (Koile, 1960). However, when psychologists in the UCC have appointments in psychology, there is perhaps more interaction than at other universities without similar overlap. Work in both a UCC and academic department involves regular interactions across boundaries and with different parts of the institution (May, 1988).

The interaction between membership in two separate departments or agencies/institutions needs to be recognized and dealt with. Your roles and their interaction may require that you educate people in both spheres about what it is you are able to do as well as what you actually do in practice. You may end up informing students or clients of the same. You will need to communicate with your superiors about the activities you are engaging in with respect to each department. You may also find that balancing roles can be a challenge at best. It may be important to emphasize what each can add to, versus take away from, the other as you are teaching others about your activities. For example, faculty and staff contribute to the institution through committee work and planning and participating in university programs (e.g., new student orientation, student activities involving faculty and staff, colloquia, and other university or departmental programs).

Holding a dual position may allow for more variety of activities including a combination of clinical, teaching, administration, research, training, supervision, and consultation. Working in both an agency and academic department may afford opportunities that working solely in one of these settings may not provide or allow. For example, this may facilitate new projects for collaboration. Finding ways of combining roles can inspire creative ideas and projects, which may not have been as obvious in an individual role, that span two different aspects of psychology. Another advantage for psychologists seeking combined careers in other settings could be ease of conducting applied research. For example, if a psychologist is working in a hospital setting and also holds a medical school faculty appointment, there may be advantages both for obtaining subjects for research and for gaining access to patients with whom research results might be applied.

There are, however, a number of drawbacks to holding multiple professional positions or roles, including increased potential for conflicts and additional stress that may arise in attempts to integrate these positions or roles. Psychologists working in academia may feel the apparently conflicting demands of the educational process and hope that it will promote their own development through a meshing of personal needs with role opportunities. Those who love teaching and learning may find the constraints to be frustrating and painful. For those who enjoy research, the necessity to work with people is often irksome, disruptive, and something of an affront to their narcissism (May, 1988). Belonging to the educational institution may present a problem that has to be managed by all.

At times, there are problems that arise from holding the dual responsibilities to an institution and to individuals. For example, UCC counselors help their institution best by helping clients. If a conflict arises between the needs of the client and the institution, state law and professional ethics mandate that clients' best interest comes first.

Acknowledgments

I thank Micah Fry and Melissa Patterson for assisting with the literature review for this chapter, and Joe Harvey for his helpful feedback on earlier versions of this chapter.

References

Arnold, J. D., & Gydesen, S. M. (1987). An evaluation of using faculty and administrators as volunteer counselors in a small college setting. *Journal of College Student Psychotherapy, 1*(4), 133–149.

Barclay, R. L., & Scheffer, B. (1986). An interdisciplinary approach to increase campus counseling services: A response to budget cuts. *Journal of American College Health, 35*(1), 41–43.

Bishop, J. B. (1986). A faculty review of a university counseling center: Knowledge, perceptions, and recommendations. *Journal of College Student Personnel, 27*(5), 413–418.

Bishop, J. B., Bishop, K. A., & Beale, C. L. (1992). A longitudinal look at faculty knowledge and perceptions of a university counseling center. *Journal of College Student Development, 33*(4), 374–375.

Flores, L. Y. & Hinkelman, J. M. (2001). Seeking a new career: suggestions from recent "survivors." Roundtable session conducted at the annual meeting Division 17 (Counseling Psychology) of the American Psychological Association, Houston, TX, March.

Koile, E. A. (1960). Faculty and the university counseling center. *Journal of Counseling Psychology, 7*, 293–297.

Lacher, M. (1981). On being a clinical psychologist at a small liberal arts college. *Clinical Psychologist, 34*(2), 9–10.

May, R. (Ed.). (1988). *Psychoanalytic psychotherapy in a college context.* New York: Praeger.

Rodolfa, E. R. (1987). Training university faculty to assist emotionally troubled students. *Journal of College Student Personnel, 28*(2), 183–184.

Scanlon, C. R., & Gold, J. M. (1996). The balance between the missions of training and service at a university counseling center. *Clinical Supervisor, 14*(1), 163–173.

Szasz, T. (1974). *The myth of mental illness.* New York: Harper & Row.

Tryon, G. (1980). A review of the literature concerning perceptions and preferences for counseling center services. *Journal of College Student Personnel, 21*, 304–311.

Suggested Reading

American Psychological Association (1995). *Education and training beyond the doctoral degree: Proceedings of the American Psychological Association National Conference on Postdoctoral Education and Training in Psychology.* Washington, D.C.: Education Directorate, American Psychological Association.

Anthony, R., & Roe, G. (1998). *Curriculum vitae handbook: How to present and promote your academic career* (2nd ed.). San Francisco: Rudi Publishing.

Goldfried, M. R. (2000). *How therapists change: Personal and professional reflections.* Washington, D.C.: American Psychological Association.

Kilburg, R. R., Nathan, P. E., & Thoreson, R. W. (Eds.) (1986). *Professionals in distress: Syndromes and solutions in psychology.* Washington, D.C.: American Psychological Association.

Kottler, J. A. (1993). *On being a therapist* (rev. ed.). San Francisco: Jossey-Bass.

Maslach, C. (1982). *Burnout: The cost of caring.* Englewood Cliffs, NJ: Prentice-Hall.

Sternberg, R. J. (1997). *Career paths in psychology: Where your degree can take you.* Washington, D.C.: American Psychological Association.

Woods, P. J. (1976). *Career opportunities for psychologists: Expanding and emerging areas.* Washington, D.C.: American Psychological Association.

Suggested Web Sites

Accredited Internships and Postdocs: www.apa.org/ed/intern.html.

APA Division 12, Clinical Psychology: www.apa.org/about/division/div12.html.

APA Division 16, School Psychology: www.apa.org/about/division/div16.html.

APA Division 17, Counseling Psychology: www.apa.org/about/division/div17.html.

APA Education Directorate: www.apa.org/ed/.

APA Practice Directorate: www.apa.org/practice/.

APA Science Directorate: www.apa.org/science/.

APAGS, Graduate Students: www.apa.org/apags/.

Association of Counseling Center Training Agencies: www.accta.net, www.appic.org.

Association of State and Provincial Psychology Boards: www.asppb.org.

Canadian Council of Professional Psychology Programs: www.usask.ca/psychology/ccppp/.

Canadian internships membership in CCPPP, CPA, APA, APPIC: www.usask.ca/psychology/ccppp/can-int-table.htm.

Canadian Psychological Association: www.cpa.ca.

Canadian Register of Health Service Providers in Psychology: www.crhspp.ca.

Council of Counseling Psychology Training Programs: www-bcf.usc.edu/~goodyea/ccptp.htm.

Council of University Directors of Clinical Psychology: www.am.org/cudcp.

Credentialing Opportunities for Professional Psychologists: www.nationalregister.com/grad.html.

Mental Health Licensure Resources and many state boards' Web sites: www.tarleton.edu/~counseling/coresour/lllpc.htm.

National Register of Health Service Providers in Psychology: www.nationalregister.com.

Program Consultation and Accreditation, CoA: www.apa.org/ed/accred.html.

Psychology from ABD to Licensure, by Shoshana Kerewsky, Psy.D.: ourworld.cs.com/PsychLicense/.

State and Provincial Laws and Regulations (University of Kentucky): www.uky.edu/Education/EDP/psyinfo2.html.

Student Affiliate Group, affiliated with Division 17 of APA: www.sagweb.org.

7

Independent Practice: Alive or Dead?

DEBORAH VINEBERG

Working in private practice is perhaps the most traditional and stereo-typic role available to professional psychologists. It dates to the earli-est practices of Sigmund Freud, and carries with it the perception of prestige, personal independence, and professional freedom. Yet reforms in the health-care system and a changing marketplace have deterred psychologists interested in this career option. For example, managed health care has restricted the number of therapy sessions per year, asserted control over the rate of reimbursement, and inserted itself within the delicate relationship between patient and therapist. For these reasons, psychologists entering the field are faced with the question of whether working as a private practitioner is a real possi-bility or more likely a fantasy.

This chapter examines the challenges of developing a private prac-tice, describes why private practice remains a worthwhile and viable career option (for certain individuals), and reviews the elements you need to consider to make this endeavor a successful one.

The Changing Nature of Private Practice

I remember being told many times throughout graduate school that private practice was no longer an option for budding and entrepreneurial psychologists-in-training. Stories were told about how insurance companies had changed how psychologists practiced and that the future looked dim for those of us who had always dreamed of having a nice private office (with or without a couch) and a few dozen interesting patients.

When I began graduate school in 1994, managed health care had already exerted an impact on the business practices of hospitals and private practitioners. Many professionals in the field displayed concern about their shrinking practices, increased paperwork, and new practice limitations (e.g., length of treatment, compensation rates, coverage restrictions). Unstructured therapeutic approaches such as psychoanalytic and psychodynamic psychotherapies were quickly being replaced by short-term solution-focused or cognitive-behavioral therapy. Long-term therapy was viewed by insurers as unnecessary and, as research was beginning to demonstrate the efficacy of specific therapies for certain disorders (i.e., empirically supported interventions were gaining increasing favor), psychologists in private practice began to lose their professional freedom. Analogous to the patients undergoing therapy who resist change, psychologists in private practice dug in their heels to maintain their practices. Juxtaposed with the popular Nike theme at the time "Just do it," the message from established practitioners was clear: "Just *doing* it" involved doing virtually anything *but* private practice.

Perhaps the changing environment was most devastating to professional psychologists who had been in the field for more than 10 years and who had come of age in a time when no one was looking over their shoulders. Up to that point, only their patients, their conscience, and the ethics board held them accountable. However, I knew no other world than one that included managed health care, and so I continued believing that there had to be a way for private practice to survive.

Getting Started: How to Start Your Private Practice

Unlike many other professions where setup costs are prohibitively high, starting a private psychology practice seemed like a bargain. There was no equipment to purchase and my only real expense was to sublet office space from another psychologist. Start-up costs also included licensing fees, which vary from state to state, and malpractice insurance, which is based on which coverage plan you choose. Once this was all covered, the issue of referrals became my primary concern. Printing business cards and arranging for voicemail were small expenses, but essential. Some clinicians suggested sending out announcement letters to potential referral sources, but in retrospect this was not very effective for increasing my referrals. Although I hoped for referrals from trusted colleagues, most of the professionals that I already knew — past supervisors, former classmates, fellow interns, residents and teachers — were either trying to keep their own private practices afloat or else did not have enough new referrals coming through to spill over to me.

When opening up a new private practice, it is critical that you establish a steady flow of referrals. You may want to examine different locations in which to sublet office space, keeping in mind what kind of patients you would like to see. I ultimately decided to establish a practice in downtown Boston, in the same building that several area city hospitals had set up satellite offices. The most important step in setting up my private practice was in establishing relationships with my referral sources. Unlike the written announcements that I sent out, meeting the physicians in these satellite offices proved to be the most beneficial action I took toward building a thriving practice.

To establish good relations with referral sources, I scheduled meetings with the physicians in my building to make personal contact and introduce myself, let them know what my interests/specialties were, and inform them of what insurance plans I accepted. I was fortunate to meet a group of doctors actively looking for good therapists who were conveniently located and able to take their many referrals. I learned that each physician saw approximately 25 patients daily. Hearing this was not only music to my ears, but my availability was apparently equally tuneful to their ears as well. Primary care physicians are excellent referral sources because of the nature of their work and because of the high number of patients in their caseload.

Competition is often beneficial for the marketplace; however, I began to worry that there seemed to be an abundance of competition affecting the professional practice of psychologists in the greater Boston area. There was one level of competition between one psychologist and another, and more worrisome to me was the second layer of competition between psychologists and the plethora of other mental health care providers. Psychiatrists, social workers, and mental health counselors all functioned as "therapists." I was not sure how to differentiate myself. I tried to reassure myself that as a psychologist I was uniquely qualified to do psychological testing. Despite this being a stimulating and fascinating option, it was not the market that I was trying to target. As I grew more comfortable with myself as an independent practitioner, I realized that it was not necessary to market my skills as distinct and different from those of other "therapists." I began to realize that patients stick with therapists who are skilled, empathic, and a good match — regardless of their professional degree.

Unfortunately, during my 20 or so years of formal education, I never once took a course in business; yet running a private practice is most definitely a business venture. Interestingly, I did not avoid such classes purposefully; in fact, I would have taken a few had I known how applicable they would likely become. However, they were not included in the standard curriculum, and I was never encouraged to seek out such coursework in other departments. For those readers who are still in graduate school or are able to take classes in a university, let me advise you as to a worthwhile investment: taking a course in business may be one of the most useful electives available to you in your many years of scholastic pursuits. For some reason, business and psychology never seemed to collide, except under the heading of industrial/organizational psychology, or when conversations about managed care lead to a discussion about the downsizing of group practices, the shrinking of hospital staff, and the closing of programs. In a nutshell, discussing business always felt like it was about bad news, and almost always needed to be said in a whisper.

Some basic understanding of accounting practices, saving strategies, and tax planning is incredibly valuable for professional psychologists. For example, opening a separate business account for your practice, instead of using your personal checking account, makes it much easier when it comes time to pay taxes. It is wise to keep your business and personal finances separate for liability reasons as well. Another way to apply business strategy to your practice would be when deciding on fees. Figuring out your hourly costs, overhead, routine expenses, and the possibility of using a sliding scale will help you determine a fair and profitable fee.

Wearing Many Hats

Although I received my degree in clinical psychology, I have had to wear many hats in the 5 years since I was licensed: accountant, public relations person, cleaning lady, insurance policy expert, receptionist, real estate agent, financial analyst, bill collector, and office manager. All of these roles were instrumental in making my practice successful and enabling me to do what makes me happiest.

In terms of donning the hat of an *accountant*, I chose to do all of my own billing. This saved me quite a bit of money and forced me to stay on top of any outstanding balances. Because one third to one half of my practice consists of patients paying through insurance, the end of each month tends to be the busiest time, when I submit health insurance claim forms to various insurance companies. These standard billing forms, now referred to as CMS-1500 forms (previously referred to as HCFA-1500 forms), can be found online at www.cms.hhs.gov/forms or purchased from many major office supply stores. Completing these forms and submitting them is not difficult, but it helps enormously to have a CMS/HCFA computer program, as the same information is required for each patient's submission from month to month. Many insurance companies also have online billing submission options, which may further simplify your billing procedures. To avoid feeling overwhelmed at the end of the month, you may want to consider collecting your fee from patients on a weekly basis. I keep track of individual balances and my business expenses by using a computer program (such as QuickBooks), which I reconcile with my bank statements on a monthly basis. You may be tempted to try and do everything; but it is wise to draw the line when it comes to filing taxes. I hired a wonderful accountant who was knowledgeable about my work because he had worked with other psychologists. He was able to answer most of my questions and expertly prepare my yearly tax returns.

The issue of electronic billing begets a discussion about the Health Insurance Portability and Accountability Act (HIPAA), which came into effect across the United States in April 2003. HIPAA is designed to protect patient confidentiality and promote patient rights. In its most simplistic form, to be compliant with this legislation, psychologists now have to provide a HIPAA notice form to all patients, explaining confidentiality, access to records, and privacy issues. Many therapists have had to modify their billing practices, filing systems, and record-keeping security measures, in accordance with these new standards. It is important to be knowledgeable about the intricacies of HIPAA and the individual state-specific laws in your area, as each private practitioner is responsible for implementing these new guidelines. A more thorough description and explanation of the many aspects of HIPAA (including descriptions of legally accurate release of information forms, complete lists of confidentiality requirements, and specific disclaimer clauses for electronic billing) can be found at www.APApractice.org.

Trying to be my own *real estate agent* ended up being quite rewarding. It is worthwhile to invest some time in investigating neighborhoods, assessing transportation issues (how easy is it to access your office?), and surveying the type of clientele with the easiest access to your intended location (downtown vs. suburbs vs. rural). I was quite careful about where I wanted my office located. I realized that most psychologists in Boston were not actually working from offices in the heart of downtown. Despite there being hundreds of thousands of people working in downtown Boston on a daily basis, it amazed me how few therapists there were. So the decision to set up my private practice downtown became clear from a business perspective, as well as from a lifestyle perspective because the bonus was that my office was just a short walk from my home.

After 2 years of subletting office space and building up my practice, I decided to go out on my own. This was both exciting and terrifying. It was expensive and risky because I was spending only half of my week doing private practice and the other half working part-time at a large teaching hospital. I was so eager to have my own space that I decided the risk was worthwhile. I rented premises in the same building in which I had subleased, and began shopping for furniture. In hopes of trying to offset the cost of my new space, I spread the word that I had office space to sublet to other therapists. Once my office was set up, I realized that I began to take the role of *cleaning lady* seriously. I was focused on keeping my office looking good. Every used tissue or half-empty coffee cup needed to find its way into the trash, and I was the one to do it. Never before had I been so aware of dirty shoes, sweaty feet, and wet jackets, but it's all in the name of business.

The varying roles that a psychologist plays are superimposed onto the clinical and administrative duties that are required for a successful practice. Table 7.1 describes the basic responsibilities that a professional psychologist would perform on a regular basis.

Advantages and Disadvantages

If you dream of becoming independently wealthy, it is important to note that although a six-figure income is not the norm, it is not impossible either. Doing a few calculations revealed to me that even a half-time practice could become lucrative (20 patients per week, at $100/ hour for 48 weeks a year = $96,000). But before you get too excited about that calculation, remember that you may not be getting your full fee for all of your patients. This is especially the case if you are trying to build a practice, decide to accept insurance, or have a sliding scale. In addition, you do have to pay rent, malpractice insurance, licensing fees, professional membership dues, and taxes.

Graduate students are known for keeping long hours. Trying to balance coursework, casework, and having a life can be cumbersome. Many new psychologists are so eager to see patients that they tend to agree to see patients at all hours of the day. Although it is wonderful

Table 7.1 Common Work Duties for Clinical Psychologists in Private Practice

Clinical Duties

Providing treatment for patients

Reading articles in clinical practice area to maintain a solid educational base

Staying current with research on psychotropic medications related to patient population

Receiving clinical supervision from senior clinician or in peer group meetings

Attending local meetings to stay connected to the psychology and medical communities

Administrative Duties

Scheduling patients and informing patients of office policies and procedures (including HIPAA)

Writing progress notes following sessions

Documenting payment collected and monitoring patient's balance due

Submitting bills to insurance companies in a timely manner

Networking; meeting potential referral sources

Becoming familiar with insurance company policies

Paying business-related bills (rent, phone, etc.)

Optional Duties

Providing clinical supervision

Presenting at local, regional, and national conferences

Networking with colleagues

---

to be so flexible, take caution. It may be hazardous to you and your patients to schedule too many sessions per day. In addition, your endless flexibility may lead you to burn out very quickly. The work of a psychologist cannot be easily translated into an economic equation; where the more widgets you can produce, the more money you make.

Finding a balance is a very important element to a good practice. You may worry that patients only want to be seen before or after their workday; however, generally this is not true. Granted, there are people who truly do not have any flexibility in their schedule, but generally speaking I have had no trouble filling my midmorning and afternoon times. As soon as I put structure around my days (the hours during which I would see patients and how many patients per day), I found that I could fill all my available time slots. I am sure that the convenience of my downtown office helped tremendously because many patients could inconspicuously leave work for an hour without much disruption to their schedules.

Achieving professional balance is very personal. I tend to thrive on seeing patients back-to-back without long breaks; however, this prevents me from seeing more than seven patients per day. My brain goes a little mushy beyond seven patients. I am sure that if I took longer than 10-minute breaks between patients, I may be able to see more patients per day — but frankly I have found my balance and am satisfied with my productivity. You may come to realize that if you start seeing patients earlier in the day, you may prefer to end work a little on the early side as well. Conversely, if you start late in the day, it would likely work to your advantage to see patients into the evening hours. Some of my colleagues do not mind starting early and ending late because they take off a few hours in between to go to the gym or go for lunch. Instead of listing all the permutations of what a daily schedule could look like, I encourage you to examine what feels right for you. It is important to fill your life with more than just work, and carving out time for yourself is crucial. For example, taking vacation time, even if that means a loss of income while you are away (as you cannot bill patients if you are not seeing them), is extremely important in terms of taking care of yourself.

An advantage of private practice is that you can select what types of patients you would like to see. You have much more input over patient selection than if you were working in a large clinic- or hospital-based practice. This flexibility allows for specialization or, conversely, gives you the freedom to create a diverse practice with patients varying diagnostically, socioeconomically, and racially.

Advice for Students

Many major metropolitan cities in the United States are already "saturated" with professional psychologists. So choosing a city in which to set up a practice should not be based exclusively on supply and demand. It is important to examine the role of geography in making decisions about where to practice.

I initially considered living in a city that popped up on my "less-desirable list," but then realized how ridiculous this actually was. I made sure to pick a city that I was going to *like* living in, regardless of the therapist-per-capita statistics. My logic behind this was that all of the cities with saturated markets were also likely to be cities to which many different types of people gravitated. The assumption was that the more people there were, the more therapists they would need. I concluded that the market would handle this professional overpopulation without my needing to intervene. All I could do was to continue to pursue something about which I felt passionate.

As you leave graduate school, internship, or a postdoctoral fellowship and contemplate a move, one of your top concerns should be to choose a place to live, a place where you think you will be happy. Moving to a city that you despise for a fantastic job might make perfect business sense, but in this field, unless you are satisfied with your own life, it becomes very difficult to help patients reach contentment and make important choices in their lives.

If there wasn't room for another psychologist in this country, I was determined to find out the hard way. Although you may toy with the idea of using your years in graduate school and hundreds of hours of clinical training to enter the business world (after all, they really do pay a decent salary!), I chose to give myself a year to try and establish a private practice. With all of the doubt instilled in me by most of the psychologists I came into contact with up until that point, this felt safer than committing to private practice for life. I reasoned that if it did not work out after a year, then I would entertain other avenues.

I believe that we each need to go after our dreams. Professionally speaking, I think that you need to try things, and when they feel right, you need to grab them. I knew that being a therapist was right for me, I felt passionate about it, and loved the challenges and rewards of working with patients. Despite the guarantee of a steady and comfortable salary offered in other settings, I was determined to figure out a way to make my dream of having my own private practice really happen.

Final Checklist

I have listed below many of the large and small tasks involved in establishing a private practice. My hope is that this checklist will act as a reference guide and a reminder that building a practice is both challenging and exciting.

- Decide where you want to live. Private practices are not portable!
  - Obtain a license to practice in the appropriate state.
- Get a phone number with voicemail.
- Print business cards.
- Set up meetings with referral sources and send out letters.
- Investigate different locations for your office:
  - Decide if you want to sublet space or rent your own office.
  - If you do rent your own space, you will need to obtain property/liability insurance.
- Understand the business side of setting up a practice:
  - Legal aspects
    - Consider sole practitioner versus limited partnership versus corporation.
    - Obtain malpractice insurance.
    - Understand HIPAA regulations and print necessary forms.

  – Financial aspects
    • Open a separate business account.
    • Set your fee.
  – Accounting aspects
    • Hire a good accountant for advice.
    • Use the accountant to prepare your annual income taxes.
• Familiarize yourself with billing issues:
  – Obtain billing software and necessary forms.
  – Decide how you will keep track of your income and your expenses.
• Set lifestyle priorities:
  – Choose your hours and set a limit on the number of patients seen daily.

No One Ever Said It Was Going to Be Easy

I hope that at the very least I have provided you with an alternative view of the challenges and rewards of private practice. My practice is incredibly fulfilling to me and I now know that it was the right choice. Reflecting on the discouraging advice I was given during graduate school, I realize how much harder this made me work. There are still hurdles that lie ahead; new mandatory HIPAA guidelines, the possibility of relocating to a new city, the transitioning world of health care. Although at times these potential changes worry me, I need only reflect on the wonderful practice that I have had the opportunity to create, the lives that I have touched, the people that I helped and cared for over the last 5 years, and the fullness of possibilities that lie ahead. If you are determined to create a private practice, if this is what you dream of professionally, I challenge you to join me in this adventure.

References

CMS Forms (2004, April). Retrieved on April 28, 2004 from www.cms.hhs.gov/forms.
HIPAA for Psychologists (n.d). Retrieved on April 28, 2004 from www.APApractice.org.

8

Group Practice: Adapting Private Practice to the New Marketplace

COREY J. HABBEN

As I set out to find my first job as a new clinical psychologist, I spent a good deal of time thinking about what kind of practice setting would be best for me to launch my career. I probably looked at every setting you can think of, and probably a few you have not considered. I looked at everything from a professional think tank to university jobs to a prison for sexual offenders to a VA hospital. You name it, I probably donned a dark suit and interviewed for it during my final days as a predoctoral intern. As it turned out, my first job was with a group psychiatric/psychological practice. I worked there for 4 years and, as I came to realize, it ended up being the best place for me as a new psychologist to start a career. Throughout this chapter, I hope to outline for you why a group practice may be the best place for a new practicing psychologist. If you are considering this as part of your professional future, then there are some issues you should consider prior to getting started.

The intent of this chapter is not to direct you toward starting or building your own group practice; the APA Practice Directorate's *Building a Group Practice: Creating a Shared Vision for Success*, a component of the "Practitioner's Toolbox Series," is a good resource (1995) if that is what you seek; also see Budman and Steenbarger (1997). Similarly, I am electing *not* to share with you wearisome discussions using arcane jargon about superfluous topics such as horizontal versus vertical integration, *pro forma* income statements, or limited liability companies versus Subchapter S corporations. My experience as a new psychologist is that we prefer hard facts and basic direction rather than "seminar-speak." Rather than inundate you with business jargon, it is my intent to help you answer for yourself two basic questions: should I join a group practice and, if I do, what will it be like? To answer these two questions, you must first consider a series of smaller questions.

Why Join a Group Practice?

Just in case you were wondering, a group practice is exactly what it sounds like: a group of practitioners who share resources to provide services under the same organization. *How* these resources are shared, *how many* and *what type* of providers make up the organization, and *what kind* of services are three major factors that can lead to variability among different group practices. For example, there are small group practices of a few psychologists, or larger multidisciplinary group practices with a variety of clinicians such as psychiatrists, psychologists, social workers, and master's-level counselors. There are generalist group practices and specialty group practices. Nevertheless, group practitioners differ from solo or independent practitioners primarily in that solo practitioners use their own resources to provide services by themselves.

When I was in college and graduate school during the 1990s and managed care became the driving force that it did, I regularly heard the same refrain from psychologists that "the days of starting your own independent practice are over." According to many senior psychologists, it was relatively easy to graduate with a doctorate in psychology and "hang a shingle" (as it is so often said), develop a nice practice, and do quite well. To say that the days of solo practice are over is a bit short-sighted; there are many parts of the country, particularly in rural areas, that are in such need for licensed quality psychologists that a moderately industrious new psychologist could probably make short work of setting up a successful practice. Unfortunately, for whatever reason, today's new psychologist tends to want to live in or near a populous city and appears to be less willing to move to smaller communities with names like Ricketts, Iowa or Bovill, Idaho. It is probably more accurate to say "the days of setting up a private practice on Michigan Avenue in Chicago or on Central Park West in Manhattan are over ... for now, at least." Whatever the reality is, too many factors have made solo private practice a challenge that many new psychologists do not want to (or, quite simply, cannot) take on at the beginning of a career. This does not mean that you cannot work in a private practice setting. Enter, group practice.

The *sine qua non* reason for joining a group practice is that you want to work in a private practice setting. You want to be able to provide your services, whether psychotherapy or otherwise, in the private sector and most likely with an outpatient population. You prefer a smaller, more independent office setting to a larger institutional, government, agency, or organizational setting. If these are all true, then there are several specific advantages to joining a group practice as a new psychologist.

Advantages to Joining a Group Practice

Shared Risk and Investment versus Solo Risk and Investment

Unless you are fortunate enough to begin your career with a good deal of capital to invest, the prospect of starting a new practice by yourself in today's marketplace can be risky and very labor-intensive. The majority of new psychologists begin their career without an income, a license, an office, or referral sources. Starting a new practice, at least from a business perspective, can be compared to starting a new restaurant; there are a lot of upfront costs, you may have to tolerate periods of time with no income while you work very hard to build a business, and there is always the possibility that you can lose a good deal of money. When you join a group practice, you share the risk, expense, and work. Furthermore, you may often be joining a practice that is already established with an existing referral base, visibility in the community, support staff, and office. You do not have to do the hard work of building a new practice because someone has already done it for you.

Building Your Practice Management Skills

There is a good chance that you would like to open up your own practice later in your career. Working in a group practice provides you with direct exposure and experience with the day-to-day rigors of managing a practice. If you want to work in a private practice setting, you need to learn how to establish and run a business, how to manage staff and office expenses, how to deal with third-party payers, how to generate referrals, and many other realities of running a practice. Joining a group practice affords you the opportunity to gain experience and grow in these areas while somebody else is running the business. Psychology graduate school has trained us to be psychologists, but not necessarily to be experts in business. Working in a group practice can provide you with the training and knowledge of running a business that you probably never learned in graduate school. Additionally, there is more security in working with a practice that is already established that you would not have in a practice that you would try to build yourself.

Working alongside Other Colleagues and Professionals

One major complaint that you will often hear from solo or independent practitioners is the feeling of isolation that goes with working alone in a private practice. This reality can be felt in many ways. What does a solo practitioner do when he or she wants to consult about a case, process through a difficult session, or just converse? In a group practice, you have peers right down the hall from your office. What does a solo practitioner do when a referral is necessary? In many group practices, you can refer your patient to a psychiatrist or another professional who works in the same office. You can also easily consult with this other professional face-to-face and maintain records in the same chart while setting up appointments at the same location. What does a solo practitioner do when referrals for new patients are needed? A solo practitioner will always need to get his or her referrals from an outside source; a group practitioner can get a steady stream of referrals from other practitioners in the same office. There are many advantages to having other professionals in the office, both large and small.

The Financial Advantages: Assumptions versus Realities

Another common assumption is that a solo practitioner earns more per year because he or she keeps all of the money generated by the practice. While it is true that an independent practitioner does "keep" all of the generated revenue, he or she also has to pay *all* of the expenses. Whereas a group practice may share the cost of expenses (such as office space, office staff, utilities, computers and software, and countless other expenses that arise), a solo practitioner has no help in shouldering the load of these expenses. Some solo practitioners manage this by keeping overhead costs at a minimum; they may serve as their own receptionist, biller, business manager, and carpet sweeper. When you consider solo versus group practice, you eventually have to ask yourself whether you want to hand over a sizable portion of your revenue to cover expenses that are paid solely by you, whether you want to minimize these expenses somewhat and add more work and headaches to your already busy schedule, or whether you want to hand over a sizable portion of your revenue to others and let them take care of the headaches so you can focus your energy on being a clinician.

If my shamelessly skewed example did not illustrate clearly, I gladly handed over a portion of my revenue to a group practice. Knowing that somebody else was marketing, scheduling, answering phone calls, billing and receiving payments, keeping managed care contracts current, filing charts, buying computers and copying machines and scotch tape and envelopes, sending and receiving faxes, vacuuming (you get the picture) ... knowing that I did not have to do any of this on the weekend was reason enough for me. When you compare the money an independent practitioner pays for expenses and the money a group practitioner pays to the practice, the difference is often not as great as you would assume (the possible exception would be psychologists who start up a practice in their home and then have their spouse do all the busy work and write *everything* off as a business expense, but that is a whole different chapter).

Group Practice Does Actually Allow for "Independent" Practice

Another common assumption about group practice is that you are not able to practice independently as you would in a solo practice. The fact is that a group practice setting still allows you to act more independently than most practice settings. There is usually much more flexibility in the hours or days that you work that you would never see with a government, agency, or institutional job. Depending on the needs of the practice, you can usually determine which types of patients you see. You are usually seen as an individual psychologist rather than a staff member. As long as you are seeing as many patients as the practice deems necessary, you can usually see as many patients as you are able if you wish to increase your income; a group practice is directly invested in your generating more revenue. As such, there are no absolute ceilings to income as you would find in many other psychology positions.

Disadvantages to a Career in a Group Practice

A group practice provides a new psychologist a nice balance of private practice perks (such as more flexibility and greater earning potential) and some protection from the downside of solo practice (such as increased financial risk and isolation). Still, as with any job, there are disadvantages to working in a group practice. One disadvantage can be the reality that you are working for a business and yet you often do not have control over many elements *of* the business. For example, you cannot independently change the fees, hire new office staff, or determine how many other providers work with you in the practice. Furthermore, you are usually removed from the process of billing and payment collection and you mostly have to trust that the process is being handled ethically and accurately. While some practices will be quite receptive to the input of clinicians, others may be less receptive and ultimately all business decisions are up to the individual who owns the practice. While this lack of control is even more standard in other types of psychology positions, it can sometimes be a source of frustration in an environment in which your income is often directly tied to your individual performance. This can lead to the same sort of frustration that can come from renting a residence; investing yourself into something that you ultimately do not own.

Another disadvantage of a group practice is more a common disadvantage to *any* private practice setting. Unlike many other psychologist positions, you are never certain what your income is going to be for a given year, month, or pay period. Because your income is usually tied to whatever payments are received by patients and third-party payers, your payments can often fluctuate from paycheck to paycheck. Similarly, any extended period of absence (such as vacation time) is often followed by a noticeable drop in pay. A common private practice axiom is that "cash follows charges." In other words, a month of seeing numerous patients will usually be followed by a spike in pay a month or two later; conversely, a 1 or 2 week period of seeing no patients will usually be followed by a significant drop in pay. The unpredictability and variability in pay can become quite wearying over time.

A final disadvantage to a group practice setting is the relative invisibility of a local practice in the overall psychological community. A good group practice may be somewhat well known in a local community, but is all but unknown anywhere else. As you develop in your career as a psychologist, future potential employers will be reviewing your professional experience as it is listed on your curriculum vitae. A psychologist from another region or state will often instantly recognize a university, major hospital, even a community mental health

Table 8.1 Advantages and Disadvantages of Joining a Group Practice

Advantages

- You share the risk, investment, and work; rather than assume it all by yourself
- You can build practice management skills for your own future practice
- You work among other professionals and avoid professional isolation
- You have greater ease of referrals (both to and from you) and continuity of care
- You do not have to worry about directly managing and paying for overhead costs
- Group practices with multiple providers often provide flexibility to practice more independently

Disadvantages

- You have less control over practice decisions (e.g., fees, staff, providers)
- Your income varies and is unpredictable (also true with independent practice)
- Group practices have little name recognition outside the community

center. Unless they are from your area or they know someone associated with your group practice, they will have very little idea what kind of setting your group practice was. An esteemed university can elicit instant credibility; even the best group practices cannot provide the same sort of professional "respect by association." See Table 8.1 for a brief overview of the advantages and disadvantages involved in starting your career with a group practice.

Starting a Career in Group (or Private) Practice

How Do I Join a Group Practice?

As a new psychologist, you will usually gain a great deal of experience in the art of looking for employment. The path to finding a position with a group practice is, in some ways, no different from the path to finding a position in any other practice setting. Some group practices will post a position in national publications (e.g., *APA Monitor*); you will particularly see this with practices in more isolated or rural areas, which have a harder time recruiting new psychologists out of their urban wonderlands. As many group practices prefer to hire someone local, they will advertise in regional publications, such as a state psychological association newsletter or Web site.

However, perhaps the best-kept secret is the number of group practice jobs available that are never advertised. There are many group practices that are victims of their own success; they have more patients this year than they did a year ago, and twice as many as a few years ago, and every provider seems to be booked up and new appointments are being scheduled a month or two in advance. There are many group practice owners who would love to bring on another provider and yet do not have the time to search for a new psychologist. As a result, many new positions with a group practice are found through informal channels. Someone with a group practice calls a colleague and asks if they know of anyone looking to join a practice in a certain area, or a curriculum vitae crosses the right desk at the right time. Keep in mind that a group practice is not as limited by funding or budgets or available "slots" like many employers of psychologists are; they are only limited by their need for another provider. If it is cost-effective (or better yet, profitable), then there is always room for another provider.

Because of this, it is important to do two things. First, you should let anyone and everyone you know that you are looking to join a practice and to pass the word. You would probably be surprised to discover how many psychologists join a practice because an informal conversation turned into a phone call, which turned into an interview and eventually a new job. If you are a new psychologist, you have probably heard a hundred times the importance of networking. Let this be time number 101: the more networking you have done, the greater your chances are that one of your acquaintances can pass your name to a potential employer. I spent the last 6 months of my internship applying for just about every position in psychology you could imagine. As it turned out, I joined a group practice because my training director heard about a group practice looking for a new psychologist and passed on my name. Incidentally, I learned about this as I was boxing up my office to leave on the last day of my internship. The 6 months of busting my hump sending out vitas and interviewing turned out nothing of value (finding a good job as a new psychologist without a license is a very tough sell), and yet I ended up with a wonderful group practice near my favorite city. All of this happened because I networked and the right person passed my name on to a group practice looking for a new psychologist.

The second thing to do, in addition to the tried-and-somewhat-true method of scanning position announcements in various psychology publications, is to identify any and all group practices within a 60-mile radius of where you would like to live and send them your vitae and letter of introduction. Tell them that you are available and would love to join their practice if they are looking to add a psychologist. Sell yourself as someone who could make quality of care, revenue, and life in general better for them by hiring you. Let them know that you would like to meet with them to discuss this further. You may send 20 of these letters out and 19 may end up in the trash, but one of your vitas may stay on someone's desk and resurface when opportunity and necessity come together.

How Do I Earn My Income?

Just as there are many different types of group practices (e.g., small vs. large, psychological vs. multidisciplinary, generalist vs. specialty), there are also several different ways in which a group practice determines how you are compensated. The common denominator is that you are expected to generate a certain amount of revenue and the practice keeps a portion of your revenue to pay expenses while paying you the remainder. The variability among practices arises primarily from the different ways to determine how much revenue you are expected to generate, how the practice keeps a portion of your revenue, and how you are paid. Although there may be other factors that can make group practices differ, you will be faced with some important decisions as a new psychologist based on how the group practice is structured. As such, you will need to be familiar with some of the more common differences in structure.

Compensation and Percentage versus Fixed Income

A common approach to compensating a psychologist member of a group practice is to pay the psychologist a percentage of whatever revenue he or she generates while the practice "keeps" the remaining percentage. Income is directly tied to whatever the provider is paid by patients and third-party payers (note: not what is billed, but what is received). For example, imagine that a new female psychologist joins a group practice that charges $120 for an hour of therapy. If she sees an average of 25 patients per week for 50 weeks (our hypothetical psychologist deserves a couple weeks vacation), she will have billed (or, charged her patients) $150,000 in 1 year. Unless she works in a practice that only sees patients who pay 100% out-of-pocket and on time every week, her practice will not receive $150,000. Insurance company write-offs, managed care contracts, late payments, and other variables will make that number smaller. Let's assume that her practice does pretty well and collects 80% of what it charges. In this case, our new psychologist's practice will receive 80% of what she billed, or $120,000. From this, the practice keeps a percentage and pays the psychologist the remainder. In our example, our fellow new psychologist works at a practice with a 65%/35% split (i.e., she keeps 65% and the practice is "paid" 35%). She is ultimately paid $78,000 for that year. Using the same numbers, she would have made $62,400 for seeing 20 patients per week or $93,600 for seeing 30 patients per week (Table 8.2).

Table 8.2 Three Approaches to Compensation of a Group Practice Psychologist[a]

	20 Patients/Week	25 Patients/Week	30 Patients/Week
Practice split[b]	$62,400/year	$78,000/year	$93,600/year
Fixed monthly charge[c]	$54,000/year	$78,000/year	$102,000/year
Fixed salary[d]	$78,000/year	$78,000/year	$78,000/year

[a] See text for further illustration of these examples. All examples are based on a group practice psychologist who (1) charges $120/hour for therapy, (2) works 50 out of 52 weeks per year, (3) after third-party (e.g., managed care, private insurance) write-offs receives collections of 80% of original charges per year, and (4) consistently sees either 20, 25, or 30 patients per week.
[b] For this example, the practice receives 35% of all payments and the provider retains 65%.
[c] For this example, the practice charges the psychologist a fixed fee of $3,500/month.
[d] For this example, the psychologist receives a fixed annual salary of $78,000/year.

Another approach is for the group practice to "charge" the provider a fixed amount each month like a landlord charges rent. The psychologist is expected to pay this amount and is allowed to keep any income that is received in excess of the fixed amount. In the previous example in which our new psychologist was seeing 25 patients per week at a group practice, let's assume that the practice expected her to pay $3,500 per month to cover all of the practice expenses and she could keep whatever she made beyond that amount. Remember that she received a $120,000 payment that year. At $3,500 per month, she needed to pay $42,000 total in a year to the practice. This left her with a yearly income of $78,000. However, she would make $54,000 for seeing 20 patients per week or $102,000 for seeing 30 patients per week. As you compare this approach to the previous "fixed percentage" example, you can see that this approach was the better option as she saw more patients per week, and definitely the poorer option as she saw fewer patients per week (Table 8.2).

A third approach is for the practice to pay the new psychologist a fixed salary much like you would see with a hospital, community mental health center, or university counseling center. The psychologist would be working as an employee of a group practice and would be expected to provide services for a certain number of hours per week. The salary would be paid whether she saw 35 people in a week or only 5. Let's assume that a hypothetical practice offered to pay our hypothetical new psychologist $78,000 for a year of work. She would make $78,000 whether she saw 20 patients per week or 30 patients per week. Some practices will offer incentives to encourage providers to generate more revenue, such as providing bonuses if certain benchmarks are exceeded. This is also done to discourage the psychologist from taking the salary and seeing as few patients as possible (Table 8.2). Please note: The numbers provided in the preceding hypothetical examples are not necessarily representative of standard charges or incomes for group practices. They were provided more as a means of illustration.

There are certainly other approaches to compensating a psychologist in a group practice, as well as variations on the three preceding examples. For example, one group practice may offer an increased percentage for the psychologist once a certain revenue target is met (e.g., the percentage changes from 65%/35% to 70%/30% once the provider generates $100,000 in revenue). Some practices may tie the performance of the whole practice into income, almost like a profit-sharing program. Some practices may have *variable* required charges to the practice based on the practice expenses (e.g., instead of charging the psychologist $3,500 per month, the charge changes each month based on operating expenses). Whatever the case, anytime you are considering a job with a group practice you should get a good sense of how the psychologist is compensated, what it bills patients, what percentage the practice normally receives as payment, and how many patients you will (or can) be expected to see per week. (Note: It is also a good idea to get this in writing.) From there, you should take some time to crunch numbers and estimate what you should expect to make in a given year. It is also a good idea to determine the practice's formula for compensation and then figure out how much you would expect to make if you saw 10, 15, 20, 25, 30, and 35 patients per week. From there, you can decide what sort of arrangement would be most advantageous or comfortable for you and for the practice.

One common question posed by new psychologists considering joining a new group practice is: "What is a normal percentage split for a group practice? 60%/40%? 70%30%?" Unfortunately, it does not appear that much, if any, empirical data are collected regarding common or fair splits for today's group practices. The easy answer is that the percentage split is whatever the market will bear in that practice's location. This is not a very good answer, however, because some group practices offer very fair and competitive splits whereas other practices will all but take advantage of new psychologists naiveté and rob them blind. In my experience of talking with and listening to new psychologists for the last 5 years, it appears that 65% seems to be a close estimate of a mean for what many psychologists are "keeping" in their respective group practices. This is in no way scientific nor is it by any means the standard; you will always find someone in another practice with a higher percentage and a lower percentage. Nevertheless, it should be considered that any split in the 50 to 60% range should definitely be reconsidered, and any split in the 70% range or higher can be considered quite fair and competitive in today's marketplace. A split somewhere in the 60 to 70% range tends to be the most common. Ultimately, you need to make the decision of what is fair.

Employee versus Independent Contractor

A tax attorney could provide you with detailed legal distinction between employee status and independent contractor status. As a new psychologist considering employment with a group practice, you will want to know the basic and surface-level differences between the two and understand how this may have an impact on you. The primary thing to consider is that an employee of a group practice has withholdings such as federal and state taxes, social security, insurance, and retirement deducted from his or her pay. The employer often pays for some benefits. At year's end, a group practice employee receives a summary of income and withholdings as a W-2 form. An independent contractor, on the other hand, is responsible for paying all taxes and benefits and receives a summary of income each year as a 1099 form. This often means that the independent contractor pays taxes on a quarterly basis. It is up to this individual to be sure and set aside a portion of each check to cover this tax bill.

If you are considering a position as an employee, you want to consider the "total compensation." People tend to focus on the salary and pay less attention to the benefits. In considering total compensation, you want to estimate the total value of the position when you consider base salary, medical insurance, life insurance, disability insurance, malpractice insurance, retirement (and whether or not the employer matches contributions), vacation, and any other benefits. In other words, take the projected salary and *add* the value of the benefits to determine the total value. If you are considering an independent contractor position, you will want to consider what your income will be and then deduct all of the previously mentioned benefits. Remember that you will be paying for your own insurance, vacation, retirement, and other expenses. To put it more simply, take the projected salary and *subtract* the value of the benefits to determine the total value.

This leads to a very important point. Regardless of what kind of practice you ultimately join, any new psychologist should definitely find a good accountant. You will need someone to complete your taxes that will only become more complicated as you become more involved in practice. Additionally, you will want to consult with your accountant whenever you are considering a new position to get an informed perspective of the tax and income implications. Talk to a veteran psychologist whom you trust and ask for a referral for a good accountant. Of all of the professional expenses I have, I consider the money I pay to my accountant each year to be some of the best money I spend.

Contracts

In addition to a good accountant, it is also a good idea to find a good attorney. If you are asked to join a group practice, whether as an employee or independent contractor, you will most often be required to sign a contract. It is ideal to be able to review this contract with an attorney, particularly one familiar with group practice contracts, to be sure that there are no potentially harmful clauses. Every contract is different, although there tend to be standard clauses in group practice contracts.

As you consider the contract, pay particular attention to certain terms. For example, what is the length of the contract? Stability is nice, but it is usually best not to lock yourself into a contract that goes beyond 2 years unless you are absolutely certain you will want to stay for that long. You can always negotiate a new contract at the end of 2 years. Similarly, what kind of termination clause does the contract include? Are you allowed to terminate prior to the end of the contract? If so, how much notice is required? Can your employer terminate you? If so, how much notice is specified? Because of abandonment, you will certainly never want to terminate a contract with only a 2-week notice, although having to provide a 6-month advance notice of termination can all but lock you in to a contract without any "out."

What are your duties and responsibilities and how are they defined? Is it specified how many patient contact hours are required? Is your compensation agreement clearly specified? Is there a "no-compete" clause? If so, is it enforceable in your state and is it reasonable? Are you restricted from any other work outside of the practice? No-compete clauses are fairly standard, although they should not be so unreasonable as to make it practically impossible to work anywhere within a 30-mile radius for a long period of time. A 2-year no-compete clause of up to a 5-mile radius is common, although this can be affected by availability of services, population of the surrounding market, and other factors.

As you can see, there are many factors in a contract that would require much more detail and consideration than this chapter could begin to review. If you cannot consult an attorney on a potential contract, at least run the details by an experienced and respected clinician who can advise you about what to keep and what to negotiate. Remember that when a contract is proposed to you, it does not mean that you have the choice of signing or not signing. Do not forget your option to offer and negotiate certain clauses. This includes not only clauses such as no-compete clauses or terms such as contract length, but also compensation and benefits. One of the most frustrating reasons that new psychologists do not earn what they deserve to earn is that new psychologists often do not try to *negotiate* what they earn. Many employers are fairly willing and able to negotiate with you, particularly if you are wanted for the position. Do not be afraid to negotiate certain issues; as long as your requests are reasonable and respectful, the worst you will hear is "no." It need not determine whether or not you get the job.

What Is a Typical Day?

There is enough variability among group practices that there is probably no standard for a "typical day." However, if you are working as a clinical psychologist in a group practice, then you will most likely spend the overwhelming majority of your time providing direct services (whether it is therapy, assessment, or some other service). A much smaller portion of your time will be dedicated to administrative tasks, such as chart work, completing paperwork for third-party payers, returning phone calls, meetings, or consulting with other clinicians. Some practices may include time for case conference meetings or guest speakers. It is not uncommon for a psychologist in a group practice to devote 75% of available time to direct service provision and the remaining 25% to other administrative tasks.

Many practices will provide you with the opportunity to have a flexible schedule. Although some practices may require you to work a routine schedule, many practices allow you to schedule patients at varying hours. In an effort to provide a wider range of hours and to break up monotony, I kept a schedule that would include a 9 A.M. to 5 P.M. day, and 10 A.M. to 6 P.M. day, a 1 P.M. to 9 P.M. day, and so on. I also had the flexibility, if I so chose, to add some hours on certain days to compensate for a day I may have taken off for a baseball game or an extended weekend. During the summer months, I would occasionally schedule three patients in the morning, take the afternoon off to go biking in nice weather, and return to see four patients in the evening. Because I was not bound to a fixed schedule, I was able to elect to do this. In this setting, you are not bound by a schedule; you are primarily driven by the need to see a certain number of patients.

This leads me to one final point about your schedule. Because of the flexibility a practice setting can provide, it is often up to you to decide how many patients you see and on what schedule. Certainly, most practices have a minimum number of direct service hours you will need to meet; likewise, your maximum number of patients will be limited by the number of patients available to you. Nevertheless, you should expect to face the question: "How many patients will I see per week? And, how many will I see per day?" The answer to these questions will vary from person to person, but you should always assess your primary values as you ponder these questions. Many psychologists wish to balance professional and personal life, in which case you will need to have a fixed limit of patients you plan to see per day and week. To the same extent, some psychologists place a primary value on production and income, in which case it would be more necessary to see as many patients as possible within reasonable limits. Taking this into consideration, just remember, if you want to work in a group practice and still maintain a minimal-stress lifestyle, do not complain that you are making less money. If you instead plan to see as many patients as you can in a week to maximize income, do not complain that you have no life or any time for anything beyond work. Make your decision based on your values and accept the consequences. Finally, remember to pace yourself. Maintaining a "nine patients a day with one 30-minute lunch break" schedule may seem easy the first few years, but makes you vulnerable to early burnout as your career develops. Your career should be viewed as a marathon, not a sprint.

Final Tips and Comments

Perhaps the simplest way to express the advantages and disadvantages of working with a group practice is to say, "The good news is that it isn't your practice; the bad news is that it isn't your practice." Nevertheless, a group practice can provide a new psychologist with an excellent start of a career in clinical practice. Do not be afraid to contact a local group practice and forward your vitae with a letter of introduction expressing your interest and availability. Talk with other members of a potential group practice to get their input about the practice environment. Do not be afraid to negotiate if and when you are offered a position. If you do not have an accountant, be sure that you have one shortly after you join a practice. Be diligent with keeping track of what you bill and what payments you receive because human and computer errors can affect your income. If you have any interest in working with children, couples, or families, then you will have a significant advantage in today's current environment. Many practices see a great number of children and families and yet many psychologists still prefer to focus on adult individuals. Finally, remember that you may not have direct control in a group practice but you do have influence. For example, if you feel a sense of professional stagnation, offer to set up a monthly case conference or grand rounds with the rest of the clinical staff.

As with any job in psychology, much of your success and satisfaction depends on what *you* do. An ideal group practice offers enough flexibility and security that you have enough freedom with "what you do" to continue to grow beyond your graduate training; both as a new psychologist and as a professional.

References

American Psychological Association Practice Directorate. (1995). *Building a group practice: Creating a shared vision for success.* Washington, D.C.: American Psychological Association.

Budman, S. H., & Steenbarger, B. N. (1997). *The essential guide to group practice in mental health: Clinical, legal, and financial fundamentals.* New York: Guilford Press.

Suggested Web Sites

American Psychological Association Practice Directorate: www.apa.org/practice.
Division 42 Online—Psychologists in Independent Practice: www.division42.org.

9

Community Mental Health Centers: Opportunities for Supervising Empirically Validated Treatment Protocols

JULIANNE M. SMITH-BOYDSTON

Finding New Avenues in Traditional Settings

When I began exploring jobs or postdoctoral opportunities during my internship year, I was amazed at the range of possibilities available to me. This came as quite a shock, after becoming accustomed to structured courses and practica, to hear advisors tell me that I could actually choose a career route that suited my interests! My first searches concentrated on structured postdocs with a mix of research and clinical work. I never even imagined working at a community mental health center (CMHC), because they had seemed prohibited by graduate and internship faculty as career options, even though I had worked at a CMHC for my advanced practicum training. But as I examined a wider range of possibilities close to favored geographic areas, I found a position in a CMHC that gave me the blend of experiences that I wanted. It gave me the flexibility to mix clinical work, supervision of staff and students, and program evaluation. In this chapter, I will outline aspects that make CMHCs a very unique professional experience for professionals in the field.

Since the beginning of my employment, I have learned that CMHCs are rich with history regarding services to adults, children, and families. They were originally established across the United States to treat community members in the least restrictive environment and without a constraint in ability to pay. Federal mandates to the CMHCs since the 1960s show the importance of community-based services for those clients who would have formerly been placed in state hospitals. These centers traditionally work at an ecological level, examining the relationship between the individual and environment and intervening at a systems level. A variety of clients from the community are treated at CMHCs, which make them very fertile environments to intervene with a range of presenting problems, from adjustment disorders to severe mental illness. I have been amazed at how "cutting edge" these centers have been in the history of mental health in the United States!

CMHCs around the country provide a range of services that are individualized to their particular communities. These services include case management and community outreach, medication management, individual, group, and family therapy, family support and education, day or partial hospitalization programs, emergency services, and residential treatment programs. One of the strengths of these settings is the range of professionals working together on treatment teams. Oftentimes, treatment teams will comprise psychologists, counselors, social workers, psychiatrists, and nurses. A Ph.D. psychologist in this setting may hold different types of positions in a CMHC. Although psychologists have traditionally held service provider positions, which may include psychological assessment as well as individual and group treatment, these positions are becoming increasingly rare as they have become less cost-effective. However, this has resulted in more opportunities for psychologists to balance administrative and supervisory roles as team leaders, supervisors, research program evaluators, and clinical directors. Your graduate advisory faculty may perceive CMHCs as a setting where psychologists "disappear from the world" into microcosms of obscurity, never to be heard from again. However, with the diverse needs of CMHCs, psychologists are able to be more creative about their roles and fitting their position to a broad range of interests. Traditional views of CMHCs as static environments are gradually being replaced by a realization of a broader range of career possibilities.

A strength-based tradition, primarily from social work, is consistent with current "positive psychology" trends in the American Psychological Association (APA) to employ more optimistic and systems-oriented ways to intervene, particularly with difficult clients. With mandates to serve those who are at risk of hospitalization, CMHCs also have a history of evaluating the success of their treatment programs. However, until recently, there has been a division between academic settings and applied work. With the APA current emphasis on disseminating empirically supported programs (programs that have shown to be effective through research trials) CMHCs are an ideal setting to validate programs with clients with comorbid psychological disturbances. Furthermore, CMHCs are federally mandated to evaluate programs and are arenas to train new professionals in the field. Using empirically developed programs and evaluating treatment outcomes will become increasingly essential in educating the public and managed care/insurance companies about effective uses of time and money for treating mental illness. Depending on the needs of a community and the interest of the psychologist, the "sky is the limit" for developing programs guided by empirical protocols.

Developing and Expanding a Program of Interest

As an example of a potential validated program that has worked well in a community setting, my initial position was as the team leader for the multisystemic treatment (MST) of juvenile offenders (Henggeler et al., 1998) program. This program has just recently been disseminated into community programs and our CMHC was one of the dissemination sites. As a part of this position, I supervised master's-level MST therapists and served as the liaison between MST services and our CMHC. The MST program is a community-based, intensive treatment program used with juvenile offenders as an alternative to out-of-home placement, particularly incarceration. The primary goal of MST is to eliminate or greatly reduce the frequency and/or severity of youth's referral behavior. To do this, MST works to empower caregivers with the skills and resources to address difficulties with problem youth independently, as well as to enable the youth to cope with systemic issues. MST also relies on the collaboration of all systems (i.e., family, school, peer, and neighborhood) involved to meet these goals.

Working with this program has been an amazing experience. My CMHC was able to participate fully in the MST dissemination project with intensive week-long training, weekly consultation with our own MST consultant, and quarterly "booster" trainings on specific clinical topics. In addition, therapists were rated monthly by families on their own therapeutic adherence to the MST treatment principles. Therapists also rated supervision practices, which helped consultants provide feedback about my own skills in order to improve therapists' skills. In this way, the program combined clinical and research efforts to evaluate the effectiveness in this setting. This increased my skills in program development as a part of a larger project and allowed me some independence in thinking about future projects and connections with the community.

There were several pros and cons about disseminating this type of program into a CMHC setting. On the positive side, the program was very exciting and brought some hope to referral sources and families who had "failed" other treatment programs in the system. In addition, the research aspect of the program helped to look at indicators of success and failure of the program. There were also some stressors associated with bringing this type of program to a CMHC setting. The protocol for treatment was very different from traditional treatment in this setting. A traditional approach includes using therapists, case managers, and youth specialists cooperatively on the treatment team. Because the MST approach was unusual in that one clinical case manager incorporated the work of the three other positions (i.e., therapist, case manager, and youth specialist) in order to streamline the process for families, administrators and staff had to be trained regarding the resulting differences. It was also important to address the potential burnout of therapists by developing ways to keep them producing effective outcomes yet remaining relatively unscathed by the intensity of their work. In addition, it was critical to maintain connections with our community partners, as we depended on them for positive outcomes. Finally, financial issues were ever-present for funding the program in the long term.

Needless to say, it has been a very steep learning curve for a new psychologist to face each of these challenges. An exciting part about being the MST team leader is training and supervising talented master's-level social workers and psychologists. Because the program is intensive, comprehensive, and evaluative of progress, it is critical to work closely with the team to achieve positive outcomes for youth and families. In addition, it is necessary to make strong connections with community partners, including the juvenile justice system and community resource centers. Regular staff and community meetings can help to keep communication open and also to be able to find out about new opportunities for the program or for particular clients. Since my training as a psychologist did not provide me with much experience in case management, I learned a great deal from my team about how to fulfill basic needs for families while achieving powerful treatment outcomes. The best part is that I feel like I can talk confidently about the successes and weaknesses of the program, and feel that I am doing treatment that is "on the edge" of treatment progress for children and families. And, amazingly enough, I am working in a CMHC!

In addition, with the success of MST in our area, there have been many demands to increase treatment length and to broaden our referral criteria. This has led our program to do some things that MST services are beginning to investigate, such as developing a continuum of care for clients that is MST focused, and using this protocol for youths with comorbid psychiatric difficulties (Henggeler, Schoenwald, Rowland, & Cunningham, 2002). Our connection with the juvenile justice system also led to further creative blending of treatment services, such as forensic assessments and treatment of youths at the detention facility. It was the regular meetings, consistent positive results, and helping staff accomplish goals that have led to increased connections that have met the needs of the juvenile justice staff as well as our CMHC. As a result, other communities are very interested in learning more about our success to potentially adopt a similar program in their area.

Cutting a Piece of the Pie

As previously noted, one of the strengths of working at a CMHC that I find particularly appealing is the vast client base that may create opportunities to specialize in certain areas. At my CMHC, a majority of the referrals in the child and family area include children with disruptive behavior disorders, including attention-deficit/hyperactivity disorder (ADHD), oppositional defiant disorder (ODD), and conduct disorder (CD). Since this is an area of special interest to me, I was able to create a standardized assessment and treatment battery for use in our center. These assessment and treatment batteries are based on materials that have shown effectiveness for these behavior problems (Anastopoulos & Shelton, 2001; Barkley, 1998; Barkley, Edwards, & Robin, 1999; Barkley & Murphy, 1998; DuPaul, Power, Anastopoulos, & Reid, 1998).

As you might realize, having the knowledge base through graduate courses and practicum experiences is not always enough in creating new programs or strengthening ongoing programs. Oftentimes there are pressures to remain with the status quo because it may be more comfortable to people. However, there is an important process if a psychologist is interested in expanding areas of interest. First, you should do the job you are given to the best of your abilities and then watch for opportunities that arise for you to use your strengths to benefit others. It may involve volunteering to help others, doing complimentary educational talks or workshops, and asking to attend meetings with key individuals who are making center decisions. For example, I have worked with child and family center staff and provided them with tools to screen for possible ADHD difficulties, as well as criteria to consider when referring for a more comprehensive assessment. This has been helpful to the therapists and psychiatrists in screening for difficulties and recognizing when to refer to the ADHD clinic. Having standardized data will allow our center to compare results we find in assessments with other disruptive disorder clinics around the nation. Changes like these have been easy to advocate because I can justify how they meet agency goals or mission statements. This is a way that I have not "disappeared in the CMHC black hole" because I have tried to keep current on published research and foster connections with academic colleagues by e-mail or connecting at conferences to make sure our protocols match current treatment practices.

Training students is another valuable opportunity in a CMHC, particularly if the mental health center is located near a training college or university. Psychologists can fulfill this interest in several ways, such as volunteering their time, becoming an adjunct professor at a university, or writing pertinent duties into a position description. As stated previously, it is critical to focus on how training students can be an asset to the agency for developing new ideas, retaining staff, and doing valuable assessments and treatment. Fortunately, my CMHC already had an existing program with the University of Kansas that I could continue to enhance. I have had the pleasure of working with social work students, advanced child clinical psychology practicum students, and child and adult psychology interns.

As I move further and further away from my own graduate training, I relish the input from graduate students on our training teams. Social work and psychology practicum students have worked in the CMHC team concept doing assessments as well as individual, family, and/or group treatment. Students have also experienced the range of community connections possible in treating clients in the CMHC. Because our site was also interested in training psychology intern students, I have assisted in developing our internship consortium and coordinating internship training tracks and didactics to blend with other formal staff training. These duties require me to examine the current literature in the areas of diagnostics, treatment, and ethics of practice across different professions. In addition, I have had the opportunity to design formal training workshops for professionals to attend on topics such as ethical dilemmas in psychology, fundamentals of diagnostic assessment and treatment, and assessment and treatment of ADHD in children, adolescents, and adults. There have also been multiple chances to present to community groups or at conferences regarding effective treatment for a range of populations.

As my position has become more diversified, breaking down a typical week into particular components can be difficult. However, my core position comprises 50 to 75% of my time as the MST team leader. This includes group and individual supervision of the MST therapists, regular contact with their cases as necessary, administrative duties such as staff meetings and treatment plan reviews, liaison with community members (particularly social services and juvenile justice personnel), and a few assessment or treatment cases. There has also been additional supervision with staff conducting assessments as well as individual and group treatment at the Juvenile Detention Center. Program evaluation also is part of my position, particularly as it relates to showing our treatment progress and ability to apply for grants.

Approximately 25% of my time has been defined as "student liaison," which includes working with the child clinical program at the University of Kansas and our psychology internship consortium. Through this position, I coordinate the ADHD clinic and provide individual and group supervision to graduate practicum students and review reports and charts. For the internship, I assist in developing training programs for the interns, coordinate the child track and training seminar, and supervise students. Other interests such as training workshops and research projects are undertaken as time permits. It has been beneficial to have a connection with the university because it opens opportunities for students to provide assistance in program evaluation as a part of their training research.

Training Background

The training that I received in graduate school and during my predoctoral internship year was great preparation for this position at a CMHC. My graduate training in clinical psychology followed a generalist training model and emphasized training as a scientist and practitioner, so I attended didactics and clinical practica covering the range of adult and child assessment and treatment. During my training, I also began to specialize by working with children and adolescents with disruptive behavior disorders. My predoctoral internship training rounded out these skills in work with children and families, focusing on disruptive behavior disorders including ADHD and conduct disorder.

At the end of my internship experience, I examined a number of programs that had the potential to meet the requirements for supervised postdoctoral hours, including formal and informal postdoctoral programs. At that time, I was not sure in what area I wanted to establish myself, but I was interested in continuing with empirical programs that would be linked to academic settings if not directly housed within an academic department. As stated previously, although I had only a minimum amount of exposure to mental health centers through practicum experiences in graduate school, I decided on working at a CMHC. It was appealing because it gave me more independence, but with necessary supervision. It also provided me with the ability to create additional duties that interested me and benefited the center. These were attractive training aspects that this position could provide for me, whereas the formal postdoctoral programs I examined could not.

The training and experience that I had accumulated previously was very useful in fitting into this position at the CMHC. My advice to other new psychologists would be to resist the urge to rule out CMHCs as a possibility for a potential work setting. As I have described, this setting can include a very active examination of state-of-the-art assessment and treatment with adults and children. As a new psychologist, it is important to examine the position description and discuss with the potential site its range of ongoing activities, mission statement, and connection with the community. As stated above, psychologists could be hired primarily for assessment and treatment of adults or children and families. In addition, there are potential uses for psychologists as team leaders supervising other master's-level psychologists and social workers on a general team or for specialty programs. Depending on the training aspects of the center, psychologists can also be involved in staff development and student training on site. They may also be used for their research expertise in developing empirically validated programs or evaluating ongoing programs for assessment and treatment. There can also be some unique arrangements established between the CMHC and other community partners for a psychologist. For example, I know of a psychologist who serves part-time as a team leader at the CMHC and part-time as a coordinator of a mental health treatment program within the school system. Table 9.1 summarizes the potential work duties in a CMHC for new psychologists.

Table 9.1 Potential Work Duties for Psychologists Working in CMHCs

Clinical Activities
Completing psychological assessments
Providing individual, group, and/or family treatment
Participating in a multidisciplinary treatment team
Completing treatment updates for clients

Administrative/Supervisory Activities
Serving as team leader to manage clinical team/director of clinical activities/manager of a specialty clinic
Serving as a liaison with community agencies
Attending staff meetings
Providing individual and group supervision of staff
Training staff in validated treatment protocols
Evaluating staff performance
Creating standardized assessment and treatment batteries
Managing funding issues of treatment programs

Program Evaluation Activities
Selecting appropriate empirically validated programs
Writing grants and other funding proposals
Developing clinical and research protocols
Evaluating treatment outcomes (indicators of success and failure)
Comparing results with other research findings
Reporting findings internally and to grant funding agencies
Presenting results at external conferences

Miscellaneous Duties
Training graduate clinical practicum students regarding assessment and treatment
Serving as a liaison with graduate training program
Serving on boards of community agencies
Providing educational workshops for staff and community members

Securing a Position and Diversifying Your Work

Securing a Position

There can be several ways to secure a position in a CMHC. The first quandary may be learning of a position opening. Positions may be found in the *APA Monitor* or APA Web site, job search Web sites, psychologist list servs, or local newspapers of favored geographic areas. However, professors and colleagues may be the best way to hear about positions, through "word of mouth." I learned of my CMHC position from my academic advisor who knew this was a favored geographic area and a professional area of interest. Positions may fill quickly, so you need to find ways to be visible, have information updated and prepared to send, and keep track of information sources.

LIFE AFTER GRADUATE SCHOOL IN PSYCHOLOGY

Of course, already being a member of the community can be very positive because you may be familiar with the client base and services available. Also, having connections with professionals that work with the CMHC can be very positive in receiving recommendations regarding your work. It can also be possible to send in your vitae if you find a position that is appealing, and see if there is a good match between your skills and the requested position. You will want to examine the position and see how it may fit with your own stated goals. Some things for any new psychologist to keep in mind are the geographic location, pay scale, benefits, range of staff, tone and hierarchy of the center, and stated description of the position, as well as day-to-day functioning. An advertised position may not meet all of your objectives in each of these areas. However, this is when your resourcefulness may pay off in modifying a position to meet your training needs as well as the goals of the center.

Diversifying Your Position

After gaining a position, a new psychologist can gain a sense of the true day-to-day functioning of the CMHC and begin to look at ways to possibly expand a role. Part of this journey is discovering your own interests, and possibly receiving additional training as necessary. Then you need to become very familiar with the goals of the agency and the functioning of the administration. Things begin to happen when the psychologist is able to look for opportunities by attending meetings, volunteering, and talking with community members about areas of need or improvements. Once you have an idea, then it is important to advocate for the need, how it can be met, and resources needed as well as ways to evaluate the program at a later point. It may even be possible to begin with small changes to show competency (i.e., joining a discussion group about changes and making some recommendations), and then work up to larger changes or the addition of new programs. Throughout the process, it is important continually to compare what you are doing with your personal training goals. If there is too much of an imbalance between these two things, you run the risk of getting caught in a "rut" or, after several years, realizing that you do not enjoy what you are doing. These times of self-reflection provide good opportunities to update your vitae and see where you have been as you pave the next steps in your professional career.

Advantages and Disadvantages of Working in a CMHC

One of the key strengths (as well as primary difficulties) in finding a position in a CMHC is that every center is unique in its funding resources, clientele, and treatment programs to fit the needs of its individual community. Therefore, a new psychologist has to look very closely at the community that houses the CMHC, the particular job description, and duties required by the psychologist. As with other positions, new psychologists need to examine if these duties will meet their own training goals. Also, working at a CMHC can be overwhelming at times because psychologists are challenged to be knowledgeable about a range of client difficulties, and are often seen as the "expert" on the team. In contrast, community mental health is an excellent training ground for psychologists to learn about a range of disorders and possibly establish their own specialty areas. However, a disadvantage of working at a CMHC could be additional duties that are added to your load that meet the needs of the center but may not include flexibility for you to generate separate "pet projects." This point is highlighted in poor economic times, such as the past few years, when systems including the mental health system are being forced to do more with fewer resources. Psychologists need to be creative in proposing new programs and justify the clinical and fiscal benefits to the center. Connections with community partners can also be effective in looking for sources of funding, which may include city, county, state, or federal funding or grants. Because of this, a nonprofit agency like a CMHC can be a particular asset in finding potential funding. In addition, there are often opportunities to evaluate and improve ongoing programs, as well as create or strengthen connections with community partners. It is also important at certain intervals to evaluate your "fit" with the system and whether it is meeting your needs or whether pressures have moved you in an undesirable path that is different from your intentions. At this point, you can then reevaluate your goals and find a setting that better meets your needs. In my position, I have been afforded the flexibility to pursue my clinical, program evaluation, and training interests. I have seen others in these settings who have preferred a more academic setting and those who have been interested in private practice. It all depends on the ongoing match between your goals and the goals of the agency.

In summary, working at a CMHC can be a very enriching experience. Depending on the needs of the community and the creativeness of the new psychologist, a multitude of roles can be established ranging from a therapist with direct client contact to clinical director supervising a team of professionals. CMHC positions have been often overlooked by new psychologists, but I hope that I have identified ways that these positions can be very meaningful and establish your career path. If this chapter leaves you wanting to learn more about positions in CMHCs, please look at the references and the Web site suggestions at the end of this chapter, particularly if you are interested in particular geographic areas. Good luck in your career search!

References

Anastopoulos, A. D., & Shelton, T. L. (2001). *Assessing attention-deficit/hyperactivity disorder.* New York: Kluwer Academic/Plenum Publishers.

Barkley, R. A. (1998). *Attention-deficit hyperactivity disorder: A handbook for diagnosis and treatment* (2nd ed.). New York: Guilford Press.

Barkley, R. A., Edwards, G. H., & Robin, A. L. (1999). *Defiant teens: A Clinician's manual for assessment and family intervention.* New York: Guilford Press.

Barkley, R. A., & Murphy, K. R. (1998). *Attention-deficit hyperactivity disorder: A clinical workbook* (2nd ed.). New York: Guilford Press.

DuPaul, G. J., Power, T. J., Anastopoulos, A. D., & Reid, R. (1998). *ADHD rating scale. IV: Checklists, norms, and clinical interpretation.* New York: Guilford Press.

Henggeler, S. W., Schoenwald, S. K., Borduin, C. M., Rowland, M. D., & Cunningham, P. B. (1998). *Multisystemic treatment of antisocial behavior in children and adolescents.* New York: Guilford Press.

Henggeler, S. W., Schoenwald, S. K., Rowland, M. D., & Cunningham, P. B. (2002). *Serious emotional disturbance in children and adolescents: Multisystemic therapy.* New York: Guilford Press.

Suggested Reading

Kazdin, A. E., & Weisz, J. R. (1998). Identifying and developing empirically supported child and adolescent treatments. *Journal of Consulting and Clinical Psychology, 66,* 19–36.

Mechanic, D. (1998). Emerging trends in mental health policy and practice. *Health Affairs, 17,* 82–98.

Schoenwald, S. K., Brown, T. L., & Henggeler, S. W. (2000). Inside Multisystemic therapy: Therapists, supervisory, and program practices. *Journal of Emotional and Behavioral Disorders, 8,* 113–127.

U.S. Department of Health and Human Services (1999). Mental health: A report of the Surgeon General — Executive summary. Rockville, MD: U.S. Department of Health and Human Services, Substance Abuse and Mental Health Services Administration, Center for Mental Health Services, National Institutes of Health, National Institute of Mental Health.

U.S. Department of Health and Human Services (2001). Youth violence: A Report of the Surgeon General- Executive Summary. Rockville, MD: U.S. Department of Health and Human Services, Centers for Disease Control and Prevention, National Center for Injury Prevention and Control; Substance Abuse and Mental Health Services Administration, Center for Mental Health Service: and National Institutes of Health, National Institute of Mental Health.

Suggested Web Sites

Center for Mental Health Services (CMHS): http://www.mentalhealth.org/cmhs/about.asp.

Information on Resources per State: http://www.mentalhealth.org/publications/Publications_browse.asp?ID=185&Topic=State%2FTerritory±Resources.

National Institute of Mental Health: http://www.nimh.nih.gov/.

President's New Freedom Commission on Mental Health: http://www.mentalhealthcommission. gov/.

Surgeon General's Reports: http://www.mentalhealth.org/cmhs/surgeongeneral/default.asp.

10

Forensic Psychology: Exciting Career Opportunities in the Legal Arena

SHAWN ROBERSON

Forensic Psychology Defined

Forensic psychology receives a substantial amount of attention in the popular media. However, the general public often narrowly perceives it as "profiling" or one specific skill instead of the wide array of activities that may be involved. According to the Specialty Guidelines for Forensic Psychologists (American Psychological Association, APA, 1991), "Forensic psychology means all forms of professional conduct when acting with definable foreknowledge, as a psychological expert on explicitly psycholegal issues, in direct assistance to courts, parties to legal proceedings, correctional and forensic mental health facilities, and administrative, judicial, and legislative agencies acting in an adjudicative capacity" (p. 657). *Adjudicative* is a general term meaning to settle through judicial means. There is obviously a broad range of practices related to forensic psychology, but this chapter specifically focuses on the career of a criminal forensic examiner, that is, a psychologist who conducts clinical evaluations of criminal defendants to answer specific legal questions.

Unfortunately, students and recent graduates in psychology are often unaware of the diverse employment options available in the forensic arena. The number of career opportunities has increased substantially in recent years. Historically, clinical forensic examination has been the mainstay of employment. Defendants with a history of psychological treatment or exhibiting a mental illness are often court-ordered to be examined for competency to stand trial or mental state at the time of the alleged offense. If adjudicated incompetent to stand trial, or found not criminally responsible due to mental illness, the defendant might be ordered for inpatient mental health treatment at a forensic hospital. Psychologists may also be requested by a federal or state court, or retained privately, to examine a variety of civil or criminal legal issues (i.e., custody proceedings, competency to be executed, civil commitment, etc.). Work within corrections, law enforcement organizations (i.e., police departments, FBI, etc.), or consultation with attorneys also provides avenues for employment. Trial consultation, discussed in Chapter 19, can be an exciting and potentially lucrative career.

Educational and Professional Training Opportunities

Educational Programs

For those interested in pursuing a forensic psychology career, choosing the appropriate training or academic program is fundamental. There are some specific doctoral level degree programs in forensic psychology, such as combination programs where you earn a doctorate in clinical psychology and a degree in law; or a clinical or counseling doctorate with specialized training in forensics. However, based on the limited number of such programs, most professionals attain Ph.D. or Psy.D. degrees in counseling or clinical psychology prior to undertaking specialized training in forensic areas (e.g., during internship and postdoctoral work as described below). Consult the American Psychology–Law Society (APLS) Web page or other APA resources to identify potential degrees in which you might be interested. Do not forget about the programs in Canada, where an extensive amount of forensic research and practice is conducted.

Research Areas

Virtually a limitless number of forensic topics can be researched; however, finding the avenue to conduct forensic research sometimes requires initiative because of the limited number of professors studying related topics. Contact local forensic professionals or state organizations that might be interested in a partnership of producing research. For example, my employer, the Oklahoma Forensic Center, was one of the sites where data were gathered for the norms of the MacArthur Competence Assessment Tool–Criminal Adjudication (MacCAT-CA), an assessment instrument for evaluating adjudicative competency (Poythress et al., 1999). Adjudicative competency is a broad term referring to a defendant's ability to understand and participate in judicial proceedings, including during trial, plea-bargaining, sentencing, etc. Graduate students and clinical professionals were both part of the team led by a university professor in this undertaking. Joining local or national professional organizations may also help to network with potential coauthors from any distance. Do not be discouraged if the opportunities do not seem readily apparent; do a little footwork and find some projects to become involved in.

Internship Training

Practicum or internship experiences can serve as a catalyst to further training and are often the cornerstone to developing a career. In my case, completing an internship that offered specialized forensic training provided an opportunity to procure a position as a forensic examiner immediately after graduation. Even if your internship does not provide an immediate opportunity for employment, it can provide a springboard for further postdoctoral training prior to obtaining a fully paid position. There are many APA-accredited internship sites that offer training in forensic psychology; see Ax and Morgan (2002) for a discussion of training opportunities in forensic psychology. Forensic hospitals, federal and state prisons, and community mental health centers that conduct outpatient forensic evaluations all provide excellent opportunities. In many instances you might discover that an internship consortium of several agencies allows for training in multiple areas, with an emphasis in a specialty area such as forensic psychology. Consult the APLS Web page, the Association of Psychology Postdoctoral and Internship Centers (APPIC) Directory (or www.appic.org), speak with forensic psychologists, and contact local and national forensic organizations to find out more about training opportunities.

Postdoctoral Training

There are a limited number of postdoctoral programs accredited by APPIC. Postdoctoral training provides an ideal vehicle to obtain specialized skills in a number of forensic activities while working toward licensure. In states where licensure is required to be a forensic examiner, postdoctoral education may be one of the only avenues to work in the area prior to licensure. Although you delay the start of your career by a year, you will gain invaluable skills that set you apart from other candidates for such positions once licensed. Postdoctoral programs emphasizing criminal forensic work, for example, may provide training in court-ordered evaluations, therapeutic services for forensic patients, participation in mock trials, and courses at a law school.

Continuing Education

Continuing education is often available locally and nationally and may be in the form of state forensic meetings, workshops, and national conferences. Division 41 sponsors education during its annual conference and the national APA meeting. Membership in local groups or national organizations provides information on opportunities for continuing education that can fulfill licensure requirements and provide relevant training.

Attaining Employment

Qualifications

The required background needed to practice can vary from state to state, but usually includes a doctorate in psychology. Fortunately, there are some opportunities for gainful employment after your degree while seeking a license. In many states, employees with a doctorate in clinical or counseling psychology can refer to themselves as psychologists for the state and perform the job duties of a full-time forensic examiner without being licensed. In other states, a license or state certification as a forensic examiner may be required. Obviously, private practice would require a license and the appropriate experience. If conducting private evaluations in multiple states, be careful you are not practicing without a license and know the relevant requirements prior to undertaking any professional activity in another state. Not doing so could result in professional sanctions or legal liability.

Researching the Possibilities

There are a number of methods for discovering potential avenues to employment in forensic psychology. First, examine relevant publications such as the *Monitor on Psychology*, the Division 41 newsletter, and publications from other relevant divisions and associations. Call local professionals, organizations, or any other potential employer such as large county jails. I, for example, discovered my position by calling my employer (who was in a different state) and conveying my interest in working for them. It may also behoove you to pursue employment with your internship or postdoctoral program. Most of the forensic examiners at my hospital were in the predoctoral internship program prior to obtaining their degree.

Developing Your Application

Given the variety of duties that forensic psychology positions can require, your application should reflect the area you wish to pursue. For example, if you are applying for a job as a forensic examiner, it is important to highlight your report-writing and assessment skills, knowledge of psycholegal issues, and ability to provide expert witness testimony. If, on the other hand, you are applying for a position as a treatment provider for sexual offenders, some of those skills might not be as important, whereas therapeutic experience would be more relevant. It is important to know the job description, as well as any anticipated changes in those organizations, before submitting an application. For example, familiarize yourself with the role of the forensic examiner in the judicial system in that state. Learn about relevant state laws and how they pertain to the prospective job. State statutes regarding adjudicative competency and other forensic topics are available in libraries or on the Internet. Explore the different careers in forensics and tailor your training based on your interests or the availability of such jobs.

Interviewing

The key factor to consider during interviewing is to present yourself as a skilled professional, committed to developing a career in forensics, with specialized training in the area desired by your employer. Highlighting the duties you can immediately perform for your prospective employer (with limited supervision) is one effective means of conveying the assets you have to offer. For example, my former supervisor, Dr. Jeanne Russell, indicated that there are several subtle qualities she believed important when screening prospective examiners, aside from background and training. One such quality might be termed the "naïve" factor. Malingering (i.e., feigning mental illness) is not uncommon among criminal defendants, and it is important that an examiner have a healthy degree of skepticism and can provide a critical analysis of data. Knowledge of assessment instruments to evaluate malingering can also set a candidate apart; as would having a dissertation on a forensic topic. Another key factor is the candidate's interpersonal style and ability to represent the organization in a professional manner. A candidate should demonstrate poise, as well as evidence that he or she will not be easily distracted in stressful situations, or intimidated by public scrutiny, difficult defendants, or aggressive attorneys.

Choosing among Offers

Of course, as with any job you should consider the salary, setting, typical duties, and opportunity for advancement. A key factor in my opinion is the amount of independence in practice and decision making the position will provide. Will the facility support you as a professional when going to court? Will you be allowed time to prepare and will the other professionals in your organization, who may be providing treatment, support your findings? Another consideration might be the ability to conduct private practice.

A Week in the Life of a Forensic Examiner

As a forensic psychologist at a state forensic center, the majority of my time was spent conducting and writing evaluations of adjudicative competency for district courts. Since becoming the department director, I continue to do several evaluations a month, but have increased my role in forensic treatment programming and administration. One day I might drive across the state to a county jail and evaluate a defendant on an outpatient basis or provide expert testimony. Another day I might act as a member of the Oklahoma Forensic Review Board to discuss the conditional release of a patient found not guilty by reason of insanity. There are a number of very interesting activities involved in this career, as described below and found in Table 10.1.

Forensic Assessment

Assessment of "competency to stand trial" is the most frequently requested form of adjudicative competency by courts (Melton, Petrila,

Table 10.1 Common Roles for a Director of Psychology Working at a State Forensic Center

---

Clinical Duties

Evaluations for competency to stand trial
Evaluations for future dangerousness
Development of Conditional Release Plans
Report writing
Expert witness testimony
Competency restoration treatment programming

Supervision Duties

Supervision of predoctoral interns
Development of internship seminars
Preparation of presentations/invited talks

Administrative Duties

Committee memberships (Oklahoma Forensic Review Board, Hospital Executive
  Management Team, etc.)
Department oversight and budgeting

Miscellaneous Duties

Consultation with legal professionals
Consultation with community mental health centers
Development of forensic manuals and suggestions for legislative proposals

---

Poythress, & Slobogin, 1997). In many jurisdictions (but not in my state), courts also simultaneously request an evaluation for mental state at the time of the alleged offense (i.e., criminal responsibility or the "not guilty by reason of insanity" plea). Competency to stand trial relates to the defendant's current appreciation of the charges and the ability of the defendant to assist his or her attorney; whereas criminal responsibility relates to the defendant's mental state when the alleged crime occurred. Other psycholegal evaluations may focus on risk assessment (i.e., the evaluation of future dangerousness), competency to be sentenced (after being convicted), competency to accept a plea bargain, and competency to waive the *Miranda* warning. A forensic examiner at my site typically completes between two and four evaluations each week for competency to stand trial, with the majority conducted at an inpatient forensic hospital or a large metropolitan county jail. We also routinely conduct risk assessment evaluations.

There are three main aspects involved in completing the criminal forensic evaluation for competency to stand trial: preparation (e.g., reviewing records), the clinical interview and occasionally psychological testing, and report writing. Preparation usually requires the least time, followed by the interview that lasts on average between 1 and 3 hours, but can sometimes be much lengthier. Report writing is the bulk of the work and can take up to 4 or more hours for a single report.

The competency to stand trial evaluation begins with a review of available background information, such as the criminal allegations, past psychological reports, medical records, etc. In some cases, it may be pertinent to contact the defense or prosecuting attorney and interview the attorney to learn about the likely evidence to be presented at trial. Any available documents regarding prior mental health treatment, recent behavior, or other psychological data may be useful in determining the extent of the defendant's symptoms and cooperation with the evaluation. It is also sometimes necessary to interview collateral sources (co-workers, family, etc.). In evaluations of criminal insanity, collateral sources are essential.

Next, I interview the defendant to assess for the presence of a mental disorder or deficit and how that might affect the legal questions at hand (e.g., knowledge of the charges, ability to assist counsel, etc.). Although there clearly is, and should be, a typical methodology for completing a forensic evaluation, the diversity among defendants can require vastly different tools to arrive at appropriate conclusions. For example, extensive testing or consultation with medical professionals may be necessary if there is a physical condition or cerebral trauma. In other cases, a language interpreter or sign-language assistant could be required. Most of my interviews consist of three elements: a mental state examination, an assessment for psychological symptoms/history, and a competency interview. The mental status examination and assessment for symptoms evaluates all relevant areas of functioning, including (but not limited to) treatment history, orientation, memory, intellectual functioning, mood, anxiety, psychosis, and substance abuse. The defendant is also questioned about his or her knowledge of the legal charges and potential penalties; understanding of facts in the case and the likely defense; relationship with attorney; and understanding of general legal information. A relatively uncomplicated evaluation for adjudicative competency can be conducted and written in as little as 6 hours. More complex cases can require days, depending on the amount of background information and the extent of interviewing and assessment required.

The most striking difference between civil and forensic evaluations is probably the rate of malingering (i.e., faking mental illness or problems). Research has estimated that defendants in forensic evaluations malinger some form of psychological symptoms approximately 15 to 20% of the time (Rogers, 1997). Simply taking a defendant at his or her word and based on presentation, as would be typical when evaluating symptoms in therapy, can be a grave mistake. I have evaluated a number of defendants who possess the ability to feign symptoms of mental retardation, psychosis, or other disorders. For example, one defendant I evaluated was incredibly skilled at behaving (and speaking) as if mentally retarded. However, his alleged offense was building a somewhat sophisticated pipe bomb, which did not match with his presentation. Further research into the case revealed multiple facts indicating he was malingering, including a third-party source that stated he had no speech impediments during his developmental years.

The third component of a forensic assessment may be psychological testing. Some professionals feel that "objective testing" provides an advantage during forensic evaluations and should be routine in every case. Based on my experience and training, I believe that psychological testing is only warranted when it provides useful information not obtained during the interview that is needed to answer a specific question. For example, if intellectual functioning appears to be extremely low and might impair competency, an intelligence test might be required. If the defendant appears to be malingering but the evidence is not clear, the Test of Memory Malingering (Tombaugh, 1996) or the Structured Interview of Reported Symptoms (Rogers, Bagby, & Dickens, 1992) might provide further data. I believe one of the most common mistakes made by forensic evaluators is that of using assessment instruments when they are not required or when the defendant's motivation and effort are poor. If a defendant puts forth little effort or is dishonest, almost any assessment will provide inaccurate results.

Report Writing

Finally, but equally important, is the report that conveys your findings to relevant legal participants. This piece has special importance, in that it should clearly explain the results with adequate depth and relevance. In fact, a well-written report may decrease the likelihood an examiner will be required to testify. Without testimony, the report is often the only mental health evidence examined by the trier of fact to arrive at a decision. Thus, there should be detailed information about the issues, citing all of the relevant data that should have been considered. Finally, pay attention to detail and do not turn in cursory work with misspellings or grammatical errors. For examples of forensic reports refer to Melton et al. (1997) and Grisso (1988).

Expert Witness Testimony

I view the most interesting and exciting portion of my job to be expert witness testimony, a topic I pursued early in my career as my doctoral dissertation studied this topic. A new forensic examiner would be wise to examine relevant literature prior to taking the stand for the first time (e.g., Blau, 1998; Brodsky, 1999; Hess & Weiner, 1999). Another good method for learning about the process is observation. As an intern, I was provided with opportunities to observe several of my supervisors testify. Such experiences can help you become familiar with the process and courtroom etiquette. In addition, observation of a supervisor's skills (whether good or bad) can provide insight into the nuances of direct and cross-examinations. Attorneys may attempt to impeach an expert's testimony in a variety of ways, including, but not limited to, witness bias, attacks on credentials, contradictory theoretical evidence, and inconsistencies in testimony (see Brodsky, 1999, for more information regarding attorney's tricks of the trade). The more an expert knows about the possible avenues of attack, and effective methods for preventing or rebutting them, the better prepared and effective the expert will be in providing an opinion.

Expert witness testimony can often be stress provoking, if not downright paralyzing to some individuals. Most psychologists are not subjected to the scrutiny of a public forum where they must explain and defend their clinical findings in an adversarial arena. Although your dissertation defense provided you a similar experience, you most likely were not subjected to as rigorous an examination as that offered during cross-examination. In addition, you may be surprised to learn that, not infrequently, nationally known experts will be hired and you could find your opinion at odds with that of renown colleagues. Although being in front of a courtroom of people during a heated cross-examination can be uncomfortable, it also provides an excellent opportunity to hone both diagnostic and public-speaking skills. Preparation is an important factor and often takes much longer than the actual testimony. It would be wise to develop a plan for conveying the findings and carefully consider your opinion based on the data. The testimony may heavily influence legal decisions profoundly affecting the lives of others. Psychologists should also be leery of an attorney who attempts to use an expert's opinion to win the case by urging conclusions not warranted by the data.

Expert testimony is sometimes required, but in the majority of cases, the attorneys or courts stipulate to the findings without testimony. As previously indicated, I firmly believe that solid report writing can decrease the number of times a forensic examiner is required to testify. Since entering the field, I have testified on about 20 of the 500 evaluations I have completed. Testimony typically lasts anywhere from 5 minutes to 4 hours, which can seem much longer during cross-examination.

Training and Administration Duties

A forensic examiner may also have a number of responsibilities in addition to court-ordered evaluations. For example, as the director of psychology, I have several administrative duties, including the oversight of departmental staff and reporting on productivity. I serve on the Oklahoma Forensic Review Board, the hospital's Executive Management Team, and other committees. I am responsible for developing competency treatment programming and forensic training, and was a coauthor of the Oklahoma State Forensic Manual (Burkett, Lanier, Russell, Hall, & Roberson, 2001). Finally, I typically have at least one supervisee from our internship program and provide seminars on forensic topics, as well as consultation to legal personnel.

A Career in Forensic Psychology

Students interested in researching the field of forensic psychology can obtain information from several professional organizations on both the national and local level. Nationally, Division 41 of the APA, known as the APLS, is one of the most well known organizations; as is the American Academy of Forensic Psychology (AAFP). APLS sponsors the journal *Law and Human Behavior*, arguably the foremost journal in the field. In addition, Division 41 offers national conferences, programs during annual APA meetings, and a quarterly newsletter publication, among other activities. Locally, there may or may not be formal associations, depending on the state. For example, Missouri has a biannual meeting and a yearly conference for research and training. Graduate students interested in forensic psychology are encouraged to become student members in relevant organizations where they have the opportunity to hold offices, network with others, and learn about the field.

Key Factors in Advancing a Career in Forensics

Attention to detail, professionalism, and the ability to convey psychological findings in a relevant manner are all important for career advancement as a forensic examiner. If your work is less than thorough, you can be guaranteed it will come back to haunt you later, probably in front of an audience. Learn to convey your findings in a clear and useful manner. Legal professionals have often cited the use of psychological jargon as the most frustrating aspect of dealing with experts (Corder, Spalding, Whiteside, & Whiteside, 1990). Finally, understand the adversarial nature of the legal arena and remember that challenges are not personal. The same attorney that vigorously attacks you on the stand might later ask you to lunch or offer you work. Also, a psychologist is not a finder of fact in legal matters; rather, you are there to provide expert assistance to the court and answer relevant questions.

Pitfalls to Avoid

There is probably no other career in psychology that will result in more scrutiny of your work. Keep up-to-date with the literature and important developments in the field. You should know what your assets and liabilities are when taking the stand, as well as have a thorough understanding of the results you plan to present. Also, be aware of how your previous work may be used against you. For example, I was once questioned about my dissertation during the sentencing phase of a death penalty case. The attorney attempted to convince the jury that because I had studied the factors involved in persuasive testimony; I might be trying to manipulate the jury into believing my findings.

The most disturbing problem I have discovered is that of the "hired gun." Some forensic examiners, or other psychologists entering the legal arena, fall into the routine of working only for the defense or prosecution. Even more bothersome, some experts' clinical judgment can be affected by the views of the side that retained them or the monetary compensation. Unfortunately, this may lead to an unfavorable reputation as a witness who is willing to "sell" an opinion to the highest bidder. If an expert's findings are effectively characterized as biased, all credibility will be lost in the eyes of the legal decision makers.

Advantages of a Career in Forensic Psychology

Forensic psychology is a fascinating field, which is probably why it is often the topic of Hollywood movies and media coverage. You will not likely be bored with a career in forensics, and just when you think you have seen it all, another interesting case comes around. There is a variety of work available, including civil and criminal cases, and numerous types of assessment, treatment, and consultation services. With some state jobs, as well as private practice, you can have the opportunity to do something different every week.

Another advantage forensic psychology offers is excellent financial opportunities in light of the downsizing of mental health care in many states. Based on my experience and conversations with colleagues, state forensic examiners (i.e., those working in a hospital or state agency) earn an entry-level salary of $40,000 to $50,000; and private practitioners typically earn hourly rates between $100 and $350. Of course, one must be licensed and gain a reputation and experience to develop an independent practice. Even if you hold a full-time organizational position, you can substantially supplement your income with outside private evaluations, if those are not prohibited by a conflict of interest. For example, examiners at my hospital are not allowed to conduct private evaluations for competency to stand trial or criminal responsibility because of their role as state examiners. However, there is the opportunity to perform other types of forensic evaluations and trial consultation (e.g., cross-examination planning; jury selection; and conducting mock trials for legal strategy).

While many specializations in psychology have been negatively impacted by government cutbacks or insurance regulations, forensic psychology has continued to grow in many areas, and there is no managed care or providers whose approval must be sought. The salary for forensic examiners is competitive and the potential for private practice excellent. In addition, I feel that my role as a state examiner provides me with an enormous benefit of objectivity unencumbered by financial concerns. That is, my continued employment does not depend on the satisfaction of attorneys with the end result. The court is my client, and I am free from the burden of one side being dissatisfied with the findings and that affecting the availability of work.

Disadvantages

Working in an adversarial setting is not for the timid. The legal arena is an environment quite unlike that of the therapeutic relationship, and often the personality characteristics that lead people to choose a career in psychology do not mesh with the role of a forensic examiner. There will almost always be one side that is not pleased with your findings and who will attempt to discredit your results. Be prepared for attacks on your credentials, skills, and background. You must enjoy a certain amount of adversarial banter if you are going to subject your work to the critique of attorneys trained to argue. Also, be aware that you may experience a higher number of complaints filed with the state board, as forensic work can subject you to legal action when dealing with peoples' civil rights. When substantial money is involved, such as in insurance malpractice cases, contractors may be hired to investigate your background or your reports may be sent to other experts in the field for review. Custody evaluations are probably the best-known type of forensic work to result in litigation against practitioners.

Closing Thoughts

Forensic psychology offers a variety of interesting career opportunities and continues to emerge as an important area in our discipline. There are numerous educational and training programs, as well as professional organizations, for those students interested in pursuing a career in forensic psychology. It is never too early to explore the possibilities and tailor your professional development to facilitate future employment opportunities.

References

American Psychological Association. (1991). Specialty guidelines for forensic psychologists. *Law and Human Behavior, 15*, 655–665.
American Psychological Association. (2002). *APPIC directory.* Washington, D.C.: Association of Psychology Postdoctoral and Internship Centers.
Ax, R. K., & Morgan, R. D. (2002). Internship training opportunities in correctional psychology: A comparison of settings. *Criminal Justice and Behavior, 29*, 332–347.
Blau, T. H. (1998). *The psychologist as expert witness* (2nd ed.). New York: John Wiley & Sons.
Brodsky, S. C. (1999). *The expert, expert witness: More maxims and guidelines for testifying in court.* Washington, D.C.: American Psychological Association.
Burkett, W., Lanier, P., Russell, J., Hall, T., & Roberson, S. (2001). *Oklahoma forensic mental health services.* Oklahoma Department of Mental Health and Substance Abuse Services.
Corder, B. F., Spalding, V., Whiteside, D., & Whiteside, R. (1990). Expert witness testimony in sentencing phases of trials: survey of judges, attorneys, psychiatrists and psychologists. *American Journal of Forensic Psychology, 8*, 55–62.
Grisso, T. (1988). *Competency to stand trial evaluations: A manual for practice.* Sarasota, FL: Professional Resource Exchange.
Hess, A. K., & Weiner, I. B. (1999). *The handbook of forensic psychology.* New York: John Wiley & Sons.
Melton, G. B., Petrila, J., Poythress, N. G., & Slobogin, C. (1997). *Psychological evaluations for the courts: A handbook for mental health professionals and lawyers.* New York: Guilford Press.
Poythress, N., Nicholson, R., Otto, R. K., Edens, J. F., Bonnie, R. J., Monahan, J., & Hoge, S. K. (1999). *The MacArthur competence assessment tool-criminal adjudication: Professional manual.* Odessa, Florida: Psychological Assessment Resources, Inc.
Rogers, R. (1997). *Clinical assessment of malingering and deception* (2nd ed.). New York: Guilford Press.
Rogers, R., Bagby, R. M., & Dickens, S. E. (1992). *Structured interview of reported symptoms: Professional manual.* Odessa, Florida: Psychological Assessment Resources, Inc.
Tombaugh, T. (1996). *Test of memory malingering: Professional manual.* Toronto: Multi-Health Systems, Inc.

Suggested Web Sites

American Academy of Forensic Psychology (AAFP): www.abfp.com/.
American Psychology–Law Society (APLS): www.unl.edu/ap-ls/.
RSR Trial Consultation and Forensic Psychology: www.rsrconsult.com.

11

Military Psychology: An Army Clinical Psychologist

JOSHUA N. FRIEDLANDER

When asked to write this chapter, I told one of the editors that I had only been in the Army as a psychologist for 3 years and wondered if I were the right person for the job. He explained to me that it was precisely because I was in the early stage of my career that I would be an appropriate choice. This conversation prompted an evaluation of my young career as an Army clinical psychologist. Upon reflection, I felt that I did have something to say about my experiences that may be helpful for other young psychologists, whether they are in the military or not. One central issue to consider lies in the very language itself of an "Army clinical psychologist" versus "a clinical psychologist who works for the Army." This differentiation was brought to my attention when I was applying for a scholarship from the Army to study clinical psychology and raised during my internship year. (*Note:* In this chapter, the term *clinical psychologist* refers to title and duties, not academic discipline. The Army welcomes and encourages applicants from clinical and counseling psychology programs for its clinical psychology residency program, for example.) It is a question that continues to inform my daily reflection and future aspirations. I address this answer more explicitly at the end of this chapter, and would ask the reader to keep this question in mind. To give the reader a sense of my experiences and conclusions, I review in turn, my initiation to the Army in graduate school, residency training, my first tour in Korea, and my second tour at Walter Reed Army Medical Center, and finally my deployment as part of Operation Iraqi Freedom.

Initiation

Careers as an Army clinical psychologist typically begin at the graduate school or internship level, although positions are sometimes available at the postdoctoral level. When I entered graduate school, the Army was the only branch of the military that offered a scholarship program at the graduate level. I contacted my local Army recruiter to find out how to apply. The scholarship program is the F. Edward Hebert Armed Forces Health Professions Scholarship Program (HPSP). It offers scholarships in a range of health professions, including clinical psychology. Most recently scholarships have been offered for either 1 or 2 years. However, this is subject to change, and I encourage readers to contact their recruiter as soon as they are considering the program. I was enrolled in a Psy.D. program at Nova Southeastern University in Florida and applied during my 2nd year for a 2-year scholarship to begin during my 3rd year. There is also a graduate program in clinical psychology at the Uniformed Services University of the Health Sciences in Bethesda, Maryland. This program offers complete funding for the entire graduate career.

Applicants need to meet the following criteria: (1) they must be a citizen of the United States; (2) they must be enrolled in an accredited school granting a doctoral degree (Ph.D., Psy.D.) in clinical or counseling psychology located in the United States or Puerto Rico; (3) they must be enrolled in a training program that is accredited by the American Psychological Association (APA); and (4) applicants must meet the prescribed eligibility criteria for appointment as a commissioned officer. These scholarships include commission as a second lieutenant (2nd LT) in the Army Reserve, full tuition for all essential costs of graduate education, including tuition and required materials, from the time of enrollment in the scholarship program, and a monthly stipend. It is not currently retroactive.

Enrollment in HPSP incurs an obligation of applying to all three Army internship sites and obligation to attend an Army internship site if the candidate is selected. There is no guarantee that an HPSP student will be accepted to an Army internship site. The prospective intern does not need to be an HPSP student to apply to an Army internship site, or any of the other military internship site. Regardless of whether the student was an HPSP student or not, the same 3-year, post-internship service obligation is required.

Currently, internship sites are available at Eisenhower Army Medical Center in Augusta, Georgia, Tripler Army Medical Center in Honolulu, Hawaii, and Walter Reed Army Medical Center, in Washington, D.C. All three are fully accredited by the APA. All three share similar training goals with different training emphases available at each site. All the residencies maintain membership in the Association of Psychology Postdoctoral and Internship Centers (APPIC). They do not typically require in-person interviews. Upon beginning the internship the student is promoted to rank of captain in the Medical Service Corps, and assumes all the responsibilities and benefits of that rank. A 45-day active duty training period, before beginning the internship, is encouraged by the Army, pending permission from the graduate school. This training is typically performed at an Army health-care facility.

Obviously, applying for the scholarship was a big decision. My decision was based on a few factors. First, I was concerned about the quality of the training. Speaking to past residents convinced me that the training was intensive, followed a generalist model, and was well respected outside the military. An additional high priority concern was that it felt as if I would be effectively signing my life away, or at least for a few years. At the time, this was not a significant deterrent to me, as I was not attached to a particular region of the country and had no significant personal ties that would be negatively affected. Of particular benefit are the monetary and health-care benefits, at least in the first few years of employment. This is not a factor to be weighed lightly, given the high cost of graduate school, nor was it one that I felt should take precedence over other issues, namely, the quality of training and lifestyle impact. I decided to pursue the application for the scholarship, and it was awarded in February prior to the academic year it would commence.

A requirement for all scholarship recipients and interns is participation in Officer Basic Course. This is a 3-month course for officer training at Fort Sam Houston, Texas, and is usually completed after graduation from the internship. This is an intensive training program in military academics and field training. In my case, a 6-week intensive course was offered, which I completed during graduate school. If you have not had prior military service, it is a rapid, and sometimes daunting introduction to basic soldier skills and the culture of the Army. This is very important because most of your time working will be in Army culture. Usually this is quite different from most nonmilitary cultures, especially graduate school, with respect to its emphasis on structure, hierarchy, discipline, group cohesion, and relatively less emphasis on individual needs. I learned, as I expect most do, to come to a different understanding of my individual needs versus that of the group. Overall, I thought the experience was excellent. It gave me an appreciation and respect for the experiences of the nonmedical soldiers of the Army, and a sense of how I fit in, personally and professionally with the Army.

Residency

I completed my internship training at Walter Reed Army Medical Center in Washington, D.C. It remains the culmination and cornerstone of my graduate education. At Walter Reed, interns are referred to as "residents" to put them on par with the physicians. The priority of the residency program is to train the residents in skill development under a "general practitioner model" while providing empirically supported clinical services. The residency is a 13-month program, which begins in mid-June. It has been accredited by the APA since 1958 and was recently renewed in 2000 for a full 5-year period. There is a focus on conceptualization of intervention from a biopsychosocial approach. This focus is underscored by frequent multidisciplinary case conferences. The residency emphasizes development and mastery of "core" clinical skills of adult assessment, psychotherapeutic interventions, which range from brief to long-term therapy, and consultation skills across a variety of patient populations, including active-duty soldiers and their family members. Patient populations are drawn from the outpatient clinic, the inpatient psychiatry ward, and throughout the hospital in the behavioral medicine service. Each resident has one or two core supervisors throughout the year and additional supervision from the chief of each rotation.

Currently, there are four rotations: inpatient psychiatry, neuropsychology, health psychology, and military psychology. The training is conducted by Army clinical psychologists as well as by civilian psychologists. Typically, residents spend 2 days per week at each rotation, and the remaining 3 days working in the outpatient psychology clinic. The inpatient psychiatry rotation concentrates on adult assessment consultation to the inpatient psychiatry ward. This involves administration, scoring, and interpretation of objective and projective personality tests, including the Rorschach, Minnesota Multiphasic Personality Inventory-2 (MMPI-2), Millon Clinical Multiaxial Inventory-3 (MCMI-3), Personality Assessment Inventory (PAI), and Rotter Incomplete Sentence Blank (RISB), among others, for purposes of differential diagnosis and disposition. The neuropsychology rotation trains residents in consultation with a variety of medical providers and insurance providers for assessment of neuropsychological functioning. A specialty service in dementia screening is also a part of this rotation. A full battery is typically administered, scored, and interpreted by the resident.

In the health rotation, residents are exposed to the range of consultation services in a major medical center. Many opportunities are available, including providing psychological screening for admission to a weight-loss program, leading groups on weight-loss strategies, performing assessment for patients recently diagnosed with breast cancer, working with prostate cancer groups, providing intervention for hypertension reduction, working with a menopause group, providing psychological consultation to surgeons for patients considered for gastric bypass surgery, conducting smoking cessation interventions, participation in a weekly health psychology seminar, and providing consultation to the Psychiatric Consultation Service.

The military rotation focuses on providing services to active-duty personnel at Ft. Meade, a support hospital to Walter Reed. This rotation emphasizes military consultation, responses to command about particular soldiers, and provision of individual and group intervention. The types of military consultation range from suicide/homicide risk assessment, recruiter and drill sergeant evaluations, fitness-for-duty evaluations, security clearance evaluations, and conducting psychological autopsies. Residents also become exposed to the administrative responsibilities of a small behavioral health clinic.

In addition to individual intervention, the residency stresses competence in delivery of services in a group format. This typically takes the form of groups focused on depression management, anxiety reduction, anger management, and an interpersonal process group. The residency incorporates a twice-weekly assessment seminar and has also been able to attract nationally known presenters on such topics as the MMPI-2, the Rorschach, suicide assessment and management, cognitive-behavioral therapy, psychological aspects of breast cancer treatment, psychopharmacology for psychologists, and outcome assessment. The residency program benefits from other military residencies in the area in the form of shared training experiences. The department also maintains status as an APA-approved provider of continuing education programs for psychologists.

I found the breadth and depth of the training excellent across the board. The benefits of training at a major medical center, such as Walter Reed, are the volume and breadth of the training opportunities. For my own needs, I was able to develop competence in personality testing and neuropsychological evaluation. In addition, I was exposed to several possible career tracks in the military and the civilian sector. When I was interviewing for internships, I interviewed at a VA, medical center, college counseling center, and a community health center. In comparison, I think Walter Reed had a wealth of training opportunities and, in particular, exposed me to a breadth of patient populations (outpatient, inpatient, active duty, civilian family members, adolescents, children, and retired geriatric populations) not found at many other sites. I emerged from the residency more confident and competent than when I entered.

Aeromedical Psychology

In the last few years, every psychology resident has been encouraged to attend training in aeromedical psychology. This is a 3-week course sponsored by the Surgeon General at Ft. Rucker, Alabama. The program prepares psychologists to provide consultation and support to flight surgeons and commanders regarding assessment, treatment, readiness and retention of aviation personnel, consultation to commanders about accident investigation and flight evaluation boards, education and training to aviation personnel on human factors, stress and fatigue, and other safety issues. In addition, the residents are exposed to possible career tracks in applied research in this field.

Types of Assignments

During the spring of the graduating year, residents are involved in determining where they will be placed for their first assignment. This is a negotiation process that occurs between residents at all three internship sites and the psychology consultant to the Surgeon General. All efforts are made to balance the interests of the residents and the needs of the Army. There are many different types of assignments. In general, the assignments are at major medical centers, smaller medical centers in support of major medical centers, combat stress control units, divisions, and in the intelligence community. Assignments vary in length of service from 1 year, considered a hardship tour, to the more typical 3-year assignment. Types of responsibilities vary depending on the setting. In major medical centers, such as Walter Reed, there are typically 11 psychologists, both active duty and civilian. Typical responsibilities have been outlined above. In addition, there are usually increased administrative responsibilities, such as an emphasis on research and development of new treatment or consultation services.

In a support hospital, the psychologist may be the only psychologist on staff along with a psychiatrist and social worker. These positions typically demand more focus on clinical services with relatively less emphasis on research and require additional administrative responsibilities such as supervision of behavioral health technicians and tracking outcome performance data for the mental health clinic. Young psychologists in these settings are faced with honing their professional skills (particularly as leaders within the Army community) and refining their clinical skills. In addition, opportunities are available to present training programs to commanders and soldiers about suicide prevention and to work with substance-abuse programs.

The Army encourages continued professional development in the form of licensure and completion of board certification in professional psychology. Once licensure is achieved and state requirements maintained, the psychologist does not have to change licensure depending on where he or she is stationed. Depending on the duty station, payment for licensure materials is possible. There is additional compensation for board certification.

First Assignment: 121st Hospital, Seoul, South Korea

My first tour was at the Army hospital in Seoul, Korea. I selected this tour because of my desire to expose myself to the great range of assignments that the Army had to offer. Because I selected a 1-year tour, that would mean I would complete my obligation at another site for the remaining 2 years. Thus, I would have two assignments during my 3-year obligation instead of one, which is typical. I was one of two Army psychologists in South Korea. I worked in the psychiatry department and performed the entire range of services for which I trained during my residency in addition to a few additional services, with which I had little or no experience. These additional services included conducting a psychological autopsy, performing two critical event debriefings (following a soldier's suicide and following a helicopter crash), consulting to the substance-abuse program, and providing supervision. This year was critical professionally as it forced me to act as a sole provider. This had benefits of increased self-reliance, development of my clinical skills, and development of leadership ability.

Second Assignment: Walter Reed

When it was time to choose my next assignment I selected and was elected for a position at Walter Reed, which was my first choice. After completion of a hardship tour, the Army tries to reward one's service with placement at a site of your choosing, dependent of course, on the Army's needs. At Walter Reed, I held a position among the health rotation. I was aware of the growing place of psychologists in primary health care, and this afforded me the opportunity to play yet another, different role. Again, I viewed this as a great opportunity to expand my professional expertise and to help me decide if I wanted to pursue application to the health fellowship in subsequent years.

Upon my arrival to Walter Reed, I was considered part of the faculty. Although in the beginning this was a little awkward, because I had trained there, it has since developed into something that I enjoy. I have begun to assume responsibilities of the faculty in terms of training of the residents, development of research protocol in the healthcare environment, and promotion of the role of psychologists in primary care. I particularly enjoy my interaction with residents. Because of these experiences, a position as director of residency training would be an appealing future role.

Operation Iraqi Freedom

At 6 months into my assignment at Walter Reed, I was assigned as a PROFIS (Professional Officer Filler System) officer to Ft. Hood's Combat Stress Control Unit (CSC). PROFIS assignments are a means of augmenting an existing unit's personnel from other resources. Should that particular unit have a mission, the PROFIS officer will report with that unit. In this case, I was allotted about 1 week to gather necessary military and personal supplies and report to Ft. Hood. At Ft. Hood we were trained for 1 month before we were deployed to Kuwait and eventually Iraq. Training included instruction in protection from biological and chemical agents, instruction in weapon proficiency, and receiving the necessary immunizations, including anthrax, for work in a hostile environment. Depending on circumstances, some psychologists will never deploy in their careers. Circumstances include the state of world affairs and whether you are assigned to a unit that deploys frequently or are attached (as a PROFIS officer) to such a unit. Nonetheless, in states of war, all military personnel have the possibility of being deployed.

The mission of a CSC is to sustain military performance, prevent stress casualties, and to treat stress symptoms (U.S. Department of the Army, 1994). I had direct experience with two levels of care within CSC: "prevention" and "restoration." Prevention teams have a clinical psychologist, social worker, and two behavioral health technicians. Depending on the location of the division's mental health resources, the prevention team may be the first available mental health resource for soldiers. The team is stationed near the front line in brigade-support areas. Prevention teams typically work with issues of battle fatigue, operational stress, homefront issues, and suicidal and homicidal risk. Prevention teams also provide classes on stress management and anger management, among other topics, and conduct critical-event debriefings. If there are division mental health services available, they would typically manage cases of suicidal and homicidal risk and clients with psychiatric diagnoses who need ongoing services. Often, prevention teams will travel in convoys to outlying camps with no psychological support services. Depending on the location of the CSC teams, they too, may be the targets of enemy fire, either at their camp or on convoys.

If soldiers cannot be managed at a prevention team, they will be referred to a restoration team. The restoration team can offer a holding facility for up to 3 days. The restoration team is staffed with a psychiatrist and comprises a psychiatric nurse, occupational therapists, and behavioral health technicians. The personnel are subject to modification given available resources.

Six months into my deployment working with a prevention team, I moved to the restoration team. The program at the restoration team included structured focus groups (e.g., anger management, stress management, communication skills), process groups, occupational therapy groups, and personal time. As a psychologist, I performed a variety of functions, including leading the process group, conducting and supervising intake interviews, conducting psychological testing, providing disposition recommendations to command, and providing psychological consultation to the hospital. The mission of the restoration team is the same as that of prevention teams: to preserve fighting strength and, ultimately, to return the soldier to the unit. I was also able to contribute to the clinical and research literature by beginning several writing projects to improve clinical work and psychological assessment with soldiers in a combat environment. (See Table 11.1 for a representative list of responsibilities of an Army clinical psychologist.)

Postdoctoral Fellowships and Career Advancement

Fellowships are offered in three areas: health psychology, neuropsychology, and child psychology. Currently, Tripler Army Medical Center (TAMC) in Hawaii offers all three fellowships, Walter Reed offers the neuropsychology fellowship, and Madigan Army Medical Center (MAMC) in Tacoma, Washington offers the child fellowship. Upon completion of the fellowships, the Army requires an additional service obligation.

Table 11.1 Responsibilities of an Army Clinical Psychologist

Clinical Responsibilities

Outpatient individual therapy: Brief and long term
Outpatient psychological testing: Objective and projective personality testing
Mental status examination
Security clearance
Drill sergeant evaluation
Fitness for duty evaluation
Inpatient psychological assessment
Aeromedical psychological evaluations
Consultation to the substance abuse program
Marital therapy
Group therapy for weight loss and lifestyle improvement
Group therapy: Interpersonal process group
Psychological screening for gastric bypass surgery
Psychological screening for breast cancer patients
Psychological treatment for smoking cessation
Neuropsychological battery administration and interpretation
Dementia screening
ADHD evaluation
Child developmental evaluation
Children: Intellectual evaluation
Suicide assessment briefing
Psychological autopsy
Critical-event debriefings
Battle fatigue briefings

Administrative Responsibilities

Evaluate performance objectives for outpatient mental health clinic
Contribute to multidisciplinary team meetings
Supervise psychology residents
Supervise behavioral health technicians
Coordinate and conduct continuing education classes
Hospital administrator
Act as on-call mental health professional for hospital admission

Research Responsibilities

Develop research ideas
Write grant proposals
Collect data
Analyze data
Write reports

Military Officer Responsibilities

Maintain physical fitness standards
Maintain soldier readiness

Career advancement in the military is competitive and depends on the needs of the Army and the qualifications of each individual. In general, clinical psychologists, like other officers, are promoted based on achievement in their clinical specialty and their achievement as military officers. Promotion to the rank of major typically occurs after 7 years, followed by promotion to lieutenant colonel after 13 years, and finally promotion to colonel after 19 years. (For a more complete history of the role of the clinical psychologist in the Army, consult Gal & Mangelsdorff, 1991.)

Personal Reflection

It has been about 6 years since I accepted the scholarship that began my initiation into the Army as a clinical psychologist. In retrospect, I have no regrets about the choices I have made personally or professionally. I have endured unpleasant aspects of my assignments, such as taking enemy fire, time away from family and friends, long hours, and limited professional support. However, each of these hardships also enriched me personally and professionally. I can say in retrospect that these "hardships" were "good training opportunities," as one of my supervisors used to say.

In addition, I finally have come to a better appreciation of the title Army clinical psychologist. In my mind, I am different from one who practices clinical psychology for the Army. The difference, in my opinion, lies in my primary identification, as an Army soldier or as a clinical psychologist. As a graduate student, I could intellectually understand the difference, but did not have the experience to flush out this slight but important distinction. At this point, I have accumulated some degree of experience. I believe this difference is important because it affects how a psychologist connects to soldiers and to Army culture, in general. In my opinion, an Army clinical psychologist's first identification should be as a soldier within Army culture, and second, albeit a close second, as a clinical psychologist. I believe that from this common and shared position, a clinical psychologist can intervene more effectively. If your primary identification is as a clinical psychologist and secondarily as an Army soldier, your sense of community and connection with the other soldiers will not be as strong, and the clinical work may not be as effective as it could be. This is not to suggest that clinical responsibilities are secondary. Rather, I am suggesting that clinical responsibilities can be informed and strengthened by a shared bond of the Army community with the soldier. In this way, you can be an effective Army clinical psychologist.

As of this writing, I will have to decide whether I will pursue a career in the Army or not, as my obligation is nearing an end. Again, I seem to find myself in a position similar to the one I was in during graduate school, where I was weighing the advantages and disadvantages. I am nearing the end of the early stage of my career in the Army and as a clinical psychologist. While it has been a relatively short time of 3 years, they have been a rich 3 years. I have done things I was not sure I could do, expanded my professional expertise, developed personally, participated in my nation's history by supporting my government in Operation Iraqi Freedom, and deepened my sense of membership, pride, and responsibility to the United States of America. Regardless of my future in the Army, I know that I am ready to continue and succeed in the next stage of my career as a clinical psychologist.

Disclaimer

The views expressed here are the author's and are not necessarily those of the U.S. Army or the Department of Defense.

References

Gal, R., & Mangelsdorff, A. D. (Eds.). (1991). *Handbook of military psychology.* New York: John Wiley & Sons.

U.S. Department of the Army, Headquarters. (1994). Field manual no. 22-51, 29 September. Washington, D.C.: Department of the Army.

U.S. Department of the Army, Headquarters. (1998). Field manual no. 8-51, change no. 1, 30 January. Washington, D.C.: Department of the Army.

12

Correctional Psychology: Looking beyond the Bars

SHELIA M. BRANDT

When most people think of psychologists working in correctional environments, they think of what they see on television or in movies: a psychologist (usually portrayed as young, bright, and filled with unresolved inner conflict) working in a dimly lit cell trying to "figure out" the inner psyche of a brilliant criminal before some intense and high-pressure deadline (e.g., execution, death of another victim), only to be thwarted at every turn by a corrupt prison official. Although this scenario may contain some elements of truth, it is not an accurate reflection of a career in correctional psychology.

In reality, correctional psychologists find themselves using their psychological expertise in performing a wide range of duties. For example, not only do correctional psychologists complete psychological evaluations, as suggested above, but they also conduct psychotherapy and crisis intervention, provide employee assistance, participate in the personnel selection process, and serve as consultants for institutional decisions and policies related to the correctional climate. The goals of this chapter include illustrating the different types of settings within the correctional field, examining the roles of psychologists working in corrections, discussing the ethical and professional challenges unique to correctional environments, and exploring the need for and importance of psychologists working within correctional systems.

Roles of the Psychologist in the Correctional Setting

Although most people think of a prison when they think of providing psychological services within a correctional setting, this is really an oversimplification. Psychologists who define themselves as correctional psychologists may be working in prisons and jails, correctional receiving centers, correctional treatment centers, community corrections centers, or state hospitals. The term *correctional psychologist* itself can cause confusion. For the purpose of this chapter, the term is defined as any psychologist working within a correctional setting, regardless of degree (i.e., MA/MS, Ph.D., Psy.D., or Ed.D.) or degree specialization (e.g., clinical or counseling psychologist).

Further, there are organizational differences within correctional settings that can have a significant impact on the role and duties of the psychologist. Weinberger and Sreenivasan (1994) provide an overview of the four basic organizational systems found across correctional settings. The most common system is where the department of corrections (or in the case of federal prisons, the Bureau of Prisons [BOP]) provides both mental health services and security needs for the institution. A second type of setting is one in which the department of corrections is responsible for the security needs, but the mental health needs are provided by a separate mental health agency. This model is employed when mental health services are contracted out. The psychologist works in the prison, but is an employee of the separate mental health agency rather than the department of corrections. Next is a setting in which both the security and mental health needs are provided by the department of mental health or similar human service department. This model is frequently seen in state hospitals with forensic units where offenders may be sentenced in lieu of prison or committed for treatment until such time that the individual can be transferred to prison. Finally, there are mental health facilities in which an agency of mental health provides the mental health services while the security needs are met by the department of corrections. Again, these types of settings generally involve individuals who have been convicted of crimes but are in need of treatment during the course of their incarceration. As a psychologist who has worked in all four types of environments, I can attest that the organizational structure not only impacts the experience of the offender but it greatly shapes the duties, expectations, and potential role conflicts of psychologists working within a given system.

Traditional Psychological Services

Given the organizational diversity of correctional settings, it follows that the services provided by psychologists within these environments also span a broad spectrum. Thus, when exploring the duties of psychologists (or, more globally, the role of psychology), it is best to organize the roles and responsibilities along a service-based continuum. Fagan's (2003) three-level conceptual model will serve as a frame of reference for the first section of our discussion of "traditional" psychology services provided within correctional settings.

The first level of services includes services that are available to all offenders (Fagan, 2003). The goals of such services are to detect mental health issues or diagnosis, refer inmates deemed to have significant mental illnesses, and provide long- or short-term treatment for offenders in general. These services include screenings for new arrivals, psychological evaluations and management of mentally ill inmates, crisis intervention, suicide prevention, and skill building (e.g., anger management, stress management, parenting skills training, and relapse prevention). Although correctional psychologists do provide individual psychotherapy, group psychotherapy may be utilized more frequently than it is by psychologists working in other settings. Two major factors likely contribute to this difference. First, the typical correctional staff psychologist may be responsible for more than 500 inmates (Fagan, 2003). Second, many inmates will often share common mental health issues (such as criminal thinking, anger management, etc.).

Crisis management is often thought of as the area in which psychologists "earn their keep" within the correctional environment. Crises may be individual in nature (e.g., discovery that a spouse is filing for divorce, death in the family, trying to manage parent–child problems during incarceration) or secondary to incarceration or factors within the institution. For example, if an institution makes changes that affect inmates' experiences of incarceration, there is usually an increase in the amount of crisis services utilized by inmates (even if only briefly). Some examples of such changes can include reduced recreation equipment or hours, real or perceived decrease in access to health services, decrease in visiting time, or changes in phone or mail access. Whether the crisis situation is more personal for the inmate or related to a more global issue, the common theme is one of helplessness. Aside from being the primary providers of crisis intervention services, psychologists are often called upon by administrative staff to either help facilitate the delivery of difficult news or changes inmates may perceive as negative.

In keeping with Fagan's (2003) model, the next category (i.e., Level 2 services) contains similar activities to those mentioned in Level 1, yet the programs and services are offered for specific groups of offenders who possess similar mental health needs or other characteristics. For example, psychologists participating in Level 2 services may be providing drug treatment to a group of offenders with substance use disorders, facilitating trauma or grief groups with female offenders, or conducting support groups for inmates with HIV. Level 2 services also include those services that psychologists may provide to institutional staff, through either psychoeducation or a formal employee assistance program (EAP) after a shared experience such as an institutional crisis (e.g., riot) or natural disaster. For example, I spoke with staff after the terrorist attacks on September 11, 2001 and provided information on how to help staff and their families cope with the attacks.

Fagan (2003) conceptualizes Level 3 services as either consultation or interventions that are systemic, as opposed to directly delivered to the inmates or even staff. Further, in these roles psychologists serve as consultants or treatment "extenders" as opposed to "providers." For example, Fagan discussed that psychologists may be asked to use their interpersonal and conflict resolution skills to mediate disputes within departments or between employees, provide their opinions about the social climate of the institution, or consult about the psychological impact of changes in inmate housing within the institution. Two other areas within Level 3 include supervision and training of staff.

Certainly, doctoral-level psychologists provide clinical supervision for new psychologists, master's-level psychologists, or psychology students; however, the majority of supervision provided by psychologists is to mental health paraprofessionals. There is a trend in correctional settings to employ nondoctoral mental health providers in the provision of direct services, some with relatively limited mental health training. These paraprofessionals include correctional counselors, correctional treatment specialists, and addictions counselors. As a result, doctoral psychologists are finding themselves more frequently in positions utilizing their supervisory, program development, evaluation, and administrative skills (Morgan, Winterowd, & Ferrell, 1999). Psychologists are also called on to develop or provide training for other staff in the institution (Harowski, 2003). For example, psychologists may be asked to design training programs to raise the awareness of staff regarding mental illness, managing job-related stressors, identifying suicidal indicators, conflict resolution, and developing leadership and communication skills in correctional managers.

The preceding section has focused on psychologists performing primarily "traditional" psychological duties (i.e., direct service, consultation, and training) within correctional environments. Not all of these opportunities are provided within every correctional institution because the range and intensity of psychological services are driven by the clinical need, mission of the facility, level of funding, and type of institutional staff (Fagan, 2003). Nevertheless, it is clear that there are ample opportunities for psychologists to utilize their clinical skills in correctional environments.

Nontraditional Psychological Services

This section explores a few of the more "nontraditional" activities, trends, or career paths in which psychologists are involved within the correctional field. Although these responsibilities are not thought of as primary psychological duties, they utilize the psychologist's expertise and specialized skills.

For example, many correctional facilities have specialized "teams" that are mobilized during various institutional emergencies. Examples of these teams include, but are not limited to, hostage negotiation, disturbance control, crisis response, and critical incident stress debriefing. While the leadership roles of psychologists vary across these teams, psychologists work with each of these teams for their specialized skills with regard to assessment of personality types, crisis deescalation skills, violence, and other risk prediction assessments and knowledge of trauma impact.

For those interested in expanding their knowledge base of psychopharmacology, correctional settings offer exciting opportunities for psychologists to take active roles in these interventions. Given that many correctional facilities use contract psychiatric providers who are not located on site, psychologists are often responsible for medication referrals, direct consultation with the psychiatrist or other physicians regarding medications to be used, and medication monitoring including assessment of any side effects or general effectiveness of the intervention. Although psychologists must not go beyond their professional competencies, they are often the institutional "expert" by the nature of the staffing regarding psychotropic interventions. It is predicted that this aspect of practice is likely to expand and become more of an independent function as psychologists pursue and achieve prescription privileges, as happened in 2002 in New Mexico (Goode, 2002).

"Telehealth," or the use of technology such as video conferencing, telephones, and fax to provide "virtual" appointments (Nickelson,

Magalletta & Ax, 1998), is a growing medium for the delivery of psychological services in corrections. The benefits of telehealth include the provision of services that may not be geographically available, eliminating the need to transport an offender into the community for services, and using distant professionals to bridge language or other cultural differences (Holton, 2003). Given that the psychologist is the on-site provider, his or her role in the effectiveness of the medium is crucial. Specifically, the psychologist often serves in a triage capacity, assessing the inmate's presenting symptoms in light of past mental health history, treatment, side effects, and other information available in the on-site file. It is often the psychologist's responsibility to convey this information to the provider on the other end of the telehealth connection.

A "Typical" Week in the Life of a Correctional Psychologist

As already discussed, the duties of psychologists working in corrections vary greatly. Many of the factors affecting how the day is spent include type of facility (e.g., receiving center versus prison), length of sentence of the inmates, and position of the psychologist (e.g., line staff psychologist or administrator). For example, for most psychologists employed in correctional settings the emphasis is on the provision of direct services or activities related to those services (Hawk, 1997). However, it has been my observation that the farther "up the chain" we go, the more the paperwork and administrative tasks increase exponentially. As such, it is hard to capture a "typical" routine for a correctional psychologist but some of the following factors seem to be common across positions and settings.

The day begins with entering the institution, which in itself is a major activity. Depending on the facility, this entails some combination of the following: showing proper identification, obtaining keys, radio, body alarm, or other equipment, passing through a metal detector, and possibly having personal property searched. In some institutions, the morning may begin with a morning meeting, rounds, or the roll call for officers if there is salient mental health information to pass on.

Inmate clients, scheduled in advance, will likely arrive at the psychologist's office or other designated meeting place via controlled hourly movements, a pass system, escort, or on their own, depending on the security level. Obviously, if an inmate is scheduled for an appointment and does not arrive, it is not as simple as a no-show in the free world. It is important that the housing unit be called to locate the inmate for the purposes of accountability. Further, unlike traditional treatment settings, the vast majority of the interruptions to services are not related to no-shows. In corrections, psychologists may find their appointments delayed by institutional lockdowns or counts where movement is prohibited or sessions prematurely terminated if they need to respond to a call for help or institutional emergency. On the other end of the continuum, it is very common for psychologists to have impromptu appointments, which result from staff members reporting that an inmate is engaging in disruptive or concerning behavior (e.g., crying, yelling, uncooperative behavior with staff, self-isolation).

In addition to seeing both scheduled and unscheduled inmates, conducting group therapy or psychological assessments, there are also several consultative duties throughout a week. For example, psychologists are expected to make special housing unit (SHU) or segregation rounds (i.e., when inmates are placed in "the hole") and keep custody staff abreast of potential mental health concerns. Other weekly meetings may include departmental or interdepartmental meetings, department head meetings, Affirmative Action meetings, and staffings with medical or the consulting psychiatrist and housing unit teams (e.g., review of inmates' programming needs and accomplishments). For psychologist supervisors, clinical supervision is also an ongoing responsibility. Less frequent responsibilities may include assisting with hiring through personnel interviews or providing training for new staff.

In summary, while correctional psychologists provide many "traditional" psychological services with their respective inmate populations, the correctional environment also provides unique and interesting opportunities not found within other settings. Table 12.1 provides an overview of the major duties performed by correctional psychologists.

Challenges and Obstacles in Careers in Correctional Psychology

The most fundamental challenge involves defining and understanding the role of the psychologist within the correctional environment or, more aptly, the multiple roles of the psychologist. As mentioned earlier in the chapter, the duties and expectations of psychologists are greatly influenced by the organizational structure in which they practice. For example, in some correctional settings, psychologists' duties are quite compartmentalized in terms of providing direct services. In these settings, psychologists do not get involved in any of the specified correctional management or security procedures aside from maintaining the security of their work areas. Yet, on the other end of the continuum, psychologists may be expected to perform, or have the

Table 12.1 Common Work Duties for Correctional Psychologists

Clinical Duties

Conducting intake assessments or classification of new inmates

Performing psychological evaluations when there is a specific referral question from institutional staff or the courts

Providing crisis intervention and violence risk assessments

Facilitating individual and group psychotherapy and psychoeducation

Managing and referring inmates taking or in need of psychotropic medications

Monitoring and assessing inmates in segregation

Evaluating suicide risk

Implementing and monitoring suicide watches

Training and Supervision Duties

Providing annual staff training in mental health issues

Supervising and conducting performance evaluations for mental health professionals and paraprofessionals

Training and supervising practicum students, interns, and volunteers

Consultation Duties

Assisting in employment interviews with job applicants

Analyzing and presenting potential effects of institutional changes (i.e., housing) on the institutional climate

Consulting as a mental health expert for hostage negotiation or disturbance control teams

Staff Services

Coordinating employee assistance program or community referrals for staff and their families

Providing critical incident stress debriefing to staff and their families after institutional crises

Serving as conflict resolution specialist or mediator for staff or departmental conflicts

Administrative Services

Attending departmental, department head, and segregation meetings or morning rounds

Maintaining a list and working knowledge of inmates with significant mental health issues coming into, within, or leaving the institution

---

ability to perform, the same security duties as other correctional staff within the institution. For example, in the Federal Bureau of Prisons, psychologists attend the Federal Law Enforcement Training Center and receive training in inmate discipline, self-defense, contraband searches, and use of force training including required proficiency with firearms.

Some authors have argued that this level of involvement in security duties may undermine traditional therapeutic goals and the relationship between the inmate and the therapist. This is the basis for the frequent but oversimplified "treatment versus security" argument

(Clingempeel, Mulvey, & Repucci, 1980; Weinberger & Sreenivasan, 1994). While examining this debate, Dignam (2003) goes on to suggest that it is more useful and accurate to view duties within the correctional environment as occurring on a "management–treatment" continuum as opposed to mutually exclusive categories. Clearly, the roles and responsibilities of the correctional psychologist can be ambiguous and, at times, confusing.

A second challenge in correctional settings, also ethical in nature, is the age-old question of "Who is the client and who is it our duty to serve?" This question has been comprehensively addressed by several authors (Brodsky, 1980; Clingempeel et al., 1980, Dignam, 2003; Monahan, 1980). All of these authors recognize that the answer to the question is that the two are not mutually exclusive. This is especially true in correctional environments where the overall mission is focused on safety and security with treatment or rehabilitation functioning as less important priorities. Dignam (2003) stated that the true "client" depends on what the clinician is "doing." For example, when a clinician is providing individual therapy, the inmate is the primary client. Yet, if a psychologist is conducting a court-ordered evaluation, the court is the primary client. Other "clients" with a vested interest in the services provided by correctional psychologists include, but are not limited to, families of the offender, society, the warden of an institution, taxpayers, correctional staff, families of the victims, etc. Dignam (2003) reminds us that viewing interests as competing (i.e., society's interest vs. offender's interest) only muddies the ethical waters. It can be argued that these interests have similar long-term goals (i.e., all parties).

Another challenge, often cited as one of the reasons professionals do not want to work with inmates, is related to the truthfulness and motivation of the inmates. While certainly this is a concern, I would argue that psychologists are faced with this issue no matter where they practice, albeit to a lesser extent. Whether it is a worker's compensation claim evaluation, a mother in therapy facing losing her children in light of her alleged drinking, an employee mandated to therapy by an employer, or an inmate having conflict with a cellmate, psychologists must use their assessment skills and clinical judgment to determine what, if any, services are needed by their clients. Aside from the obvious criminal justice issues, inmates are faced with many of the same mental health issues as all of our clients: marital difficulties, depression, the need for stress management skills, grief, and anxiety about the future.

A final but very real challenge that can become an insurmountable barrier if ignored by the clinician is the numerous diversity issues found in correctional settings. A few of these issues include ethnic background and race, which can have a very practical impact on communication with inmate clients, age of offender, rural versus urban offender, socioeconomic background, and religious affiliations or beliefs. Although space prohibits a full discussion of these factors in this chapter, anyone pursuing a career in correctional psychology should be well versed in the understanding and appreciation of diversity as well as culturally competent to practice with a diverse population. Specifically, the clinician must be willing and able to work with individuals who have often had life experiences vastly different from theirs and even those of the general population.

Rewarding Aspects of Correctional Psychology Careers

After reading the last section, you may be asking yourself, "Why would any psychologist want to work in correctional settings?" Although the primary mission of the correctional environment, as defined by today's standards, appears to be punishment, a secondary mission is very congruent with an underlying tenant of psychology. Specifically, Hawk (1997) reminds us that the mission of *psychology* (italics added) within a prison system is to assist in the rehabilitation and reintegration into society by offenders. She goes on to observe that the correctional field is rich with opportunities for psychologists to utilize their expertise to influence the development of correctional policies.

Although historically, there may have been a strong stigma about working in correctional environments, this trend seems to be less evident. Further, there are greater opportunities for psychologists in corrections than there were years ago. It was not until after World War II that the discipline of psychology began to show interest in the correctional field (Magaletta & Boothby, 2003). This interest was bolstered by legal opinions that reinforced inmates' constitutional rights for access to a wide range of mental health services provided by trained mental health providers (*Inmates v. Pierce,* 1980; *Ruiz v. Estelle,* 1980). In the 1980s, the emphasis on drug abuse treatment became a fiscally supported priority after the Anti-Drug Abuse Act of 1986. These judicial and legislative actions, coupled with the mass deinstitutionalization or transinstitutionalization (the idea the mentally ill were removed from hospital care-based settings only to be incarcerated) of the mentally ill, have resulted in several opportunities for psychologists to provide clinical services for an underserved population. However, while the number of inmates (particularly those with mental illnesses) continues to rise, the estimate of the psychologist-to-inmate ratio appears to be half of that observed in the 1980s (Boothby

& Clements, 2000). Thus, the need for mental health service providers remains quite high.

Further, psychologists who work in correctional environments are not only providing needed clinical services, but they also are actually performing a public safety function. More than 95% of all offenders eventually return to their communities (Hawk, 1997). Thus, treating inmates with mental health conditions in the prison is more likely to result in more predictable and rational behavior in the community (Wilkinson, 2000).

In addition to the benefits to the inmates (i.e., Constitutional right, improved mental health upon release), there are several staff issues that influence psychologists to work in prisons (Hawk-Sawyer, 1997). As an example already stated in the discussion of Level 3 services, psychologists often provide initial assessments, support, and referrals for staff working in correctional settings. They may provide more intensive counseling and debriefing to the staff and their families after disturbances at a facility or natural disaster. Psychologists may use their expertise to provide training for staff on everything ranging from how to handle conflict and stress in the correctional workplace (which is always abundant!) or specific interpersonal skills for managing and interacting with inmates.

Developing a Career in Correctional Psychology

So how does one develop a career as a correctional psychologist? Most psychology graduate students know that the logical answer to that question is, "take a course." However, it is not that simple when dealing with correctional psychology, because graduate courses in correctional psychology are not widely available (Harowski, 2003). In fact, a survey of predoctoral interns completing their internships in predoctoral correctional settings found that only 7% of the interns reported completing a course in correctional psychology prior to their internship year (Pietz, DeMier, Dienst, Green, & Scully, 1998). There are even fewer graduate programs that offer any type of specialization or emphasis in correctional psychology. Although specialty courses may be limited, correctional psychologists working within the field recommend several core areas in which to strengthen one's knowledge base and gain experience. Specifically, potential correctional psychologists are advised to establish competence in psychological testing, diagnosis, and treatment of personality disorders (Boothby & Clements, 2000). It also serves as a benefit to develop crisis intervention skills, familiarize yourself with substance abuse treatment and group therapy models, utilize empirically documented treatment interventions, and gain as much experience as possible with racially and culturally diverse populations (Magaletta & Boothby, 2003).

In addition to the academics, interested individuals are encouraged to complete a practicum or volunteer in a correctional mental health setting. This type of experience will allow you to observe the treatment context in which services are delivered. However, Magaletta and Boothby (2003) caution that there is a great amount of diversity in the quality of the experience and supervision in some of these less formal placements. As such, the expectations and competencies should be clearly set forth before arriving at the institution.

If you are seriously interested in exploring correctional psychology as a career avenue, then it is particularly helpful to use the internship year to explore the correctional environment. As far as predoctoral internships are concerned, the Federal Bureau of Prisons probably offers one of the most accurate portrayals of life as a correctional psychologist. With that said, there is great diversity in the training experiences of the interns. Interns may gain experience at medical centers for prisoners, in the general population, with male or female offenders, with inmates with serious mental illnesses or substance abuse/dependence disorders, or with inmates suffering from chronic medical illnesses or HIV (Harowski, 2003). Several authors (Ax & Morgan, 2002; Harowski, 2003; Magaletta & Boothby, 2003) argue that the internship is the ideal opportunity to gain experience in corrections because the intern is engaged in clinical work that provides exposure and opportunities to work with inmates while surrounded with ample supervision, didactic instruction, and support. Further, the intern can gain exposure to the climate and pace of the work within the correctional environment while obtaining a well-rounded training experience that will generalize outside of corrections if the intern determines correctional work is not a good fit.

If you are without past correctional experience but interested in exploring a career in correctional psychology, do not lose heart. Most jails and prisons have strong volunteer programs or at least an interest in getting "free" services for the inmates. Consider taking advantage of opportunities such as this to become involved to assess your interest and comfort in providing services in the correctional setting. The Chief of Psychology or Mental Health within a facility in which you are interested is usually a good place to find some ideas about how you can gain some clinical experience in the setting. Although it is certainly helpful to speak with psychologists working in correctional settings, I strongly advise against taking a job in a jail or prison without some type of fieldwork in a correctional setting first.

In addition to taking specialized courses, seeking correctional training experiences, and actively participating in the supervision process, another avenue for developing knowledge or networking with correctional mental health professionals is through professional organizations. A few professional mental health organizations dedicated solely to correctional psychologists (Magaletta &Boothby, 2003) include the Criminal Justice Section of the American Psychological Association's Division 18, Psychologists in Public Service, and the American Association of Correctional Psychologists. Other resources that provide valuable information include the Federal Bureau of Prisons, the American Correctional Association, and the National Commission on Correctional Health Care. This author contends that it is essential that professionals, especially new professionals, participate in such organizations; not only for the dissemination of knowledge, but also for networking, mentoring opportunities, and to ensure that their voices are heard. It has already been stated that the work of a correctional psychologist can seem isolating within the correctional environment. Membership in professional organizations is a mitigating factor in this dynamic. A similar opportunity for exploring the correctional field is listservs on the Internet. Often these sites contain dialogue about current trends in the field, serve as resources for information requests, or even advertise job or postdoctoral internship leads.

Lessons Learned in Correctional Psychology

In this final section, I would like to leave you with some thoughts based on my own experience and that of other new professionals within the field. First, be prepared to sell yourself and your skills. This may be particularly true if you are a doctoral psychologist applying for a position that hires both master's-level and doctoral-level clinicians. Research recent hires and salaries and assess what skills you have that may make you more competitive than other candidates. For example, can you conduct needed psychological evaluations that other candidates may not have the competency to provide? Are you willing to design a practicum placement or similar training experience that will increase the provision of psychological services with little to no cost to the institution? This thought is reflective both of my own experience and a more widely held concern of correctional psychologists that many of the available jobs are going to master's-level clinicians as opposed to doctoral level (Morgan et al., 1999; Boothby & Clements, 2002).

Next, remember that the correctional environment is its own culture and riddled with bureaucracy. Although opportunities abound, change can be slow; in large organizations such as any state department of corrections, county jail system, or the Federal Bureau of Prisons, it is easy to lose sight of the big picture. While psychologists have a long history of advocating for their clients, they are often ill prepared for politicking, and this is a skill that is essential in working for change in the correctional field.

Remember your goals and what excites you about the field. Although I am a new professional by definition (5 years or less since receiving my doctoral degree), I have already had the opportunity to observe both correctional psychologists who have maintained their professional passions and those who have become enveloped or overwhelmed by the obstacles of providing psychological services within an institutional setting. Because it is easy to understand logically how familiarity and complacency sets in within highly structured and challenging environments, I do not judge these latter professionals. However, I challenge you to maintain professional interests and ties outside of the correctional environment.

Finally, I believe it is essential to choose a mentor within the field. Think of someone who has similar interests and career goals as well as some common life circumstances. Psychologists working within correctional environments are at high risk for professional isolation. In some settings, a clinician may be only one of a few or may even be the only psychologist on staff. Without consulting with a peer or mentor, it is easy to lose sight of clinical focus, objectivity, and perspective. The relationship between an institution and its mental health staff is a tricky one. Although the institution generally values and relies on the objectivity and expertise of its mental health professionals, often there is also a strong pull for the professional to conform or concur with the general consensus. Working with a mentor helps you maintain your own professional identity and direction and provides you with support.

References

Ax, R. K., & Morgan, R. D. (2002). Internship training opportunities in correctional psychology: A comparison of settings. *Criminal Justice and Behavior, 29*, 332–347.

Boothby, J. L., & Clements, C. B. (2000). A national survey of correctional psychologists. *Criminal Justice and Behavior, 27*, 716–732.

Brodsky, S. L. (1980). Ethical issues for psychologists in corrections. In J. Monahan (Ed.), *Who is the client?* (pp. 63–92). Washington, D.C.: American Psychological Association.

Clingempeel, W. G., Mulvey, E., & Repucci, N. D. (1980). A national study of ethical dilemmas of psychologists in the criminal justice system. In J. Monahan (Ed.), *Who is the client?* (pp. 126–153). Washington, D.C.: American Psychological Association.

Dignam, J. T. (2003). Correctional mental health ethics revisited. In T. J. Fagan & R. K. Ax (Eds.), *Correctional mental health handbook* (pp. 39–56). Thousand Oaks, CA: Sage.

Fagan, T. J. (2003). Mental health in corrections: A model for service delivery. In T. J. Fagan & R. K. Ax (Eds.), *Correctional mental health handbook* (pp. 3–20). Thousand Oaks, CA: Sage.

Goode, E. (2002). Psychologists get prescription pads and furor erupts. *The New York Times*, March 26, D1, D4.

Harowski, K. J. (2003). Multiple roles. In T. J. Fagan & R. K. Ax (Eds.), *Correctional mental health handbook* (pp. 237–250). Thousand Oaks, CA: Sage.

Hawk, K. M. (1997). Personal reflections on a career in correctional psychology. *Professional Psychology: Research and Practice, 28*, 335–337.

Holton, S. M. B. (2003). Managing and treating mentally disordered offenders in jails and prisons. In T. J. Fagan & R. K. Ax (Eds.), *Correctional mental health handbook* (p. 101–122). Thousand Oaks, CA: Sage.

Magaletta, P. R., & Boothby, J. (2003). Correctional mental health professionals. In T. J. Fagan & R. K. Ax (Eds.), *Correctional mental health handbook* (pp. 21–37). Thousand Oaks, CA: Sage.

Magaletta, P. R., Fagan, T. J., & Ax, R. K. (1998). Advancing psychology services through telehealth in the Federal Bureau of Prisons. *Professional Psychology: Research and Practice, 29*, 543–548.

Monahan, J. (Ed.). (1980). *Who is the client?* Washington, D.C.: American Psychological Association.

Morgan, R. D., Winterowd, C. L., & Ferrell, S. W. (1999). A national survey of group psychotherapy in correctional facilities. *Professional Psychology: Research and Practice, 30*, 600–606.

Nickelson, D. W. (1998). Telehealth and the evolving health care system: Strategic opportunities for professional psychology. *Professional Psychology: Research and Practice, 29*, 527–535.

Pietz, C. A., DeMier, R. L., Dienst, R. D., Green, J. B., & Scully, B. (1998). Psychology internship training in a correctional facility. *Criminal Justice and Behavior, 25*, 99–108.

Weinberger, L. E., & Sreenivasan, S. (1994). Ethical and professional conflicts in correctional psychology. *Professional Psychology: Research and Practice, 25*, 161–167.

Wilkinson, R. A. (2000). Impact of mentally ill on justice system. Congressional testimony on Offenders with Mental Illness in the Criminal Justice System submitted to the United States House of Representatives House Judiciary Subcommittee on Crime, September 21.

13

School Psychologists in Nontraditional Settings: Alternative Roles and Functions in Psychological Service Delivery

RICHARD GILMAN AND TERRI L. TEAGUE

As practitioners within one of the four recognized specialty areas within psychology, school psychologists attain specialized training in the practice of psychological science as it applies to children, youth, and families, learners of all ages, and the schooling process. As such, school psychologists provide a broad array of services, including psychological assessment, intervention, prevention, consultation, health promotion, and program development and evaluation, with particular focus on the cognitive, social, and developmental processes of learners and the learning environment. Recognizing that these processes involve a large range of contributing factors, school psychologists have advanced knowledge of theories and empirical findings in developmental and social psychology, developmental psychopathology

within cultural contexts, applied behavior analysis and behavior modification, learning strategies and curriculum instruction, individual,
group, and family counseling, and measurement theory and applications of advanced statistical methodology. School psychologists
working in school settings are required to attain the specialist degree
(National Association of School Psychologists, 2003), while the practice of school psychology in other settings requires doctoral-level
training.

Considering that the world's first psychological clinic was created
to help students with learning difficulties, the relationship between
psychology and schools is as old as the practice of American psychology (French, 1990). Thus, it is not surprising that school psychology
as a formal specialty evolved from the work of this seminal clinic, and
the majority of practitioners (approximately 85%) continue to work in
school settings (Reschly, 2000). Practitioners who work in schools are
responsible for delivering a variety of services, all subsumed under
the necessity for promoting the psychoeducational and psychosocial
well-being of students and families (Nastassi, 1998). In this regard,
school-based psychologists are responsible for the delivery of primary
(i.e., strategies designed to prevent problems from first emerging),
secondary (i.e., strategies designed to reverse or preclude harm from
identified risk factors), and tertiary (i.e., strategies designed to reduce the
severity of harm within identified individuals) levels of intervention.

Pursuing a Career in Nontraditional School Psychology

Although the employment outlook for school-based practitioners continues to be favorable (Fagan, 2002), a number of school psychologists (particularly at the doctoral level) choose to utilize their training
and skills in nonschool (i.e., nontraditional) settings. Estimates
between 5% (Reschly, 2000) and 31% (Curtis, Hunley, Walker, &
Baker, 1999) have been reported for school psychologists who are
employed in nontraditional settings on a full-time basis. There are a
number of reasons nontraditional settings are chosen. For example,
the relationship between psychological practice and the needs of
school systems is often influenced by legal requirements that typically
restrict the type and level of services that are delivered. Because
school-based psychologists are recognized as experts in administering
and interpreting various psychoeducational batteries for the purposes
of determining eligibility for placement in special education, these
activities dominate the majority of a school-based school psychologist's time, often at the expense of providing other services such as
counseling and other remedial activities (Bramlett, Murphy, Johnson,

Wallingford, & Hall, 2000; Curtis et al,. 1999; Hutton, Dubes, & Muir, 1992; Reschly & Wilson, 1995). In addition, the range of qualified administrative positions for school-based psychologists is often limited (in comparison to nontraditional settings), with the position of director or supervisor of psychological services usually the terminal position. Further, school-based clinicians must often adopt a "generalist" approach, leaving little opportunity to specialize in treating a specific difficulty (e.g., eating disorders, pediatric concerns) or for a specific age range (e.g., preschool children). Finally, practice in the school setting often restricts or limits additional revenue sources (i.e., third-party reimbursements) that may be available to clinicians in nontraditional settings.

Previous assertions by some (e.g., Matarazzo, 1987) maintained that skills obtained in doctoral graduate training programs and practiced in APA-accredited internship sites are roughly similar across psychology subspecialties. Further, almost two decades ago Abidin (1985, cited in Pfeiffer & Dean, 1988) noted an absence of data to suggest that psychological training in a given program, under a given title, is best suited for a particular setting or to perform specific services. Data to refute this observation remains nonexistent. Given these previous assertions, the absence of data to suggest that substantial training differences exist across psychology subspecialties, and the constraints that are often placed on school-based psychologists, there is a growing realization that school psychology is defined less by the setting in which it is practiced and more by the competencies that the practitioner holds (Ysseldyke, Dawson, Lehr, Reschly, Reynolds, & Telzrow, 1997).

This chapter briefly describes five specific nontraditional settings that exist for school psychologists, as well as some reasons school psychologists choose these particular settings. The five nontraditional settings are private practice, residential institutions, neuropsychological settings, pediatric settings, and early intervention or child guidance centers. Following these descriptions, considerations for practicing in nontraditional settings, as well as suggestions on how school psychologists can best prepare for and secure positions in such settings are discussed.

Nontraditional Areas of School Psychology

Private Practice

Of all nontraditional areas in school psychology, private practice is perhaps the most appealing but also the most demanding (in terms of time commitment, financial resources, etc.). Typical daily and weekly activities will vary according to a number of factors including the clientele served, specific needs of the community, and specialization of the clinician. Whatever the reason, entering private practice is largely a function of choice, depth, and flexibility of specific roles that may or may not be granted to the school-based psychologist. That is, while the core functions of assessment, consultation, and group and individual interventions are practiced in both school and clinical settings, there are differences in the manner in which these functions are practiced in each setting (Medway, Hagan, Hartye, & Hosford, 1988). For example, due to legislative mandates, assessment-related activities constitute the largest activity and amount of time for school-based clinicians. Private practitioners, who are not directly tied to such mandates, may determine that psychoeducational assessment is less important than other functions in a specific case (e.g., implementing an individual behavioral intervention, parent consultation for a child with an elimination disorder). School psychologists in private practice may also choose to specialize in a specific area, such as child advocacy, or in treating disorders that would normally be beyond the purview of a school-based practitioner (such as providing ongoing, intensive individual therapy for sexually abused children or children diagnosed with an eating disorder).

In addition to flexibility and specialization of functions, there are a number of other reasons more school psychologists are choosing the private arena. Changes in third-party insurance reimbursement policies, the rise and dominance of health maintenance organizations (HMOs) and preferred provider organizations (PPOs), and the expansion of school psychology training programs to modify their curriculum to include nontraditional settings (e.g., Power, DuPaul, Shapiro, & Parrish, 1995) all speak to the economic incentives that await school psychologists in private practice. Methods in which these incentives are realized include providing second opinions for parents who wish to challenge the assessment findings of school-based psychologists, providing auxiliary services that may be impractical in many school settings (e.g., ongoing family therapy), and providing services to students with specific physical disabilities (e.g., spina bifida), emotional disorders, or other difficulties whose condition or age precludes them from being served in the regular school settings. Second, private practitioners serve as external consultants who are largely unhindered by the constraints often placed by the school system on the school psychologist. Thus, private practitioners often possess leverage with parents that a school-based school psychologist may not have (Pryzwansky, 1989), particularly if parents voluntarily seek the services of the private practitioner. Finally, private practitioners may be more involved in larger child advocacy efforts, where the "client" is not a specific individual or family but rather social agencies and court systems. In this regard, private practitioners have the option of becoming involved in activities such as conducting forensic evaluations or making judgments concerning adoption (Medway et al., 1988). Such roles are largely beyond the capabilities or interests of many school-based clinicians.

Residential Treatment Settings

Residential treatment centers (RTCs) are typically self-contained settings in which multidisciplinary services are provided to severely involved youth. Young people are often required to stay at the setting in order to receive these services, and, depending on the severity of the concern, the length of stay can fluctuate from brief- to long-term duration. All service delivery and intervention strategies are monitored on a regular basis.

The typical day-to-day functions of psychologists working in an RTC vary according to the administrative level held, the skills necessary to meet the mental health needs of the youths, and the type of RTC. All these possibilities serve as options that are typically not afforded the school-based psychologist. For example, the administrative positions that an RTC-based psychologist can assume can be more varied than what is usually found in a school setting, with positions ranging from clinical/program director, to research consultant, to educational director (see Morris & Morris, 1989). Further, in regard to role flexibility, in most cases children are initially tested by other staff prior to their admission to the RTC, often rendering psychoeducational evaluations as minimal responsibilities of the school psychologist. Greater emphasis is therefore placed on conducting functional behavior assessments, monitoring behavioral modification strategies, and designing and implementing psychoeducational or psychosocial interventions. Moreover, given that fewer children are served in an RTC (as compared to schools), psychologists often maintain a more of a "hands-on approach" with students under their care. Thus, ongoing and in-depth consultation with parents and teachers, program evaluation and modification, and team management are typical functions of the RTC-based psychologist. Finally, unlike the school-based psychologist, who may be the only mental health specialist in the school setting, the RTC-based school psychologist has the opportunity to interact with other mental health professionals including psychiatrists, clinical social workers, and other staff psychologists. In this regard, overlap in professional roles helps ensure that comprehensive behavioral, psychosocial, and psychoeducational services are provided.

Neuropsychological Centers

Continued advances in the medical field, improvements in neuropsychological assessment, and progress in cognitive rehabilitation strategies have all underscored the need for assessment and rehabilitation of individuals who suffer from neurological disorders (e.g., seizures, traumatic head injuries). These requirements call for a psychologist's skills in linking results from psychometric assessments to identify and address emotional, cognitive, and social deficits as a result of the disorder. As such, there are a number of functions inherent in the training of school psychologists that overlap with practice in neuropsychological settings. For example, given that the primary responsibility of neuropsychologists is to administer and interpret results of neuropsychological batteries, assessment-related activities primarily constitute their main day-to-day affairs. Although school-based psychological reports may or may not incorporate a neuropsychological component, the goal of the report is similar in that assessment data are gathered for the purposes of identifying an individual's strengths and needs, linking this information to intervention. The similarity in regard to testing responsibilities is further supported given that many of the subtests usually incorporated in a neuropsychological battery typically are used by school-based clinicians. Thus, the substantial amount of training in assessment administration and interpretation in school psychology graduate programs readily translates to clinical neuropsychological practice.

Unlike school-based psychologists who assume a more "generalist" approach in working with a variety of clinical presentations, clinic-based neuropsychologists work with a specific population that has experienced neurological insults. Thus, school psychologists in this setting are specifically trained to identify deficits from neuropsychological testing to help determine educational implications and functional adaptive behavior needs.

Early Intervention Centers

Each state's Child Find policies, stemming from the Individuals with Disabilities Education Act (IDEA) legislation, have made the identification of infants, toddlers, and preschoolers who are at risk for developmental disabilities a high priority, with early intervention a primary goal. Influenced by Child Find laws and other related educational legislation,

Early Intervention Centers (EICs) have been created in each state, with the location of EICs ranging from public school–sponsored centers to other settings (e.g., university-affiliated child guidance centers, Head Start).

School psychologists who choose to practice in EICs provide an important role in the identification and intervention process, collaborating with and providing recommendations to families and other professionals for intervention. Much like school-based clinicians, assessment-related activities (particularly assessment of developmental delays) are a primary function of EIC-based psychologists. Further, consultation with other members of an EIC multidisciplinary team (MDT), which typically includes classroom teachers, occupational therapists, physical therapists, speech-language pathologists, and in some cases medical professionals and social workers, constitutes an integral role for the EIC-based psychologist. Services provided may also include individual therapy, designing and implementing behavioral management programs for individual students or classrooms, providing teacher workshops, and in some settings conducting early childhood research or engaging in child advocacy efforts. Working with parents and other family members in designing and assisting in interventions in the home may be another role, and in some settings, conducting parent training workshops may be an expectation. Other services may be provided in an EIC, depending on the center's mission and identified needs.

Pediatric Settings

Pediatric settings share characteristics similar to EICs and neuropsychological clinics, with a primary focus on children (although with a larger age range than in an EIC) and the provision of services within the larger medical environment (as a neuropsychology practice may do). Nevertheless, school psychologists working in pediatric settings usually serve a wider range of disabilities and medical conditions than might be found in either an EIC or in clinics specializing in neurological deficits. Different pediatric settings hold different roles and responsibilities for the pediatric school psychologist, with the assessment of cognitive, adaptive, and/or behavioral or emotional functioning serving as the primary role. Depending on the setting, evaluations may include assessments before and after a medical procedure (i.e., brain surgery). In other settings, psychologists may conduct evaluations tracking the development of infants and toddlers born prematurely or with medical complications. As in EICs, psychologists in pediatric settings consult and collaborate with other MDT members and parents. In the pediatric setting, MDT members typically include motor and speech/language specialists, social workers, as well as medical professionals, particularly developmental pediatricians. Psychologists may also engage in counseling and behavioral intervention strategies to assist children and families in dealing with a specific diagnosis and adherence to treatment protocols, generally providing intervention on an outpatient basis, although intervention may occur on an inpatient basis for children who are hospitalized. Conducting child research or engaging in child advocacy efforts may also be roles of the pediatric school psychologist.

Practicing in a pediatric setting as a specialty area has also garnered much interest in the larger field of school psychology. A number of training programs currently have specialized in, or are in the process of specializing in, pediatric school psychology (see Power et al., 1995). Given the number of children who experience various medical conditions, the choice for many school psychologists to practice in pediatric settings will likely continue in the future.

Advantages and Challenges of a Nontraditional School Psychology Career

Advantages

As previously noted, the practice of school psychology in nontraditional settings allows many practitioners greater flexibility regarding the roles selected and clientele served. Although in some settings (e.g., neurological clinics, EICs, and pediatric clinics), the primary responsibility likely focuses on assessment-related activities, the function of the particular setting dictates the clientele served, type of assessment battery used, and provision of other services (e.g., individual counseling, parent consultation), all of which may fundamentally differ from what is provided in school systems. Further, other nontraditional settings (such as private practice) allow the school psychologist flexibility in type of clientele seen, services provided, and choice of specialty. Such advantages are often not afforded to the school-based psychologist. Finally, psychologists working in RTCs (and in other nontraditional settings as well) are often viewed as a "Jack [or Jill] of all trades" in that they are responsible for a number of direct and indirect diagnostic and intervention services as well as administrative functions that may not be available to most psychologists working in schools. Thus, for psychologists who are interested, there are a number of nontraditional settings that are available to school psychologists who wish to extend their practice to include a more complete range of service delivery.

Challenges

In spite of the number of advantages that are reported by those practicing outside of the school environment, school psychologists who are interested in nontraditional settings should be aware of the many challenges that may not be experienced by their school-based peers. Perhaps the most pertinent challenge is job security. The need for school-based psychologists will likely continue as long as federal mandates (most specifically, the Individuals with Disabilities Education Act) and state education policies require the services of qualified mental health professionals to help determine eligibility for special education programs and other service delivery (Curtis et al., 1999; Reschly & Wilson, 1995). Legislative protection is often not extended to nontraditional practitioners. As another challenge, economic constraints experienced by many medical centers can lead to a decrease in services considered complementary to medical care. Thus, minimizing or eliminating psychological services associated with a medical setting may be an initial cost-cutting strategy. Job security is also compromised in settings that rely heavily on grant support (such as university affiliated programs, or UAPs), where financial support and employment opportunities often extend only to the life of the grant. Similarly, continued efforts to obtain external grants (i.e., writing grant proposals) to preserve faculty lines may involve a substantial amount of time that detracts from service delivery. Thus, clinicians who are not prepared to set aside grant-writing time or have adequate grant-writing skills may find careers in these settings particularly frustrating. Securing external funding is typically not an evaluative criterion for school-based psychologists. Nontraditional settings that rely primarily on insurance reimbursement (such that may be experienced in private practice) may face situations that are not experienced in the school setting, such as difficulties enrolling in insurance registers, delinquency in remuneration, and occasional sporadic caseloads. Finally, perceptions as an outside consultant to a school team may lead to less than optimal cooperation with school personnel.

Considerations for Practice in Nontraditional Settings

Training Considerations

For clinicians who weigh the above advantages and challenges and still find nontraditional settings appealing, there are other considerations that must be carefully deliberated. Of these considerations, adequate training is foremost. Prospective graduate students should research school psychology training programs that provide didactic training of the types of nontraditional experiences that are of interest to them. Unfortunately, while most training programs provide general, broad-based training that prepares graduate students for entry into the schools, few programs provide training for practice in specific nontraditional settings. Further, the programs that offer specialization may vary widely in terms of the specific populations served (e.g., preschool children) or settings they prepare graduates to enter (e.g., pediatric hospitals). Given this concern, many students independently explore options that allow them to attain a fuller understanding of how psychology may be applied to a particular setting. Some students enroll in courses that are entirely outside of their discipline to help them prepare for a career in nontraditional school psychology. For example, students interested in private practice may enroll in a business management or marketing course, which allows for a greater understanding of strategies necessary to successfully market their practice and to maintain solvency. Further, some students interested in neuropsychological settings enroll in various anatomy and medical courses, which allows for a greater understanding of the physiological underpinnings of human behavior. Finally, many students enroll in independent study credit hours that allow them to provide basic services (e.g., scheduling appointments or conducting intake evaluations) or conduct research (as part of a research team) under the supervision of a faculty member with expertise in a particular population. These independent study experiences facilitate a comprehensive understanding of the typical functions of a psychologist practicing in a particular setting.

Internship/Postdoctoral Training Considerations

In addition to formal, didactic learning, it is also important to apply to internship or postdoctoral programs that closely match specialty interests. For example, individuals who are interested in working in a pediatric or EIC setting might seek practica or internship experiences in a UAP pediatric clinic or in hospitals that support child psychology internships. As another example, individuals who are interested in working in an RTC, pursuance of an internship at an actual RTC is important. Moreover, psychologists who wish to practice in restrictive educational or living environments (such as alternative schools or juvenile detention centers) may find it advantageous to seek additional training opportunities in these settings.

Many nonschool-based internships and postdoctoral settings often recruit and enlist child clinical psychology graduate students, primarily as a result of misperceptions or a general lack of awareness of the skills that school psychologists possess. Therefore, marketing the breadth of skills held by school psychologists (beginning at the internship level) becomes a priority. As noted earlier, a school psychologist's training is similar to that of counseling and clinical psychologists, particularly those trained to work with children. Beyond this commonality, however, the school psychologist possesses a comprehensive understanding of school environments and climates, special education laws and regulations, and knowledge of accommodations and modifications that may be implemented for students who require individualized education plans or 504 accommodation plans. This knowledge proves helpful in nontraditional settings when providing intervention recommendations, particularly as they relate to a child's learning, behavioral, or academic functioning. In this regard, internship and postdoctoral sites that allow students to apply this specialized knowledge in nontraditional settings help them prepare for the types of psychoeducational concerns they will likely experience as a professional.

Typical Workweek in Nontraditional Settings

Given the nature, clientele, and particular needs of each nontraditional setting, perhaps the most consistent, identifying characteristic of the "typical" workweek is its atypicality. This is not to say that the types and roles inherent in each setting vary to such a degree that weekly comparisons are untenable, but rather the time spent in each activity will vary depending on the population served, the setting in which services are delivered, and the time of year. As some concrete examples, professional time spent in private practice is largely devoted to assessment, consultation, and intervention activities. The time spent in each activity will vary depending on the specialty of the private practitioner (e.g., those who specialize in individual therapy vs. those who specialize in evaluating suspected learning disabilities), as well as the time of year (academic year vs. the summer months) and nature of the referral (e.g., second-opinion psychoeducational evaluations vs. parent training). As another example, practitioners working in RTCs with rolling admissions may devote most of their time in assessment-related activities one week (depending on the number of youths admitted into the center) and consultation and therapy the following week. Indeed, even within settings that provide predominantly assessment-related activities (such as EICs and pediatric settings), the amount of time spent conducting assessments will depend on a number of factors including the type of clientele referred to the psychologist and how much time is left in the funding cycle (which may call for more time devoted to grant writing). The weekly fluctuations of time spent in a particular role in nontraditional settings is very much different from that reported by practitioners in school settings. In the latter, the majority of time on a weekly basis (roughly 60 to 70%) is spent in assessment-related activities, followed by (in order) intervention, consultation, and research (Hosp & Reschly, 2002). Such flexibility in time spent across various functions is considered an additional appeal for practitioners in nontraditional settings.

Nevertheless, there are some overarching characteristics in the practice of psychology that transcend any particular role or function across settings. These characteristics largely involve time spent participating in direct services (e.g., assessment, group/individual/family therapy, etc.), documentation (i.e., writing process/progress notes, report writing, etc.), meetings (e.g., parent consultations, multidisciplinary meetings, supervision), and professional development (research activities, in-service training, attending workshops) and marketing strategies. Although again it is clear that time spent within each characteristic varies, it can be assumed that approximately 20 to 30 hours will be spent in direct services, with an additional 8 to 10 hours spent documenting the direct assessment. Finally, the remaining portion of the clinician's time will involve participation in meetings and professional development activities. Table 13.1 lists the common work duties for school psychologists practicing in nontraditional settings.

In summary, contrary to prevailing perceptions that school psychology is setting specific, the range of nontraditional settings for which school psychologists practice is considerable. As school psychologists realize the generalizability of their skills, the number of school psychology practitioners in nontraditional environments will likely increase. With this stated, the purpose of this chapter is not to minimize the impact of school psychologists who practice in the school setting. Indeed, changes in training curriculum, demands of local education agencies, and continual amendments to IDEA dictate that the roles and functions of school-based practitioners will continue to expand to include multiple functions as well (see Ysseldyke et al., 1997). In many respects, those who choose to practice school psychology are able to serve the mental health and psychoeducational needs of children and families regardless of setting. What primarily differs between settings are the flexibility in roles, choice of setting in which to practice psychological science, and types of incentives (financial and otherwise) inherent in each setting. Considering the advantages of practicing in either schools or nontraditional settings, the future of school psychology remains quite optimistic.

Table 13.1 Common Work Duties for School Psychologists Practicing in Nontraditional Settings

Clinical Duties

Providing psychological or psychoeducational assessment of children
Consulting with teachers, parents, other professionals
Designing and implementing interventions (counseling, therapy)
Implementing and monitoring behavioral intervention plans
Conducting workshops/training for parents or other professionals
Interpreting evaluation data
Writing psychological reports
Reporting evaluation results to parents and other professionals
Providing recommendations to parents and other professionals for enhancing a child's academic, behavioral/emotional, and adaptive functioning

Professional Duties

Attending departmental or multidisciplinary staff meetings
Attending conferences or workshops for continued professional development

Miscellaneous Duties

Securing external funding through grant writing
Conducting research (depending on setting)
Engaging in child advocacy efforts
Teaching/training of interns or externs
Supervising other professionals and staff members
Securing funding for services rendered through insurance/Medicaid billing

References

Adelman, H. S., & Taylor, L. (2000). Shaping the future of mental health in schools. *Psychology in the Schools, 37*, 49–60.

Bramlett, R. K., Murphy, J. J., Johnson, J., Wallingsford, L., & Hall, J. D. (2002). Contemporary practices in school psychology: A national survey of roles and referral problems. *Psychology in the Schools, 39*, 327–335.

Curtis, M. J., Hunley, S. A., Walker, K. J., & Baker, A. C. (1999). Demographic characteristics and professional practices in school psychology. *School Psychology Review, 28*, 104–116.

Fagan, T. K. (2002). Trends in the history of school psychology in the United States. In A. Thomas & J. Grimes (Eds.), *Best practices in school psychology* (4th ed.) (pp. 209–222). Bethesda, MD: National Association of School Psychologists.

French, J. L. (1990). History of school psychology. In T. B. Gutkin & C. R. Reynolds (Eds.), *Handbook of school psychology* (pp. 3–20). New York: John Wiley.

Hosp, J. L., & Reschly, D. J. (2002). Regional differences in school psychology practice. *School Psychology Review, 31*, 11–29.

Hutton, J. B., Dubes, R., & Muir, S. (1992). Assessment practices of school psychologists: Ten years later. *School Psychology Review, 21*, 271–284.

Kramer, J. J., & Epps, S. (1991). Expanding professional opportunities and improving the quality of training:: A look toward the next generation of school psychologists. *School Psychology Review, 20*, 452–461.

Lund, A. R., Reschly, D. J., & Martin, L. M. (1998). School psychology personnel needs: Correlates of current patterns and historical trends. *School Psychology Review, 27*, 106–120.

Matarazzo, J. D. (1987). There is only one psychology, no specialties, but many applications. *American Psychologist, 42*, 893–903.

Medway, F. J., Hagan, M. L., Hartye, M. A. A., & Hosford, P. M. (1988). The school psychologist in private practice. *School Psychology Review, 17*, 429–434.

Minke, K. M., & Brown, D. T. (1996). Preparing psychologists to work with children: A comparison of curricula in child-clinical and school psychology programs. *Professional Psychology: Research and Practice, 27*, 631–634.

Morris, R. J., & Morris, Y. P. (1989). School psychology in residential treatment facilities. In R. C. D'Amato & R. S. Dean (Eds.), *The school psychologist in non-traditional settings: Integrating clients, services, and settings* (pp. 159–184). Hillsdale, NJ: Lawrence Erlbaum.

Nastassi, B. K. (1998). A model for mental health programming in schools and communities: Introduction to the mini-series. *School Psychology Review, 27*, 165–174.

National Association of School Psychologists (2003). What is a school psychologist? Bethesda, MD: Author.

Pfeiffer, S. I., & Dean, R. S. (1988). Guest editors' comments: School psychology in evolution. *School Psychology Review, 17*, 388–390.

Power, T. J., DuPaul, G. J., Shapiro, E. S., & Parrish, J. M. (1995). Pediatric school psychology: The emergence of a subspecialty. *School Psychology Review, 24*, 244–257.

Pryzwansky, W. B. (1989). Private practice as an alternative setting for school psychologists. In R. C. D'Amato & R. S. Dean (Eds.), *The school psychologist in non-traditional settings: Integrating clients, services, and settings* (pp. 67–85). Hillsdale, NJ: Lawrence Erlbaum.

Reschly, D. J. (2000). The present and future status of school psychology in the United States. *School Psychology Review, 29*, 507–522.

Reschly, D. J., & Wilson, M. S. (1995). School psychology faculty and practitioners: 1986 to 1991 trends in demographic characteristics, roles, satisfaction, and system reform. *School Psychology Review, 24*, 62–80.

Tryon, G. S. (2000). Doctoral training issues in school and clinical psychology. *Professional Psychology: Research and Practice, 31*, 85–87.

Ysseldyke, J., Dawson, P., Lehr, C., Reschly, D., Reynolds, M., & Telzrow, C. (1997). *School psychology: A blueprint for training and practice II*. Bethesda, MD: National Association of School Psychologists.

Suggested Reading

Curtis, M.J., Grier, J., Chesno, E., & Hunley, S.A. (2004). The changing face of school psychology: Trends in data and projections for the future. *School Psychology Review, 33*, 49–66.

D'Amato, R. C., & Dean, R. S. (1989). *The school psychologist in non-traditional settings: Integrating clients, services, and settings.* Hillsdale, NJ: Lawrence Erlbaum.

Fagan, T., & Wise, P.S. (2000). School psychology: Past, present, and future (2nd ed.). Bethesda, MD: National Association of School Psychologists.

Suggested Web Site

Division 16 of the American Psychological Association (School Psychology) http://www.indiana.edu/~div16/G&O.htm.

III

Business Roles for New Psychologists

14

Management Consultation: Improving Organizations

JANE KASSERMAN

The Psychologist as Management Consultant

When approached about writing this chapter, I was immediately eager and enthusiastic. Why? First, I am passionate about my work. Second, I believe that, as a discipline, psychology has much to contribute to improving the effectiveness of organizations and the people who work in them. Third, the profession of management consulting is one about which psychology students and new professionals frequently know very little and, as a result, may overlook as a viable career option. By sharing some of my experiences and insights, I hope to help close the information gap and stimulate interest in pursuing what I believe is an exciting, dynamic, and vital profession.

My own path into consulting was long, circuitous, and not at all preplanned. Initially, I earned my doctorate in cognitive-experimental psychology, and worked at AT&T Bell Labs for 5 years designing computer–user interfaces. While employed at Bell Labs, I realized that something was missing in my professional life so I eventually returned to school full-time to retrain in clinical psychology. At the time, I intended to become a practicing clinical psychologist; however, I began to question my original plan during my first year of work. I was frustrated with the impact of managed care and disenchanted with the clinical work. One day, my mentor handed me a position announcement from a regional consulting firm. To this point, I had not thought about consulting as a career path and had only a vague awareness of the nature of the work. However, I was open to investigating the possibility. The more I learned, the more intrigued I became and, ultimately, I was offered and accepted a consulting position. That is how I got my start and, after 2 years with the firm, I joined the Philadelphia office of Rohrer, Hibler, & Replogle (RHR) International, where I now work.

Although my story does not offer much insight about how to prepare strategically for a career in this field, I will discuss a more targeted and planned approach, as well as review a set of competencies that will allow you to be competitive in this field. More specifically, this chapter provides an overview of the types of services that management consultants provide, suggests how you can develop a career as a management consultant, provides an inside look at the work life of a consultant, reviews the personal qualities that are important to being a good fit for this line of work, and focuses on preparing for a career in the field.

What Does a Management Psychologist Do?

In the broadest sense, management psychologists apply psychological expertise to help organizations and the individuals who work in them be more effective. There are a number of organizational settings in which consulting services are provided, including for-profit businesses, government agencies, the military, schools and universities, and other nonprofit organizations. Most of my experience as a consultant has been in the private sector, and it is through this lens that I will describe the work.

Under the umbrella of improving organizational effectiveness, management psychologists provide a range of services. Depending on the presenting issues and attendant needs, we may intervene at the individual, group, or organizational level. It is often appropriate to consult at more than one level simultaneously within an organization. In fact, I have found that some of the most interesting and challenging work I have been involved in has been multilevel in nature. What follows is an overview of the kinds of services that management psychologists typically provide to address the needs of their clients.

Individual-Level Interventions

At the individual level, consulting services typically entail assessment and coaching. Assessment-based interventions are geared toward providing guidance in (1) job selection and job placement decision making, (2) manager and executive development, or (3) successfully transitioning and integrating an executive into a new role and, in turn, improving retention. Executive coaching, which incorporates individual assessment, is provided to assist with development, career planning, or new role integration. Components of an individual assessment may include a participant interview, administration of assessment instruments (e.g., a style inventory such as the Myers-Briggs), multirater or 360° feedback (a tool used to offer insight into the executive's leadership impact as perceived by others including direct reports, peers, and boss, and administered via an anonymous survey or interview process), and other relevant background information. Because individual-level interventions always occur within the broader organizational context, it is essential that this context be clearly understood by the consultant at the outset. In addition, the consultant must gather information about the leadership requirements of the role against which the individual is being assessed, whether for selection, development, or integration purposes. This background information is usually obtained from discussions with the participant's manager and human resources representative.

Subsequent to the assessment, the consultant provides feedback to the individual and, depending on the context, key stakeholders in the organization such as the individual's manager and human resources partner. If the purpose of the assessment is to assist the organization with job selection decision making, then initial feedback will be provided to the organization. When an assessment is conducted as part of a development or integration process, feedback is generally given to the individual first and, in some cases, to only that individual, depending on what is agreed to upfront. Feedback is utilized to provide insight about the relevant characteristics of the executive, including key leadership strengths and development areas.

After providing feedback, the consultant may assist with the creation and implementation of a development or integration plan through ongoing coaching. The plan would generally include agreed-upon areas of focus and associated action steps. An example is when an executive who has been effective using a hands-on, directive leadership style is promoted into a broader leadership role where a more collaborative, team-oriented approach will be needed. Left to his or her own devices, he or she is likely to rely on his or her preferred approach, which has worked well in the past. Part of his or her integration plan would focus on this development area and include suggestions for incorporating new leadership behaviors consistent with the demands of the new role. Coaching might include regular, one-on-one meetings to discuss and review progress, behavioral observation (shadowing the executive, sitting in on staff meetings, etc.), ongoing feedback, and facilitated, development-related discussions between the executive and his or her boss.

Group-Level Interventions

At the group level, services include team development and improving intergroup functioning, for example, between departments or divisions. These interventions have an assessment component as well, and are used to identify group strengths, weaknesses, and other relevant issues that inform both recommendations made by the consultant and the ongoing consulting process itself. When working at the team level, consultants may intervene with the team leader, team members, the team as a whole, or some combination thereof. For example, the CEO who is launching a new business strategy may seek assistance in determining how the senior team needs to function to execute the new strategy successfully. In addition to working with the CEO and senior team members to define critical team behaviors, a consultant might interview individual team members — and possibly other key people in the company who interact with the team — to assess the team's current state relative to the desired level of functioning. With this understanding, the consultant would then work with the team to facilitate the development of needed team behaviors — helping the team ensure its decision-making process serves the broader strategic goals of the company, improving communication between team members, and enhancing the team's ability to manage organization-wide change, to name a few examples. Consultant-facilitated team sessions designed to attend to these kinds of issues are typically an integral part of team development work.

Organization-Level Interventions

At the organizational level, interventions become even more diverse. Organizational assessment can be designed to explore a broad range of characteristics considered important to effective organizational functioning. In contrast, a specific aspect of organizational functioning may be the focus of the assessment process — alignment with business strategy, readiness for change, decision-making processes, and management practices, to name a few. Organizational assessments are often, although by no means exclusively, conducted through the use of surveys, such as employee attitude or satisfaction surveys, culture surveys, etc. Surveys may be supplemented with or substituted by other data-gathering techniques such as individual interviews or focus groups. Feedback on survey results is subsequently provided by the consultant to key stakeholders in the organization, along with recommendations to address relevant issues that have been identified. Follow-up consultation often becomes an integral part of the process, in which the consultant partners with management to provide guidance on implementing recommended actions.

Consultants may also assist in the planning, design, and implementation of talent development and succession planning processes within an organization. Additional organizational-level consulting services include facilitation of systemic changes in the context of a merger or acquisition, the launch of a new strategy or other major business initiative, or corporate-wide restructuring. Organizations often overlook the psychological aspects of change; management psychologists can be particularly helpful in advising clients about what to anticipate and how to provide effective leadership to ensure that organizational change efforts succeed.

Where Do Psychologists Build Careers in Management Consulting?

The settings in which management consultants work can be thought of as falling into two broad categories: external and internal consultancies.

With respect to external consultancies, there are a few different types to consider. One is employment in a large, general management consulting firm that has a human capital practice arm in addition to other practice areas. These are firms like Accenture, Aon, Boston Consulting Group, Deloitte, Mercer Delta Consulting, McKinsey & Company, and Price Waterhouse Coopers. There are also national and international consulting firms in which management psychology is the core or predominant practice, for example, Development Dimensions International (DDI), Hay Group, Personnel Decisions International (PDI), and RHR International Company. Yet another alternative is joining a smaller, regional or local consulting practice. Oftentimes, these practices have been started by one or more consultants who worked in a larger firm for some period of time before deciding to venture out and create a practice of their own. Solo practice is yet another way to work as an external consultant; however, you need to ask yourself if you have sufficient knowledge and skills to ensure that you would be practicing within your boundaries of competence. If you have had the opportunity to acquire a solid set of skills in applying psychological expertise in organizational settings and actual experience doing so, then beginning your career as an independent consultant may very well be appropriate and feasible. Otherwise, there are considerable advantages to first working with other, more experienced consultants from whom you can learn about the profession and receive both guidance and support.

In contrast to external consultancies, a number of management psychologists are employed by the client organization that they serve. Such opportunities are often found in large, Fortune 500 companies that have functions specializing in organizational development or leadership development. These functions reside within the human resources department or may be stand-alone departments. Internal consulting opportunities can also be found in the public sector and other nonprofit settings.

In evaluating which type of setting is best for you, there are a number of factors to consider beyond what I have already mentioned. Your decision making should be based on your interests, needs, and preferences, so it is important to identify what those are. You should also investigate different employment settings and reach out to consultants who can discuss with you the relative advantages and disadvantages of these settings. Below I describe some common characteristics of medium- to large-sized consulting firms.

When you work in a medium- to large-sized consulting firm, you have ready access to a network of experienced colleagues and possibly early career professionals like yourself, there are opportunities to collaborate with colleagues on consulting engagements, and you will gain exposure to a range of client organizations and assignments. Additionally, formal training and development opportunities may exist to provide you with resources to support your professional growth. Larger firms can also provide opportunities to manage accounts and programs in which you supervise the work and guide the development of other consultants.

In consulting firms, it is typical that a portion of your compensation is salary based and additional compensation (or bonus) is based on consultant performance-related criteria — productivity, client satisfaction, and teamwork, for example — and group or overall firm performance. In some firms, bonus compensation can represent a substantial portion of your total income and, because it is not guaranteed, you need to be comfortable with having part of your income "at risk" from year to year. By gaining some understanding of the base salary range at a particular firm, you will at least be able to determine whether the level of guaranteed income is acceptable to you. In addition, learning about the firm's track record of performance is also important in assessing the overall level of risk. Some firms weather recessions better than others, and some have ways to ensure valued consultants are compensated adequately in a difficult year.

What Is the Work Life Like?

I work in a well-established, reputable consulting firm. Most of our clients are mid- to large-sized, for-profit corporations. My world is a business world. It is dynamic, action oriented, challenging, and unpredictable. I experience one or more of these qualities in virtually all aspects of my professional life, at nearly all times. I am engaged from the moment I start my day. A typical day for me may include checking and responding to voicemail; answering a call on my cell phone while driving to a client; consulting with an executive; reflecting on the client meeting that just occurred as I drive to the office; checking and responding to voicemail as I drive to the office; making phone calls at the office to schedule appointments, contacting our travel agency to make arrangements for an out-of-town client meeting, and meeting with an office colleague to discuss our upcoming appointment with a client; having lunch downtown with a business contact, then returning to the office and contacting a senior executive to discuss preparations for an upcoming team development off site, checking and responding to voicemail, preparing my monthly billing and expense report, taking a call from a client to arrange a candidate assessment, and checking client account reports to monitor payment of invoices; driving home reflecting on the day and running through a mental checklist of the next day's activities, and, finally, checking and responding to voicemail one last time at the end of the day.

While less frequent, there are also days when I work from home to take advantage of the time saved and stress avoided by not commuting to and from the downtown office. These opportunities allow me to focus on work that requires sustained concentration — like preparing a report for a client — and to balance the busy, sometimes hectic, days with some relative "quiet" time. I am still fully engaged (and stay in touch with the office throughout the day), but in a slower-paced, reflective manner.

Beyond what I have already stated, what can you take from these real-world descriptions of a day in the life of a management consultant? I hope that you get a sense of the variety of day-to-day activities, not simply the quantity. The breadth of activities and experiences, the range of clients and people that consultants serve, and the ever-changing nature of the work provide a rich environment for continuous learning and both professional and personal growth.

Second, there is a fast-paced intensity to the work. Executives work in a rapidly changing, competitive, and bottom-line-oriented world. Effective consultants readily adapt to this world because they enjoy the stimulation and challenge of partnering with high-functioning, results-focused executives to help them achieve their business goals. Also, those of us who work as external consultants typically serve multiple clients simultaneously, and much of the work is conducted on site at the client's location. Therefore, whether traveling by car, plane, or train, getting from point A to point B is part and parcel to the profession, particularly if you are an external consultant, and it contributes to the pace and activity level.

Third, business development will likely be part of your professional responsibilities, regardless of the size of the firm in which you work. Now, if the mention of business development causes you to have images of snake-oil salespeople, I assure you that there are a number of management consultants such as myself who had similar initial reactions. The good news is that the clients we serve have a professional need and they buy our services because they believe we can meet their needs, not because we show up at their door peddling our wares.

A final aspect of the work life that needs to be mentioned is client account and project management. When you have account management responsibility, you serve as the main point of contact for the client and are ultimately responsible for the success of the consulting program. Account managers also have administrative responsibilities (e.g., billing and receivables) and oversee and coordinate the work of other consultants involved in the account. Project management duties can vary but, at a minimum, include oversight of a particular consulting assignment within a client account.

What Personal Qualities Make You Well-Suited to Management Consulting?

You may have already decided that because you are interested in becoming a management consultant, possess the necessary credentials, and are motivated to build a career in the field, you would be well suited to the work. This may very well be true; however, if you have had little or no direct exposure to this work, I encourage you to do a self-assessment check, just to be clear in your own mind that you have not overlooked anything important in your thinking.

Table 14.1 Personal Characteristics of Management Psychologists

Find working in business settings appealing
Comfortable working with leaders of organizations
Possess strong interpersonal and relationship-building skills
Possess professional maturity and impact; confident and credible
Balance empathy with objectivity and independence of thought
Possess solid analytical and intuitive abilities
Adapt to quickly changing demands; flexible
Possess high energy level and stamina
Is conscientious and reliable
Possess continuous learning orientation; curious
Committed to practicing ethically and with integrity at all times
Committed to self-development

I have had the opportunity to work in the field long enough to witness consultants who have thrived and those who have struggled. I have also learned from the wisdom of others, far more experienced than I in these matters, about what they have come to understand to be key personal characteristics that tend to make a person more likely to be a good fit for the profession. These characteristics are summarized in Table 14.1.

Almost everything that management consultants do requires the ability to influence in some form or another. While your expertise and credentials can help you gain initial access to a prospective client, your credibility is ultimately determined in other, more subtle ways. Consulting is as much about the art and practice of selling who you are as it is convincing others of what you know. Managers and executives need to feel comfortable that you can fit into their world, "speak their language," empathize with them, and function at their pace. For these reasons, presence and impact are very important. That is, projecting professional maturity and confidence, demonstrating your energy level, listening with genuine understanding, and speaking with clarity and conviction.

To develop an accurate understanding of the person, group, or organization with which they are intervening, management psychologists must be adept at gathering, integrating, and synthesizing relevant information. They must then be able to identify the implications of this understanding and advise the client accordingly. For these reasons, having strong analytical skills is essential. However, the ability to rely on one's intuition is equally important. There is much that is unpredictable about the nature of management consulting, and this is a significant part of what keeps it both interesting and challenging. It is a common experience of consultants to arrive prepared to follow a previously agreed upon agenda with an executive, only to then find themselves having to quickly switch gears to discuss an unanticipated, emergent issue that the executive is struggling with and wants to address — now. These and similar situations require you to think on your feet, so you must be comfortable drawing upon your instincts and previous experiences in order to respond effectively in the moment.

To meet the demands of our clients, management consultants are often required to work or travel during evenings and weekends. In other words, this is not a "nine-to-five" profession with regular, predictable work hours. Moreover, the workload has a cyclical quality to it. There can be periods of intense activity that last for a number of months before the pace slows, which, thankfully, it inevitably does. And, assuming an effective business development strategy is being executed, business will eventually pick up again. The ability to ride the ebbs and flows of the marketplace requires both stamina and patience. At all times and especially during the busy periods, you need to consciously attend to yourself to ensure your personal needs are not overly neglected. Of course, what this translates into specifically will vary from one person to the next. The point is that you need to proactively manage yourself and your time. Know your own limits, and be very vigilant about not exceeding them. Otherwise, like anyone working in a demanding profession, you will put yourself at risk of burnout.

Training and experience notwithstanding, ongoing attention to one's personal development is integral to consulting. This means cultivating your self-awareness to understand your needs, motivations, strengths, and weaknesses. The fact that management consultants guide others' development is reason enough to incorporate self-development into your day-to-day practice. Beyond this, it is essential to be tuned in to how you may need to adjust your behavior to ensure you have the desired impact on any given client. If you are willing to be self-critical, accept feedback, and work on your development with a positive orientation toward self-discovery, you will be off to a good start in this profession. In concluding this section, I again encourage you to take time to reflect on your personal characteristics and compare them with those I have outlined.

How Do You Prepare for a Career as a Management Consultant?

Advice on how to prepare for a career in this profession can be a bit tricky, because there are a number of ways to prepare, yet no prototypical path. I believe this is reflective of both the developing state of the profession and the fact that the competencies needed to become a management consultant are rarely acquired through graduate training alone. So what competencies are needed?

Table 14.2 Competency Areas of Management Psychologists

Assessment at individual, group, and organization levels
Psychological testing including administration, interpretation, and feedback
Intervention design at individual, group, and organization levels
Coaching and advising to increase effectiveness and foster development
Process consultation
Group or team facilitation
Business knowledge and experience
Professional ethics and legal issues
Account and project management
Business development and networking

While the profession has not defined these in any formal way as yet, progress is being made. The Society of Consulting Psychology (APA Division 13) has developed a set of principles for education and training at the doctoral and postdoctoral level (Education and Training Committee, 2002) and, although these principles are still evolving, they are a valuable resource that can lend insight to your own planning and preparation. Table 14.2 provides a summary of fundamental competancy areas that are fairly consistent with the more detailed principles developed by Division 13.

Having listed these key skill areas and knowing that many others could be added, I also recognize that many management psychologists have gaps of some form or another that they either make the best of or work to address through their own personal development plan. Nonetheless, you should have a solid foundation of most if not all of these competencies before setting out to consult and, through ongoing on-the-job consulting experiences and training, continue to build upon them. Some suggestions for how you can go about acquiring these skills follow.

In terms of getting the appropriate education and experience, my first recommendation is that you complete graduate training in a psychology program, preferably at the doctoral level. The most common areas that doctoral-level management psychologists have trained in are clinical psychology, community psychology, counseling psychology, school psychology, educational psychology, and industrial/organizational psychology (Web site, Society of Consulting Psychology). While these disciplines differ from one another in important ways, they all offer valuable training and experience relevant to management consulting. Doctoral-level psychology programs that are dedicated to the study and practice of organizational consulting are also beginning to emerge (e.g., Alliant International University). Some schools also offer dual or combined degrees that can be particularly useful preparation, such as Psy.D./MBA and clinical/industrial and organizational degrees. Although it is not a requirement that "management consultants" be licensed, having a license provides you with an important credential that you can use to market your expertise as a psychologist. Some firms such as RHR International require consultants to be licensed psychologists or at least license-eligible when they join the firm. If you are already licensed, supplemental consulting-related training can be obtained through continuing education courses and workshops. Reading the professional literature is also a good way to augment your knowledge base.

Whether you are attending or have completed graduate school, I encourage you to look into opportunities for gaining hands-on, consulting-related experience. These opportunities can be few and far between and, consequently, require initiative on your part to uncover. University counseling centers sometimes have consulting outreach services that can provide valuable exposure to organizational dynamics, management, and the consultation process itself. Alternatively, a faculty member or colleague may know a local consultant who is willing to provide exposure and training to an interested graduate student or newly minted psychologist. Consulting-focused postdoctoral internships, while not abundant, can provide wonderful preparation and are an excellent way to supplement doctoral training, particularly if you are unable to gain this kind of exposure and experience as a graduate student. If you can swing it, another option to consider is offering to volunteer your time in exchange for a valuable learning opportunity.

Gaining business experience and, in particular, management experience is also highly recommended. If you have the opportunity to take business courses or, even better, obtain an MBA, this will serve you well. Academics aside, working in a business setting where you can experience an inside view of how organizations function is quite useful preparation. My experience working at Bell Labs, even though it was a research and development environment, gave me an appreciation of organization dynamics and corporate life, and there is no question that it continues to inform my work even as my breadth of exposure to different organizations expands. Serving in a management role is a terrific way to develop a firsthand understanding of the challenges that managers and executives face. Outside of the business world, leadership opportunities can be found in other arenas, for example, through involvement in a community group, professional association, or nonprofit institution.

Regardless of whether you are ready to begin your job search or expect to be on the market in a few years, you should start networking now. Developing relationships with practicing consultants and fellow aspiring consultants is not just helpful during a job search, but also provides opportunities to learn more about consulting, become actively involved in the profession, and build networking skills that will be invaluable to your business development efforts as a practicing consultant. You are also more apt to learn about position openings if you have relationships with people who are in a position to be aware of those opportunities. One of the best ways to begin networking is through involvement in professional associations. I recommend the Society of Consulting Psychology (APA Division 13) and the Society for Industrial and Organizational Psychology (APA Division 14, also known as SIOP), in particular, both of which also have student groups. Attending the annual conferences of these divisions is a great way to interact with and learn from consulting professionals. Additionally, supervision and mentoring services are now offered through Division 13 (see Web site for additional information). Both divisions provide job search assistance through their Web sites as well.

Preparing for a career as a management psychologist is not a lock-step process, and there is plenty of room to chart your own course in a way that fits your specific needs and interests. However, it does require initiative on your part to create opportunities that will provide you with relevant experience and help you build your knowledge and skills. If you choose to embark on the journey and remain open to the learning opportunities afforded you along the way, you can be assured of an adventure that will bring you challenge, surprise, meaning, and personal growth.

Acknowledgment

I express my appreciation to several colleagues at RHR International who provided helpful feedback and suggestions for this chapter: Paul Winum, David Astorino, Dante Capitano, Bill Hicks, Stacey Philpot, and Deborah Rubin.

Reference

Education and Training Committee, Division 13, Society of Consulting Psychology, American Psychological Association. (2002). Principles for education and training at the doctoral and post-doctoral level in consulting psychology/organizational. *Consulting Psychology Journal, 54,* 213–222.

Suggested Web Sites

American Society for Training and Development: http://www.astd.org/.
Center for Creative Leadership: http://www.ccl.org/.
Human Resources Planning Society: http://www.hrps.org/.
Leader to Leader Institute (formerly the Peter F. Drucker Foundation for Nonprofit Management): http://www.pfdf.org/.
Society for Human Resources Management: http://www.shrm.org/.
Society for Industrial and Organizational Psychology: http://www.siop.org/.
Society of Consulting Psychology: http://www.apa.org/divisions/div13/.

15

Quantitative Analysis: Life as a Quant Jock with a Ph.D. in Social Psychology

JODIE L. STEELE

I will never forget the "Wall of Rejection." I was a senior in college, about to finish my B.A. and awaiting responses from the 10 social psychology Ph.D. programs to which I applied. My friend "Jim" was about to finish his Ph.D. in social psychology at my university and had already started hearing from the 50 schools to which he had applied for tenure-track professorial positions. At first, the rejection letters for Jim's potential jobs trickled in slowly. Jim was a strong candidate for an academic position; he had a good number of publications, good teaching experience and evaluations, and had been mentored by a well-respected (and well-connected) social psychologist. Then the rejection letters started arriving in Jim's mailbox at an alarming rate; he wasn't even being considered for interviews! Perhaps as a coping mechanism, Jim decided to create a "Wall of Rejection" in his office on campus. He posted each letter on his wall, one after another, until almost all four walls were covered. The only remaining space was later covered by Jim's office mate's rejection letters.

While I was superficially amused by the Wall of Rejection, deep down, I was a little worried. Would I go through all the hard work it takes to get a Ph.D. only to have a Wall of Rejection with more pages than my dissertation? Regardless, I was determined to get a Ph.D. in social psychology. I loved (and still do love) the field, the research process, and the mental stimulation too much to give up that goal. But it was before I even started my Ph.D. program that I told myself to keep an eye out for nonacademic careers that I could use my skills, just in case the job market didn't improve by the time I finished (Jim ended up taking a job teaching high school).

About 2 years into my graduate program, I noticed that the job market had not changed much since Jim's memorable job hunt. Highly qualified recent graduates of my program were taking postdoc positions in cities they never would consider living in or staying on to work in their advisors' labs because there were no other choices. Moreover, my college friends who immediately hit the "real world" after graduation (instead of going to graduate school) were getting promotions, buying cars and houses, traveling, and moving to places they always found interesting. I began to realize that if I decided not to follow the traditional academic path, I would have a lot more of what I called "life flexibility."

I reasoned that in an academic job market, especially the tough one that pervaded the 1990s, I would have virtually no say in where I lived. If the only school that offered me a job was Western Podunk College, then that is where I would have to go. Or I could take a post-doc position at Northern Mountaintop University for a couple of years, only to pack up and move 2 years later to another temporary spot or for the new assistant professorship at Eastern Podunk.

An important side effect of getting to choose where I wanted to live was stability. I could move somewhere and stay for 10 days, 10 months, or 10 years. I was young, unattached, and felt that if there ever was a time to go with immediate gratification (as opposed to completing two postdocs and then hoping for a tenure-track position), this was the perfect time. I didn't need to be rich, only stable and comfortable (although I admit I was envious watching my gainfully employed college friends talk about the perfect negative correlation between their savings account and my own).

Thus, as I progressed in my Ph.D. program, a nonacademic job became more and more attractive. And I knew I had to prepare; I didn't expect to be able to sell myself as an experienced business-woman who happened to have a Ph.D. in social psychology. I had to have at least some experience in the business world. I began to brain-storm industries in which I thought my social psychology training could be applied. Market research immediately came to mind, as I knew that field covered attitudes and attitude change, survey and other research methodology, and data analysis; it seemed like a good outlet for the skills learned in a psychology Ph.D. program.

Test Drive:
Exploring the Nonacademic World While Still in Grad School

The summer after my second year of graduate school, after I had just completed my master's degree, I began to search for a summer internship in market research. I had heard that advertising agencies liked psychologists because of their insight into human behavior (and attitude and behavior change), so I focused a significant amount of my time sending my resume to advertising agencies. My resume attracted some attention because I had a postgraduate education, a psychology background, and was willing to work for cheap (think of it as an investment).

I ultimately accepted an internship in the market research department of a small advertising agency. Over the course of the summer, I helped conduct market research for a variety of the agency's clients: a hospital, a home builder, and a casino, to name a few (the variety of topics we covered kept me on my toes). I was pleased to find out that I was right; the research skills I acquired from graduate school translated smoothly to the business environment. I wrote, implemented, and developed surveys. I analyzed and interpreted data and recommended strategy changes based on what I found. I introduced the agency to the idea of test and control groups for some of their marketing ventures. And I enjoyed it immensely.

What fascinated me the most were the results of one of the surveys I had developed for the home builder client. The survey was given to people as they exited the model homes in a particular housing development. Among other things, participants were asked to rate various aspects of the homes and to suggest improvements. One of the things that stood out in the data analysis was that people really did not like the shower–bath combo in the master bedrooms of the model homes. They wanted a separate shower stall and bathtub. In my final report, I highlighted that finding, as it came up again and again in the surveys. Within weeks, the construction company was changing the design of their homes to include a separate shower stall and bathtub. I understand that this may sound trivial; does the setup of the bathroom really matter that much? Moreover, did I spend all this time in grad school to recommend bathroom layouts? The answers to both of those questions are arguable, but I will say this: seeing the construction company change their well-established plans because of what I found in my survey was extremely gratifying. I was seeing real changes made as a result of my research. My report wasn't getting skimmed and then filed away (and maybe later shared in a graduate class) like a journal article. People in the real world found it useful and meaningful and took action because of it.

In a more general sense, I was finally being exposed to the business world. I learned the lingo, the culture, and the expectations. The summer ended quickly, but I wanted to learn more. I figured if I spent one more summer doing a similar job and liked it, I would be convinced that this would be a good career path for me. The following summer, I accepted a part-time job at a midsized market research firm that specialized in customer satisfaction research. Again, I was exposed to a variety of industries: child care, chemical sales, computer chips, etc. and, again, I brought something unique to the MBA-educated team that I worked with. Because of my education and training in psychology, I had unique, sophisticated data analytic skills (I even taught a short weekly seminar about statistical analysis), well-practiced survey-design skills, and insights into human behavior that could help clients improve their customers' satisfaction with their products and services. Through this job, I became more adept at using Excel and PowerPoint, improved my interviewing skills, and gained more exposure to the norms and expectations in a business environment. Again, I liked what I saw. I knew this was a career path I could follow. And I realized that this wasn't just a good backup career in case the academic thing didn't work out; this was a good path to follow in its own right.

So far, I have discussed my experiences within advertising and market research firms during my graduate school years, but now that I have been employed in this world for a few years, I also know that most major companies (for example, banks, pharmaceuticals, insurance, and so on) have departments within which someone with my type of background would be very valuable. Whether it is their market research department, data analytics department, database management department, strategic planning department, productivity and quality department, customer satisfaction department, or program evaluation department, they need someone with a strong social science research background.

In summary, I found a career path in which I could fairly easily find a job, I could use my hard-earned skills, I could live where I wanted to, I could have financial stability, and I could be happy. Additionally, when I left the office, I could turn off my work life. If someone said, "Hey, Jodie, want to catch a movie after work today?" I could instantly say yes and not have to mentally go through the journal articles I had to read, the papers to write, exams to grade, and ultimately conclude that I could watch the movie for 23.4 minutes before I had to go home to finish my work.

One important fact to note is during these two summer jobs, I kept my graduate school advisor in the loop. I didn't hide my interests and opportunities from him and I didn't let it get in the way of my graduate work. I managed to balance both. My advisor was remarkably supportive, despite his desire to breed future academics. That said, I tried not to let on how seriously I was considering this career path because I didn't want him to think I wasn't also serious about my academic work. I told him and other professors in my program that it was an area in which I was interested and wanted to get my feet wet, but that's it. I'm sure they had their suspicions, but everyone was more supportive than those "rumors" you hear when you first start graduate school about how you will be excommunicated if you even have a thought about a non-academic career. For this aspect, I advise you to tread carefully. Know the people around you. Don't keep secrets, but don't put everything in neon lights. If the people around you respect you, they will respect your decisions.

Finding a Job

The Resume

Once I decided to pursue a career in business as opposed to academia, the next step was finding a full-time job. Before applying for a job, I had to develop a resume that highlighted my skills and could convince employers that a psychology Ph.D. would be an asset to their organization. The internship and part-time job I discussed above definitely helped pad my resume and highlighted my applied skills; however, putting "Jodie L. Steele, Ph.D." at the top certainly captured people's attention (or, if you're not finished yet, list the Ph.D. as "in progress" and give a realistic completion date). I broke my educational background into the three major degrees: B.A., M.A., and Ph.D. And I highlighted the topics I studied as they might relate to business opportunities. I always included a line to the effect of how psychology was the study of human thoughts, attitudes, and behavior and that consumer behavior was a subset of that. In doing so, I was indirectly telling prospective employers that I had expert knowledge of how their customers and clients might think and behave and could bring a rigorous academic perspective that they previously did not have. In other words, I made sure to answer the questions, "Why would a social psychology

Ph.D. be an asset to our business?" and "Why would a social psychology Ph.D. want to work here?" before they asked it; those questions are inevitable because you will look very different from their typical candidate.

Newspaper Listings

I used as many outlets as I could think of to find job listings. Newspaper classifieds had an abundance of listings, which I found under topics such as Research, Analytics, Statistics, Data, Advertising, Marketing, and Marketing Research. Every weekend, I would pour through the listings, circling the ones that sounded relevant and interesting. And then every Monday morning, I would go to the post office to mail off a one-page resume, a more lengthy curriculum vitae, and a cover letter to all of these places. I kept a notebook that included the jobs I had applied for, the contact information, and the date.

Headhunters/Recruiters

"Headhunters" or "job recruiters" are another great resource. Many people don't realize that headhunters are FREE! Headhunters make their money by placing people in positions and receiving a commission (from the employer) equal to a certain percentage of what your annual salary will be. From the employee (your) perspective, this is a great deal. You don't have to pay anything and it is in the headhunter's best interest to place you in a well-paying job. Another benefit is that headhunters are the liaison between you and the employer. They set up the interviews, pass along feedback, negotiate terms of employment, and make sure you get placed in a good job; they only receive their commission if you stay for a certain period of time (so if you leave the job, they don't get their commission). I highly recommend this resource. And don't be afraid to have multiple headhunters, despite what they might tell you (an individual headhunter may ask you to work "exclusively" with them). I once received a call from a headhunter who had found my resume on HotJobs.com (that and Monster.com are other good places to post your resume and look for jobs; more on that later). She was very abrupt, almost rude, and barely listened to what I had to say. In fact, if I had to pay her, there is no way I would have worked with her. Nevertheless, I figured it wouldn't hurt for her to help me with my job search, and surprisingly, she was the one who ultimately found me a job that I accepted (and enjoyed).

You can find headhunters listed in the employment sections in newspapers, in the yellow pages under "Recruiters" or "Employment," via online searches, or through recommendations from people you might know in the business world. If you are working with a few headhunters, be sure to call them once per week to make sure they are thinking of you and are looking for jobs that might suit you.

Online Job Listings

As I mentioned earlier, online job sites are another great resource. HotJobs.com and Monster.com are among the most popular. For those sites, you can post your resume for employers and headhunters to look at and also search through hundreds of job listings. If any particular job listing gives you the option of contacting the company directly (either via an e-mail with an attachment, regular mail, or telephone) as opposed to contacting them via the external job site, you should strongly consider that option. From what I have heard, the files sent via these job sites often arrive in a cluttered, disorganized, and hard-to-read fashion, so where possible, it is best to send application materials directly to the employer. You can also use the Internet to search job openings at particular companies you might be interested in working for (e.g., IBM, Coca-Cola, Accenture Consulting, etc.).

Interviewing

Through all these processes, you will hopefully start receiving calls for interviews. Some may do initial phone interviews and then ask you to come in. Others will have you come in person several times. They usually want you to come in immediately, so be prepared to do some schedule rearranging. Dress as you would if you already had a job with this company. A nice suit (for both males and females) is usually appropriate; err on the side of being too dressed up as opposed to being too casual.

The interviewer will usually spend some time telling you about the position and then will ask you about your background to gauge your preparedness for the job. Don't be shy about sharing the skills and training you bring. As a psychology Ph.D., you have so many assets and talents: primary and secondary research skills, analytic skills, proven discipline and persistence, and immense knowledge of how people behave and think. And when they inevitably ask you what a psychology Ph.D. is doing there, be honest. Make a case for how your skills translate well to the skills necessary for the job opening, but also explain the other factors that led you to decide not to pursue a traditional academic career.

While you are interviewing, you should be paying attention to the environment around you. Are people friendly? Is the layout of the office acceptable to your needs? Do you like the person interviewing you (likely to be your boss)? Remember, finding a job is a two-way street: they have to want you, but you have to want them too.

Do You Accept?

If you get an offer, don't give an answer immediately. Take some time to think about it and compare it to any other offers you might have. Is the salary what you expected (starting range can be from $40,000 to $60,000 and up)? What are the benefits (insurance, vacation time, etc.)? Is there opportunity to advance? And remember that offers are negotiable. You can ask for a higher salary or more vacation time (just don't be unreasonable in your requests). And be honest about other offers you might be entertaining; that might motivate them to sweeten the deal. Use this opportunity, now that the offer is in your hand, to ask more detailed questions about the job: the hours, what specific projects and responsibilities will you have, etc. You can also ask the employer to refer you to another employee to give you another perspective on the job. Having said all that, tread carefully. You don't want them to regret making the offer. At the same time, do what it takes to gain the knowledge necessary to ensure (as much as it is possible) that you will be happy working there. If you have any major events already planned (e.g., a vacation, wedding, etc.), mention that upfront (after the offer is made) because most company policies don't have their vacation allotment kick in until you have been employed for 3 months (but most companies are willing to work around prearranged plans if you tell them).

My Career Beyond Academe

Since completing my Ph.D., I have worked for two different companies in two different industries. What I have found is that my skills have translated well into both industries (and presumably others as well); however, being immersed in graduate school for so long makes the learning curve for understanding business-related industries more of a challenge.

Advertising/Direct Marketing

The first job I had after completing my Ph.D. was at a full-service direct marketing and advertising agency. By "full-service," I mean that the company had the ability to do everything for an advertising campaign: strategy, account management, creative development of the advertisements (ads), production of the ads, and media planning (where to place the ads).

I worked in the Strategic Planning Department, which had a subdepartment called "Data Analytics." Although the entire agency had about 300 employees, the Data Analytics group was small; there were just three of us. I was assigned primarily to the team managing the account for a huge pharmaceutical company (although I did occasional work for other accounts). My official title was "Data Analyst" but unofficially, I was known as a "Quant Jock." A lot of the advertising campaigns we ran involved some sort of response mechanism from the customer: it might be a 1-800 number to call for more information after seeing a television commercial or a survey to complete after receiving a mail package about a particular medication. These avenues for customer response translated into data for me to work with.

Analysis of the survey data was very similar to the logic and techniques used in academia. Using SPSS or SAS, I had the freedom to "play" with the survey data in the way I felt would be most useful. That is, I could conduct the types of analyses I felt were most appropriate and then present the results to the strategic planner on the team. The planner would then take those results and integrate them into the next plan for the client. Thus, the analyses I conducted helped the team decide how best to target customers during the next round of advertising. Other analyses looked at response patterns of those considered the most "valuable" customers, to see how to best grab their attention in future ads. Additionally, I would often help develop the surveys and later analyze the data from them.

I enjoyed this job a lot. It was fun to work on a variety of accounts (made each day different) and the advertising agency environment is a fun one to be in. I was surrounded by young, smart, energetic, and creative people. I also enjoyed the independence that this job allowed. While my boss was aware of the work I was doing, I was the "point person" for data analytics for certain accounts. Because most people in this industry have little knowledge of statistics, I could recommend the most relevant analyses and explain to my colleagues why they would be useful to conduct. Similar to my experience with my first internship, I could see real changes made as a result of my analyses.

Some negative aspects about this job included frustrating occasions when research techniques were sacrificed to save time and money. Thus, because we were often at the mercy of client deadlines, in-depth analyses were sometimes skipped just to get something in the hands of the clients by a certain date. Or sometimes the team or client would flat out ignore the results of the analyses because of a mandate delivered from higher up in the firm; we were required to do something despite what the data told us.

Another larger negative, the one that ultimately drove me from the firm, is that when the economy and business are bad, the advertising budget is one of the first things slashed. And when advertising budgets are cut, advertising agencies lose a lot of money. My company got hit hard by this and started several rounds of layoffs. While I survived the layoffs, I began to feel that my days were numbered, so I hit the job market in hopes of finding something more stable.

Financial Services: Consumer Research

I was fortunate to obtain a job (through a headhunter) at a large banking corporation. I have been with this company for more than 2 years and I now know from discussions with my current boss that having a Ph.D. in psychology was what got me in the door for an interview.

My responsibilities at this job are a little different. My title is "Measurement Analyst," which means I do more than data analytics (which probably makes up about 25% of my job). I am responsible for all aspects of research as it is needed in the various projects related to the bank's retail banking efforts. When there is the need for information about a policy change, a procedural inefficiency, or a new product, various people within the bank come to our group for help with research. For the projects I'm assigned to, I determine the best research method (referring to secondary research, designing interviews or focus group sessions, designing a survey, testing a pilot group, etc.) and then manage all the efforts around making sure the research is conducted effectively and efficiently. Usually an outside vendor will conduct the research (e.g., surveying customers), but I conduct the data analysis, write the report including my own insights and recommendations derived from the data, and then serve as a resource for any further work that needs to be done on the project.

A typical day for me involves working on a number of different projects in various stages of the research process. Let's use my calendar for tomorrow (at the time of this writing) as an example. The first thing on my agenda tomorrow is meeting with a colleague who wants to do a survey about employee rewards and recognition within her department. I will meet with her for about half an hour to get a feel for the kind of information she is looking to gather from fellow employees so that I can write a good, useful survey to present to her by the end of the week. Then, I will return to my desk to write up a report on the results of a series of interviews I designed and conducted with employees of my bank's Fraud Department about fraud detection techniques and processes; this report will be used by senior executives in the Fraud Department to help improve and streamline the bank's fraud detection process. Right before lunch, I'm meeting with a couple of people who are working on a project to improve bank tellers' online policy manuals to finalize the focus group moderator's guide for the focus groups we are conducting next week.

When I get back from lunch, I'll work for a while on the survey about employees' experiences as customers of our bank that I'm designing. Because I am managing all aspects of this survey project, I will also put some time into the logistics: making sure that the communications (announcements, invitations to participate) are being written, programming the survey using our online survey tool, and contacting various departments to make sure all of the questions meet their needs. I will then open up my SPSS file for our ongoing customer satisfaction survey data and do some preliminary analyses and will also start content-coding the responses to the open-ended questions. Those tasks, along with new things that will inevitably pop up, will keep me busy throughout the day. What you might notice is that the types of tasks I will be working on tomorrow are very similar to the tasks you work on in graduate school; I am just applying these research skills/tasks to, in this case, banking issues. See Table 15.1 for a summary of my daily responsibilities.

I enjoy this job because I feel that all of my education and training are put to use. More specifically, I use all aspects of my research skills on a daily basis. Additionally, I get to use my insights into human thoughts and behavior to interpret the research. Admittedly, as I indicated earlier, there was a steep learning curve for me in terms of the business itself. That is, before starting the job, I knew virtually nothing about banking, besides managing my own checking and savings accounts. So while I brought unique research and thinking skills to the bank, I had to work very hard to become familiar with the banking industry.

Was It Worth It?

Both of these jobs made me realize that there are indeed places for psychology Ph.D.s in the business world. Do I miss the academic world? Sometimes. But I try to keep my foot in academia at least to some extent. I occasionally attend psychology conferences and also teach a night class in social psychology at a local college. I try to stay at least somewhat involved and up-to-date with the academic world.

I am happy with the career path I chose for many of the same reasons I initially suspected would be attractive. I can choose where I

Table 15.1 Common Work Duties for Research and Data Analysts in Corporate America

---

Research Process Duties

Designing surveys
Designing interview scripts
Designing focus group moderator's guides
Analyzing survey data
Coding/analyzing content
Performing quasi-experimental design
Sampling
Performing secondary research interpretation

Research Dissemination Duties

Presenting research findings to peers, senior executives, internal departments
Providing *ad hoc* analyses as requested
Preparing reports summarizing research findings
Publishing key research findings on company Intranet

Consultant Duties

Recommending appropriate research methodologies
Advocating research to support decision making and change
Proactively identifying teams/areas/processes that could benefit from research
Managing projects

Miscellaneous Duties

Responding to phone calls, e-mail
Managing professional development (training, seminars)

---

want to live, I am financially stable, I see my work have immediate impact on the business, my hours are reasonable (and in the evenings and on weekends, I don't have to think about work at all), I work with interesting people, the work is fast paced, and what I do each day is a little different from the day before.

Should you move from the Ivory Tower to the glass-paneled, security-card-monitored high-rise? I have had a very good experience in the business world, but certainly there are psychology Ph.D.s out there who tried it and hated it. If you have at least some curiosity about what the business world might be like, I recommend testing the waters gradually. Try to get an internship while you're still in grad school. You might also consider taking (or auditing) business-related courses. Also, it is important to manage your own expectations. The first job you take may not be ideal, but keep in mind it is giving you valuable business experience and something other than education to put on your resume. As with other decisions you make in your life, don't make sweeping generalizations based on an isolated experience (e.g., if your boss is a jerk, it doesn't mean the business world isn't for you; it just means your boss is a jerk). But give it a shot. People will tell you that if you leave academia, it is difficult to come back. And while you may have to work a little harder, it isn't an impossible feat and the risk may be very worthwhile.

Conclusion

Whether you have your own "Wall of Rejection" or simply aren't sure the academic lifestyle is suited to you, a career in business is very satisfying, challenging, and a great outlet for the thousands of hours of training and work you dedicated to earning your Ph.D. in psychology.

16

Software User Research: Psychologist in the Software Industry

CHRISTOPHER N. CHAPMAN

Introduction

"You went to work at Microsoft? What do you do, treat stress?"
"You'll hate a job in industry; it's all just about money."

Those statements are the most common reactions I heard from psychologist friends when I changed careers 4 years ago. I had a postdoctoral fellowship in a prominent research lab, a rewarding psychotherapy practice, and the hope of an academic and clinical career that I had been working toward during 14 years of college, graduate school, and postgraduate training.

My reasons for changing were diverse. I was tired of academic politics. My research interests did not have the focus that is so important for success in academia. My family did not wish to relocate (possibly several times) according to academic position. Finally, an alternative, full-time clinical career was uncertain — it seemed to risk both financial health and emotional burnout.

After focused thinking about my skills and interests, a great deal of research, and a lot of luck, I found a position that I love. I work as a usability engineer at Microsoft, where I help design software that better fits peoples' needs and abilities. My work affords me the opportunity to learn constantly, to express my passion for helping people, to engage in varied and stimulating research, and to have a rewarding career.

In this chapter, I write about my experience at Microsoft. My thoughts are also informed by contact with colleagues at other technology companies. I hope to communicate enough about my work to enable you to determine whether it would interest you, and to suggest how you can learn more about it.

Most new psychologists in my experience are unfamiliar with the specialized research areas of usability and human–computer interaction, so I provide a broad introduction to the field and suggestions for further reading. If you do have firsthand knowledge of human–computer interaction, you may be interested to read the comments about other roles for psychologists and notes on applying for jobs.

My suggestions and recommendations here apply to psychologists at all levels. I have colleagues who have transitioned to the software industry at all stages of their careers, ranging from new graduates to tenured faculty. However, new psychologists often share characteristics that could make the software industry of particular interest: they are up-to-date on research methods, have a diverse and recent background in empirical research, are accustomed to adapting to dynamic situations, and may have enthusiasm for computer technology.

Psychologists at Software Companies

We may start broadly by thinking about many possible careers for psychologists at software companies (and I include Internet companies in this; Web sites are software). Psychologists at software companies include project managers, consultants, psychometricians, cognitive science researchers, human resources specialists, employee assistance providers, and technical writers.

In general, we may break these opportunities into four categories. First, there are positions that emphasize specific psychological training and skills, such as employee assistance, human resources, and psychometric test specialists. The first two are common to all large companies, but some readers may be unaware of the role of psychometrics in the software industry. Many large technology companies have specific curricula that allow specialists to become certified as engineers and technicians with specific skills in technology. For example, a Microsoft SQL Server administrator may wish to become certified as a "Microsoft Certified Database Administrator" (MCDBA); a Cisco network technician may wish to become a "Cisco Certified Internetwork Expert" (CCIE). These certifications are based on a mixture of coursework and formal testing. Psychometric specialists are often employed to design, develop, and validate these tests and related training materials.

Second, there are positions that are open to psychologists on the basis of general education and organizational skills. At many software companies, there is a title of "program manager" that encompasses a wide range of positions where people are responsible for managing the scope, features, specifications, and delivery of various projects. Some of these positions are highly technical and employ experts on specific technologies. Other positions are open to people from various backgrounds who have a proven ability to organize complex projects and guide them to success.

Third, there are some opportunities that engage psychologists because of previous clinical, statistical, or other experience that is important for specific projects. For example, a group within a company may focus on sales opportunities within the health-care or mental health industries; or a software company may specialize in products that are used by psychologists, such as statistical analysis packages or clinic management tools. Psychologists may be needed as consultants on these projects and as field sales representatives, especially if the customers are other psychology researchers or mental health professionals.

Finally, there are opportunities for psychologists to engage in applied research that emphasize skills in behavioral data collection and analysis. Many technology companies have dedicated research groups that offer opportunities to pursue research in artificial intelligence, natural language, cognition, perception, and other kinds of psychological and psychophysiological study; these opportunities are generally well known to academic psychologists. However, there are opportunities for applied research within product development that are less obvious to most psychologists.

For the remainder of this chapter, I will talk about the field in which I work, an area of applied research known as "human–computer interaction." It is large, diverse in scope, composed mostly of psychologists, and corresponds well with the skills that many psychologists have. Within the software industry, it is most commonly present as a particular area of specialization: "usability engineering." Although I focus on usability engineering, the other areas previously mentioned are also open to psychologists. Many of my comments about skills and job seeking apply equally to those areas.

Usability Engineering

Usability engineers study the interactions between people and computer software systems. They study interactions with traditional software programs as well as other media, such as Web sites. The goal of usability engineering is to improve software so that it is easier to use, does what people want and need, and opens new possibilities for people. Usability engineers work in a variety of settings: at large technology companies such as Microsoft, IBM, and Apple; at specialized consumer and business software companies; at consulting groups that provide usability coverage for other companies; and in software groups within other companies and institutions, where they work on projects for which the user interface is important.

Historically, usability engineering derives from the field of human–computer interaction, which is a branch of the larger field of human factors engineering. Human factors engineering arose in the mid-20th century, when it became apparent that interaction design was a critical factor affecting people's ability to use complex mechanical systems. Humans have various cognitive strengths and limitations. When these are not taken into account, a system can be created that is nearly impossible for anyone to control reliably. In classic research, human factors engineers studied the layout of complex environments such as airplane cockpits and nuclear power plant control centers. They discovered that the application of empirical behavioral research methods could lead to better designs for these controls, which led to safer systems and improved performance.

As computer technology became widespread and increasingly important to businesses and consumers, the study of human interaction with technology was extended to the study of computer interaction. One early area of research was computer interface hardware. Researchers investigated many areas of direct human–computer interaction, such as designing monitors, mice, keyboards, and other interfaces. In the early years of the software industry, developers focused primarily on traditional computer science issues such as efficient algorithms. However, as software systems became more complex, it was increasingly apparent that the industry — and individual products — would benefit from attention to behavioral issues. The field of usability engineering was born.

What is "usability"? The concept is amorphous, and the definition depends on the product in question and the goals that exist for the product. Usability engineering focuses on how people *interact* with software; this makes it different from computer science, which focuses on theory and development of computer systems. In general, usability engineers tend to think about four questions:

1. What are the goals that a user has, when interacting with a software product?
2. How does a user accomplish those goals, and how difficult is it to perform the tasks that are involved?
3. How does a user understand the processes involved with a product?
4. What are the user's cognitive and emotional responses? Is the user satisfied, excited, bored, confused, or angry?

The importance of these questions varies for different products. For example, evaluation of a new video game would be likely to emphasize factors such as whether the game is fun and engrossing. Evaluation of an accounting system would be likely to ask whether operations can be completed quickly and accurately.

Usability engineers work as part of software development teams and interact closely with team members over the course of product development. The software "lifecycle" denotes the sequence of stages in a product's history. It begins with initial planning, moves through design, development, and testing, and culminates in product release and ongoing customer support.

Early in the lifecycle, a usability engineer can help to identify problems with current products that may be addressed by a new product or version. The usability engineer can also assist the team to develop realistic usage "scenarios" (examples of how the software may be used for various tasks), based on customer data. As new software is developed, the usability engineer may examine it in various stages of completion (various "builds" of the product) to give feedback to the team. When the product nears completion, it can be tested in a laboratory with representative users. After the software product is completed and released to customers, a usability engineer may talk with customers to understand their problems, review customer support logs, and suggest ways to improve customer support and future versions.

Typical Activities in Usability

At Microsoft, I work as a usability engineer in the Hardware Division on home networking products. We make devices that allow home users to deploy networks, share network resources such as printers, share broadband Internet connections, and connect wirelessly to their networks. My job is to investigate how home users understand networks and to determine how we can improve the interaction experience with our products to better serve our customers (and win new customers). Prior to this position, I worked for 3 years as a usability engineer in the Microsoft Windows Server product line. Windows Server is a product that supports centralized services that can be used by many other people ("client systems") at a time. Servers run applications such as large databases, e-mail services, Web sites, Internet information routing, information storage, backup, and network security. In that position, I worked to make our software easier for network administrators to use.

Perhaps the most representative activity of a usability engineer is a laboratory usability study. In a usability study, people from the community are recruited on the basis of their match to a target market for the software, and are invited to come and use the new software. In a typical session, users are asked to perform representative tasks according to a predetermined plan, and are asked to "think aloud" about their actions while working. For example, in a home networking laboratory study, I might ask users to set up a new network device and configure computers to connect to it, just as if they were setting up a new product at home.

In a laboratory study, the usability engineer explains the value of the user's feedback and emphasizes that it is the software, not the user, that is being tested. The development team watches behind a one-way window. The usability engineer records data on users' ability to perform tasks, where they experience problems, what causes the problems, how well users understand the tasks, how long it takes to complete the tasks, and similar information. After a number of different people have performed the same kinds of tasks, the usability engineer provides feedback to the development team on how users are performing and what would improve the product.

However, laboratory studies are only one way that usability engineers may contribute to products. Laboratory studies represent a certain gold standard of behavioral research, but they are also costly, time-consuming, and unable to address some kinds of questions. Often there is no need to run a laboratory study; a usability engineer may be able to answer a question about whether a design is adequate on the basis of past experience with customers. It is also important for usability engineers to understand their users' thought processes and real-world work, and that information is best acquired through customer visits, field observations, interviews, or surveys. Finally, usability engineers can have large impact during the planning process; it is vital for usability engineers to be involved with software planners and developers as they detail the goals and features of a new product or version.

There is no typical week or month in this work. The software field is continually changing; every product is something new. We are always challenged to learn something new, to find new ways to understand our users, and to represent their needs to the development teams. However, during the course of a given month at Microsoft, I may perform activities like these:

- Meet with a team to review initial plans for a product that has not yet entered coding (actual programming).
- Conduct a laboratory study of a product that is nearing completion, to see how well users perform common tasks.
- Review the specifications for a product from a different group and provide feedback to the group on how customers might respond to the product.
- Invite a group of customers to Microsoft headquarters to participate in a focus group about new products.
- Visit a customer's workplace to learn about the customer's usage of our products and related technologies.
- Give a presentation of top usability issues to a product team or management.
- Coach a project manager on how the manager can better think about usability issues as part of the design and specification process.
- Collect and analyze survey data from customers.
- Engage with a group of usability engineers from other companies to discuss issues that are affecting the technology industry as a whole.

A summary of common tasks for usability engineers is shown in Table 16.1.

The Joys of Usability

There are many things that I enjoy about my work as a usability engineer. The most important is that I am still in a "helping profession"; my job is to help customers by ensuring that we make the best software possible for them. The users with whom I work — home users who want to benefit from network technology — are people who are interested in using technology to make their lives richer, simpler, and more efficient. They benefit from technology that allows them better access to information and shared resources. By deploying home networks, they also are the *de facto* managers of technology on which they and their households come to depend. By assisting them with the

Table 16.1 Common Work Duties for Usability Engineers

Product Research and Development Activities

Meeting with a product team to assess what its members need to know from customers and how user research can affect the product

Designing and conducting a laboratory study to observe participants using software products (experimental or quasi-experimental research)

Conducting a focus group to gather customers' feedback about their technology needs

Designing and deploying an online survey to assess customer needs, satisfaction, or behavior

Visiting customers' homes or workplaces to understand the context in which they use technology products

Presenting research findings and recommendations to a product team and management

Writing study proposals and research reports

Reviewing research proposals, plans, and results from other people, such as other usability engineers or market researchers

Education for Yourself and Others

Learning about technology developments for new products

Coaching a development team on how to understand customers and apply user research data in the development process

Teaching a class for new usability employees about a research method

Taking a training course to expand skills with research methodologies or technology

Mentoring a new employee to help the employee perform better and have more impact on product development

Business Activities

Contracting with an outside company that will provide specialized research services

Interviewing job candidates for usability, user research, and design positions

Developing and maintaining research plans and associated budgets

---

often-difficult tasks in networking, I help them and their households and families in many areas of life: work, study, entertainment, and other important activities and relationships that depend on information and online contact.

Another rewarding aspect of a career in usability is the continual challenge and diversity of the work. As you may infer from reading the lists of activities previously mentioned, there is no single right or wrong way to do usability work. Usability engineers are accountable for finding ways to contribute to product design and success, but there is no blueprint for doing that. In the course of contributing, we are invariably drawn into acting as researchers, interviewers, designers, writers, students of new technology, and teachers about human behavior. We are consultants who constantly seek new ways to engage with both product developers and customers to yield the best possible software systems. I have never heard a usability engineer complain of boredom in his or her job!

Finally, the software development workplace can be personally exciting and rewarding. The industry is notorious for long work hours (an inevitable result when market-necessitated deadlines conflict with everyone's desire to get a product "right"). However, it is a field that employs smart and hard-working people, that emphasizes achievement over superficial appearance, and that rewards a love of learning. Salary and benefits are good, and there are many opportunities for strong performers to learn, grow, advance, or change positions across a career.

Thinking about a Career in Usability

How do you know whether usability might be the right career for you? There are two absolute prerequisites: you must have a passion for making technology better for people, and you must have strong behavioral research skills. One thing is generally unnecessary for usability engineers: detailed technical knowledge or experience. Programming experience or other deeply technical background may be helpful for some projects, but it is not necessary to work on most kinds of software, and most usability engineers are not trained in programming or computer science.

To help determine whether usability might appeal to you, consider the following questions:

- Are you interested in technology and do you enjoy working with it?
- When using software products or Web sites, do you often think that they don't make sense? Could you suggest improvements?
- Do you enjoy working with people and trying to understand their needs and how they think?
- Do you enjoy laboratory research studying behavior?
- Do you have a strong research background, with a proven understanding of empirical methodology?
- Can you respond positively to dynamic work environments where you are responsible for finding ways to contribute amidst changing requirements and conflicting goals?

If the answers to those questions are "yes," then you might enjoy the work of a usability engineer.

Many psychologists have not worked in industry or high-tech settings before. It is important to consider the positive and negative aspects of a career in industry, compared to the more familiar realms of academic, research, and clinical careers.

Compared with academia, a corporate career offers fewer opportunities to achieve the personal status and public recognition that is afforded to professors and researchers. There is less security than you would achieve with tenure, and you have less opportunity to follow your own research interests. Work and projects are directed by the marketplace, not by the interests of science. Working hours and tasks are less flexible, and the work environment may be less idyllic than that of a college campus. On the positive side, work is clearly delineated and constrained; unlike much academic work, it does not blend into all hours of your life. Salary and benefits are likely to be better, especially early in a career; colleagues may be less likely to engage in political disputes that neglect your accomplishments; and there is a clear sense of contributing to the success of a larger group. There can be more ability to choose where you live, and you have the pleasure of seeing immediate real-world results from your work.

When compared with clinical careers, careers in industry do not offer the emotional rewards that come from direct engagement in helping people with life's crises. Clinical careers offer possibilities to work for yourself, to function at high levels of maturity, to have great flexibility in working hours, styles, and locations, and to engage in many different kinds of work, including psychotherapy, supervision, teaching, and management. On the other hand, clinical careers can be difficult to start. They are financially uncertain and the work may lead to stressful situations with difficult clients, overwhelming personal responsibility, or professional isolation. Careers in the software industry offer clearer paths to success than clinical work, they bring the delight of creating new products, and they offer possibilities to help many people, even millions of people, through attention to the human needs of technology users.

How to Prepare for a Career in Usability

There are five activities that will assist you in learning more about possible careers in usability. First, learn as much as you can about usability work. I recommend that you start by reading two books. The first book I recommend is Donald Norman's *The Design of Everyday Things* (also published as *The Psychology of Everyday Things*). Norman gives an enjoyable introduction to the ideas that underlie good technology design. If those ideas interest you, I recommend that you learn more about the profession of usability engineering in Jakob Nielsen's *Usability Engineering*. Nielsen's work is the best overview of usability engineering in practice, and his book is quite readable (unlike many titles in the field, which are reference books or academic texts). Nielsen presents the basic theory of usability along with practical suggestions and exercises for learning how to do usability research.

Second, unless you have a very strong empirical research background, such as Ph.D. from an experimentally oriented program, think about strengthening your research background. Usability engineering usually does not require advanced statistics, but it *does* require strong experimental design skills and the kind of intuition about sampling, power, and the importance of results that comes from substantial experience in behavioral research. In addition to the offerings of traditional graduate schools of psychology, you may be able to find courses that offer specific training in usability methodology at your local college or university. Such courses may be offered through a university's extension school or in various academic departments. You may wish to check course listings in psychology (cognitive), human factors, computer science, technical communications, and related areas.

Third, perform some usability research of your own. Once you begin thinking about it, it is likely that opportunities will abound. For example, whether you are currently in school or working, it is likely that you, your department, your colleagues, or a professional group will have a Web site with important content for you and your peers; or perhaps you work with software that is important for your research or professional work. After reading Nielsen's book, think about the common tasks that you would need to perform with the Web site or software, and invite a few friends or colleagues to participate in a usability study. Collect data on their task performance. If possible, find the person or people responsible for the Web site or software and share your results with them. If this is not practical, you could instead visit some popular Web sites, such as Amazon.com or MSN.com. Identify as many positive and negative aspects about the user experience as you can, and list ways that the experience could be improved.

Fourth, research the software industry and any companies that may interest you. Very large companies such as Microsoft often have a number of books written about them. Among those books, some may cover a company's work environment or follow the course of a specific project. Those kinds of titles will help you to learn what it might be like to work there. For Microsoft, Randall Stross's *The Microsoft Way* talks about what Microsoft is like for employees and whom it hires, and Fred Moody's *I Sing the Body Electronic* follows the development process for a consumer software title. If you are interested in smaller companies or consulting firms, look up information about them online: do a search at your favorite search engine, and research them in the online business database at a university library.

Finally, go online and look at job postings. Most technology companies post positions online and recruit people through online submission and review of resumes. Reading these job postings will acquaint you with the specific requirements and expectations you would need to meet to enter this career.

Three suggestions may assist with reviewing job postings. First, try a variety of key words when searching a company's database; not all companies use the same job titles or descriptive phrases. Usability engineers may be found with titles such as "usability engineer," "user testing," "human factors engineer," "user researcher," and even with generic titles such as "program manager." If you can do a keyword search, try "usability," "psychology," "user AND research," "human-computer," "human factors," and similar phrases.

Second, when reading job postings, remember that what they call a "requirement" is often not a requirement. Job postings are often written hastily, recycled from the past, or written by committee. If you read a posting that says "X skills, Y experience, and Z years of work are required," I suggest that you read it as "an ideal candidate would have X, Y, and Z ... but other candidates will be considered." The most important thing is to be able to communicate honestly and effectively how you could contribute to the success of the company.

Third, if you apply, be prepared for a very unpredictable time-frame. The private job market does not operate on the kinds of fixed schedules that are found in graduate school and academic careers. After an applicant submits a resume online, a company may call within a day or two to conduct or schedule an interview. Alternatively, an application may languish and never receive a formal rejection. It is important for an applicant to respond with flexibility and clarity to whatever situations may arise.

If you pursue a career in usability, you can be proud that you are helping to make people's lives better through technology. If you pursue other career paths, please let those of us in the software industry know when we can help you! It is only through learning about our users and their needs that we can continue our work to make software better.

Disclaimer

Opinions and statements expressed here are those of the author, and do not necessarily reflect the views, practices, or policies of Microsoft Corporation.

References

Moody, F. (1996). *I sing the body electronic: A year with Microsoft on the multimedia frontier.* New York: Penguin.

Nielsen, J. (1994). *Usability engineering.* San Francisco: Morgan Kaufmann.

Norman, D. A. (1988). *The design of everyday things* (also published as *The psychology of everyday things*). New York: Basic Books.

Stross, R. E. (1997). *The Microsoft way: The real story of how the company outsmarts its competition.* Cambridge, MA: Perseus.

17

Executive Management: Helping Executives Manage Their Organizations through Organizational and Market Research

STEVEN WILLIAMS

Management Consulting

In its simplest terms, management consulting is a very broad field that has as its ultimate goal to help executives (and their subordinates) improve the functioning of all or part of an organization (or its staff). It generally involves working closely with company executives such as chief executive officers (CEOs), chief operating officers (COOs), chief financial officers (CFOs), chief information officers (CIOs), senior vice presidents, and other executives at the top tier of the organization. Management consultants may also work with managerial staff at other levels, as well as with nonmanagerial staff. They may also work with those groups outside of but affiliated with an organization, including boards of directors, executive or finance committees, consultants, certified public accountants, executive search firms, and the like. Management consultants may spend as little time as 1 day helping an executive address a specific concern, or they may spend an entire year (or more) helping executives work through more complex issues with far-reaching implications.

Management consultation can be implemented in a variety of ways depending on the needs of the clientele. In some ways, it is akin to theoretical orientations in human service psychology in which some psychologists approach their work from a mainly cognitive-behavioral perspective, while others approach their discipline from a psychodynamic framework. Likewise, one orientation in management consulting is the use of and strong emphasis on organizational benchmarks and market research to guide organizational management decisions.

Industry Research

The collection and application of organizational research provide management consulting from an objective and empirically driven perspective. This is perhaps a considerable departure from the one-on-one executive coaching model. The use of organizational research in management consulting involves a process of collecting benchmarking data. *Benchmarking* is a technique that provides a company with a frame of reference, allowing for external (and sometimes internal) comparisons to be made so that the company can gauge its current performance and plan for the future. All too often companies have limited knowledge of how competitors, other similar companies, and individuals are performing. Benchmarking, therefore, provides industry "intelligence" on organizational practices, policies, and procedures within a specific industry or sector. It may entail, for example, amassing benchmarking data from numerous organizations about expenses and revenue, use of technology, and personnel practices such as compensation, benefits, and "perks" offered to staff.

Often, executives are uncertain of the normative practice in a particular industry and they are often left to "wing it" on their own. It is surprising to discover how many CEOs or other top executives are clueless about organizational industry norms or expectations. Not all CEOs are from Fortune 500 companies with years of experience and coaching, and even those high-ranking CEOs need professional guidance. Instead, many executives are from small or mid-sized companies that are not recognizable household names. Some of the common questions that are raised by executives include the following: How much should I compensate my staff to stay competitive in the marketplace?

What types of benefits and "perks" do employees expect to receive? Are we spending too much money on overhead expenses? How much money do other organizations generate from online sales? What policies are other companies implementing to protect themselves against sexual harassment lawsuits?

These are just a handful of the questions and dilemmas that executives face. By comparing their organization against industry norms of other organizations of similar size and type, executives (and their boards of directors) are better able to establish company policies, modify organizational procedures and practices, and justify decisions that are made.

Market Research

The collection and application of market research share many similarities to organizational research, and the two are not mutually exclusive. They both involve using objective and empirical data to shape organizational decisions, and they often employ similar methods. The main difference, however, is that where organizational research focuses on the trends and practices of other organizations, market research hones in on the organization's products, services, and customers. Which products and services are most valued by our customers? What new products and services are competitors planning? What is the most efficient way to market our new product? What is the maximum price customers will pay for a service without turning to our competitors? How much should we charge for our new service? Executives struggle with these and other questions on a daily basis, and prefer to make decisions on more than just a hunch. This market research or competitive intelligence gives executives strategic guidance allowing them to evaluate existing programs, launch new programs, forecast revenue and costs, and keep abreast and ahead of the competition. Based on my experience, the lack of appropriate market research and assessment is one of the major reasons newly formed organizations are not successful. In a nutshell, market research helps an organization evaluate the viability of its products and services, as well as evaluate customer behaviors and attitudes.

Organizational Management: Applying Organizational and Market Research to the Workplace

Management consultants, who collect and use organizational benchmarks and market research as their main approach to help executives make important decisions, also help them apply the information correctly. All too often I have seen the costly and embarrassing mistakes that occur when executives are not coached on how to use the data appropriately. For example, I have witnessed occasions when executives have made decisions based on poor research methods or small sample sizes. Similarly, I have seen executives make decisions that are *solely* based on research findings without consideration of other important factors that may have an impact on decisions.

Each organization has its unique circumstances and complexities. The role of the management consultant extends to understanding the personality, dynamics, and functioning of the organization. It also entails some understanding of financial statements, employment law, executive contracts, competitors, marketing strategies, and other aspects of an organization. And, perhaps most importantly, the management consultant must understand the "politics" that are behind the decisions and the implications that they will have for the organization. The more management consultants understand about the organizations they are working with, the better they are able to harness the research in such a way that helps them compare "apples to apples," speak the language of the executives, which helps them produce the most optimal outcome for the organization.

Professional Responsibilities and Activities

The role of the management consultant is diverse, and is often influenced by the type of setting and clientele. Perhaps the best way to illustrate a career in management consulting is by example. Here are just a few of the activities that are involved in this profession.

Research Development

Management consultants who work in this capacity are involved in all stages of overseeing the collection of organizational benchmarking data, market research, and competitive intelligence. This may include developing survey instruments, statistical sampling, data collection (via mail, Internet, telephone, or other means), data analysis, report writing, and debriefing. It often involves managing a staff of professionals who assume many of these responsibilities.

Consultation

This is perhaps the central focus of management consulting. It involves helping executives use benchmarking statistics to make important decisions. Let's examine three real-life consulting scenarios.

Scenario One. I was recently asked by a CEO of a Washington, D.C., company for a compensation and contract analysis. More often than not, a company or its board of directors requests and pays for compensation and contract analyses. However, the unique circumstances faced by this CEO prompted her to contact me directly. The CEO believed that she was considerably underpaid for someone of her years of experience and background, and that the benefits and "perks" that were in her contract also were not commensurate with that of her peers. Because her contract was up for renewal, she thought this was an ideal opportunity to negotiate a better package.

Based on CEO compensation data that I previously collected from almost 1,000 CEOs, I was able to extensively examine compensation, benefits, and terms of contracts for those CEOs whose organizations matched her organization's revenue size, staff size, company type, industry, and focus. I was also able to match her against peers with similar years of experience, degree level, and other credentials. After careful analysis, the benchmarking data suggested that she was indeed paid considerably less than her peers. The hard data were used as a negotiating tool, and her board of directors eventually agreed to a more competitive compensation package than she was previously awarded.

Scenario Two. A CFO of a large company informed me that his job was in jeopardy because the organization was not as profitable as its main competitor. For the past year, he had informed his boss (the CEO) that the net revenue projections that were determined at the beginning of the fiscal year were on par with what is expected in their industry, and that being any more ambitious would only lead to an unrealistic net revenue projection. Because it was his word against his boss's word, he did not have a leg to stand on. He asked me to perform a budgetary analysis of his organization, comparing information from its financial statements against those of similar organizations from the same industry. After meticulously examining the organization's revenue, expenses, assets, liabilities, investments, and reserves against the various line items of the financial statements from more than 500 organizations, I was able to determine that his organization's net revenue projections were indeed consistent with those of other companies in the industry, and that his net revenue projection was appropriate. He now had the objective data to convince his CEO and the board of directors that his assumption was correct. By the way, both the CFO and CEO kept their jobs.

Scenario Three. An association wanted to convert all of its hardcopy book titles to CD ROM or e-book formats. The thinking was that it would reduce excessive printing costs and that the more technologically advanced medium would appeal to its mostly young members. I was asked to conduct a market research study of the association's membership to determine various issues surrounding this decision. The market research yielded interesting results. Among other pertinent findings, the majority of members was lukewarm to the idea of books in the form of CD ROM and e-books, and members expected to pay considerably less for electronic books than they would for the same title in hardcopy print format. Hence, the organization would stand to lose substantial revenue if it made this decision, even with the benefit of lower costs associated with this electronic medium. The market research prevented the organization from moving in a direction that it would have regretted.

Training

Training involves holding educational workshops for executives on a variety of topics in organizational management. For example, for executives who are less experienced, topics may include supervising staff, budgeting, employment law, sexual harassment in the workplace, marketing, and the like. For those who are more seasoned, educational sessions may be more hands on, and include more specific topics of interest.

Employment Opportunities, Setting, and Salary

Management consulting provides numerous opportunities in a vast number of settings for graduate students who would like to pursue this career. If your management consulting orientation is organizational and market research, then your options are just as wide. Conceivably, any executive at an existing or developing business or company can make use of organizational benchmarks and market research, so there is no shortage of potential customers.

Perhaps the most common option is employment with a firm that consults with company executives. Typically, each firm has its own niche. For example, one setting may be in an executive search firm that is established to help an organization recruit and place top-level executives. This is the setting that is most likely to emphasize benchmarking data on compensation, benefits, and contracts of CEOs and other top executives. Employment law firms are another type of agency that provides legal consultation to executives. These firms often need management consultants who can arm lawyers with data that may be used as leverage in a judicial proceeding. For example, if a company is accused of sexual discrimination practices, a management consultant who works for an employment law firm may be asked to conduct a comprehensive internal study of the organization's gender-related hiring and termination practices, which may entail extensive interviewing of staff. Another possibility may be a marketing firm that specializes in helping companies collect market research on customers and investigate information about competitors. In this capacity, the management consultant works closely with the marketing team so that an effective marketing strategy, based on market research data and competitive intelligence, is implemented. Yet another setting may be a firm that is designed to help floundering organizations turn around and become more successful. In many cases, these firms take over complete operation of the organization.

Management firms also target specialized clientele or sectors. For example, some work exclusively with for-profit organizations while others work only with charitable or other nonprofit entities. Still others consult with government agencies, universities, or hospitals. A management consultant may work directly from the firm's headquarters, or may be placed at the client's organization to work more closely with the client on a daily basis until the project is completed.

Professional associations and societies are another popular setting where management consultants are found. There are numerous associations, most of which are nonprofit organizations, that have CEOs, CFOs, CIOs, and other executives as their members. In many instances, these professionals join associations to receive guidance and support in their professional roles, as well as to network with other professionals of similar backgrounds. Many of these associations require profession-based research that is used to help these members in their professional capacities.

Once a management consultant is more grounded in the field and has generated a network of contacts and clients, self-employment as an independent management consultant is a possibility. The benefit of independent consulting is that you can generate your own niche that matches your expertise and interest areas. For example, you may decide to build your own market research firm and exclusively conduct market research and competitive analyses for companies. Independent consultants may find themselves in any of the settings that were previously mentioned.

Generally, the compensation in this field is attractive but depends on several organizational and personal factors such as setting (e.g., for-profit, nonprofit, self-employed, etc), clientele served (e.g.,

Fortune 500 executives), revenue size, and geographical location of the company. Personal factors such as years of experience, degree or special certifications attained, and the payment arrangement may also have a bearing on compensation.

As a result of these moderating factors, it is difficult to pin down a specific salary that a management consultant can earn. On the lowest end of the continuum, it is not uncommon for a newcomer to earn an annual salary of approximately $50,000. Conversely, management consultants with a few years under their belts earn close to or more than a six-figure salary. According to the American Psychological Association, psychologists with a mere 5 to 9 years of experience working in management consulting fields earned an average of $123,800 in 2001 (Singleton, Tate, & Randall, 2003), and those with more years earned substantially higher salaries. Some management consultants who work for executive search firms, for example, may have compensation arrangements that are a percentage of the newly recruited executive's first-year compensation. A colleague of mine who owns his own executive search firm has a compensation agreement that paid 10% of the newly placed executive's base salary. He recently placed a CEO in a mid-sized for-profit company. The CEO's starting base salary was $900,000 (by the way, this does not include monetary bonuses and "soft money" perks such as an automobile, home mortgage expense reimbursement, country club membership, and professional liability insurance), so my colleague pocketed $90,000 for the 5-month search for just one of his clients! It is important to mention that you do not have to be employed at for-profit organizations to earn big bucks. Many nonprofit organizations pay handsomely as well. Typically, the larger the organization's revenue size, the higher the compensation.

Training and Professional Development

Perhaps the obvious training in psychology that will prepare you for a position in management consulting is a master's or doctoral degree in industrial/organizational psychology or human factors psychology. However, not all psychology graduate students pursue this path and many graduate students develop an interest in management consulting during or after graduate school. We examine how master's- and doctoral-level graduate students can leverage other coursework and psychology subfields to lead them in the career direction in management consulting.

If you are still in psychology graduate school, there are certain courses or experiences that are relevant to the field of management consulting. Some of these courses and experiences may not be obvious to you on the surface. For example, research methodology, survey development, and statistics are courses that are generally found in most psychology subfields and should become an important emphasis in your training. Proficiency at literature searches and other analytic procedures are other useful skills that are common in psychology graduate programs and tap similar skills sets for those management consultants who are engaged in generating intelligence for an organization's competitors. Experience in teaching, public speaking, defending research (e.g., thesis, dissertation, etc.), and writing are all common to psychology graduate students, and are used frequently by management consultants.

I once had a mentor who told me that most management problems are people problems, and if you can effectively manage people then the rest is cake! I have found this axiom to be true and believe that those students who take courses in clinical interviewing, psychotherapy, social psychology, and cognitive development have the beginning foundation for a career in management consulting. Many of those courses tackle human behavioral issues such as crisis intervention, conflict resolution, problem solving, group dynamics, motivation, and persuasion, all concepts used by management consultants.

If you have completed graduate school and would like to embark on a career in management consulting, you should consider taking continuing education courses to round out your formal psychology graduate school training. This may entail taking a few introductory courses in business, marketing, or consulting on a part-time basis at a local community college. Doing so will help you understand some of the basics and the often-used lingo, and will make way for a smoother transition into your first job. It will also give you added credibility in this field. If you do not have the time or money to enroll in a community college, then you should take advantage of the countless professional development seminars that may earn you a certificate of completion on a relevant topic.

No matter how much formal education you receive, you may find that most of your training and development in this area will occur on the job. The more skills that you acquire, the more options you will have in management consulting.

Advice to Students and New Professionals

The advice that I have for students is both broad and specific. First, it is important to think about your career ambitions at the earliest possible stages of your graduate training. Too often, psychology students only think about their first job during their final year of training. By that time, they have missed opportunities to take relevant coursework, develop skills, and gain exposure in management consulting.

If feasible, be open to volunteering part of your time in a management consulting setting. This can occur in a variety of ways. As a graduate student, you should think about donating at least 8 hours a week at a local management consulting firm as an intern or practicum student. I know what you're thinking, you're already too busy attending classes, holding down a part-time job, probably doing research, teaching, or clinical practicum, and spending countless hours studying! But believe me, it's worth it. These positions do not have to be advertised. You can send unsolicited requests (along with your resume) to companies, many of which would be delighted to provide you exposure in exchange for your unpaid assistance at their organization. The idea is that this pro bono work and mentoring will pay off in the future. It will afford you the experience you need, sometimes lead to paid opportunities in that area or within that organization (assuming you impress your supervisor), and provide you with an opportunity to network with others who are already established in management consulting. Remember, you have to crawl before you walk, and getting this exposure will set you apart from the pack and may give you an opportunity to "break into" the field.

Second, "think outside the box." This seems to be an overused cliché but worth repeating again in this context. Traditionally, psychology graduate students are not trained to "think outside the box" when it comes to making career decisions. Students must avoid being pigeonholed into the typical career paths. This restricted thought pattern only limits your career options. Instead, you should identify the micro skills inherent in psychology training, and learn how to apply those skills and knowledge in various settings.

As previously mentioned above, the management consulting field applies many of the skills and knowledge acquired in almost all fields of psychology, and you do not have to be enrolled in industrial/organizational psychology or human factors psychology to pursue this path. For example, the skills that underlie psychodiagnostic interviewing and psychotherapy are very similar to the skills necessary to help executives diagnose workplace issues and dynamics, manage their subordinates, increase workplace motivation, and produce change in the workplace. So take some time to identify and write down the skills, knowledge, and abilities that you have acquired so that you can determine how best they fit into management consulting.

Third, once you land that first job, always have your eye on the next job that you intend or hope to have. You need to be one step ahead. The name of the game is to acquire as many skills as possible. Sometimes your position may afford limited opportunities (especially when you are new to the field). It doesn't hurt to ask your supervisor if you can take on additional responsibilities as part of your job. I've never experienced a supervisor who was reluctant to giving a supervisee more work if the request is reasonable and realistic! Again, this gives you an opportunity to stretch your management consulting repertoire.

A Typical Week in the Life of a Management Consultant

> The best-laid plans of mice and men go oft astray.

The above proverb pretty much summarizes my work on a week-to-week basis. As much as I try to plan exactly what I would like to accomplish for the week, there are always unanticipated projects that take me away from the main projects that are already on the roster. Anyone who embarks on a career in management consulting will soon realize that flexibility is key, and that being responsive to your clients in their time of need is essential. Despite the title of this section, I admit that there is no *typical* week. But what I will try to do is summarize a handful of the activities that my week may entail.

Most of the week may be consumed by overseeing the conduct of a major financial benchmarking effort that involves the collection of company financial tax forms. This is just one type of organizational benchmarking effort. This huge undertaking involves requesting tax forms from nearly 8,000 companies and then soliciting additional financial information that is not found on these forms. Once the data are collected from as many companies that are willing to provide them to us, we must systematically verify the information and make sure it meets all of our quality control requirements. This may involve checking other sources to corroborate the data or making some direct calls to the responding company's CFO or controller. My team and I must go through this rigorous process because these and other benchmarking data, collectively, will ultimately serve as the basis for the management consulting recommendations that we make to our clients. It is, therefore, the foundation of our work. Other team members may be working on another phase of the project — entering the financial data into a database so that the information is analyzable. Again, my task is to coordinate that effort so that it is executed flawlessly.

While that project is continuing, part of my week may entail leading a 1-day workshop for a group of human resource professionals. One of my most popular workshops is on competitive staff benefits where I help human resource professionals understand which benefit offerings are most likely to attract new hires and retain existing staff. The workshop also helps companies stay competitive in the marketplace by revealing the benefits that other local companies within the same industry are offering staff.

Whenever I have some downtime, I continue working on a comprehensive compensation analysis for another client with a large staff size. I am often asked to determine whether a company is equitably compensating its staff, a very sensitive topic for most companies. This task usually takes several weeks to complete given that every full-time staff person's compensation is examined and matched against a comparable industry standard. It takes time to do this right. It is important that the unique qualifications, background, and experiences of staff are factored into the equation so that we are comparing apples to apples.

Finally, my week may involve a meeting with the senior management staff of a large company for which we have conducted market research. After giving the executives a detailed report on the market research findings and a profile of their competitors, I usually end my market research consultation with a meeting where I orally present the findings and recommendations. I find that the face-to-face meeting and the dialogue that follows help them remember the most important parts of the findings and, therefore, increase the likelihood that they will follow through with my recommendations. It has often been my experience that executives rarely read market research reports from page to page; therefore, this added component is necessary. In this meeting, I impart to them actionable ways that they can use the information to improve their business processes, marketing, and customer service.

I can guarantee you that the following week, and the week after, will bear no resemblance to what I just described. In large part, that is what makes this career so appealing. Table 17.1 illustrates a handful of duties performed by management consultants. By no means is this an exhaustive listing, and depending on the clientele and setting, the tasks that management consultants undertake may vary.

Advantages and Disadvantages

As with any career, management consulting has its pros and cons. One of the key advantages is that management consulting is a growing field, and executives are becoming dependent on its expertise. There are a multitude of opportunities and workplace settings, and this is likely to increase in the near future. Another plus is that it is an extremely lucrative career for psychology degree recipients, even for

Table 17.1 Common Work Duties for Management Consultants

Research Duties

Collecting benchmarking data in the management and human resource fields to aid with decision making by CEOs, CFOs, human resource staff, and other executives

Conducting market research to give executives strategic guidance allowing them to evaluate existing programs, launch new programs, and forecast revenue and costs

Engaging in the collection of competitive intelligence so that companies and their executives can stay abreast of the competition

Developing survey instruments and other data collection tools

Conducting statistical sampling, data analyses, and report writing

Verifying information and making sure it meets all of our quality control requirements

Service Duties

Working closely with executives to apply research and other information to make sound business and strategic decisions

Understanding the culture, dynamics, functioning, and "politics" of the organization so that recommendations to executives are more informed and tailored to the organization

Understanding the financial statements, policies, procedures, and laws affecting an organization so that appropriate direction can be given to executives

Leading workshops for various groups of human resource professionals, CEOs, CFOs, and other executives on various topics in management, contracts, compensation, and benefits

Helping companies stay competitive in the marketplace by revealing trends of other local companies of the same size and type

Imparting actionable ways that executives can use data to improve business processes, marketing, and customer service

recent graduates in psychology. Depending on your niche, clientele, and expertise, the salary ceiling is as high as what you can convince someone to pay you for your services and time.

There is a downside. Even though there are a multitude of factors that can determine whether business decisions proceed as planned, if your management consulting played a large role in a decision that took a wrong turn, you may find yourself blamed or targeted unjustly as the scapegoat. It may even be a situation where someone did not follow your advice in the manner that you intended. In the business world, some seemingly look to "pass the buck," especially when highly paid executives are involved. A worse-case scenario of this happening is that you may be subject to a lawsuit, but at the very least the same company probably will not solicit your services again and your reputation may be stained slightly. All in all, however, I do believe the advantages outweigh the disadvantages.

Reference

Singleton, D., Tate, A., & Randall, G. (2003). *2001 salaries in psychology.* Washington, D.C.: American Psychological Association.

IV

Applied Roles for New Psychologists

18

Public Health: Career Opportunities for Psychologists in Public Health

MONICA L. BASKIN

Overview of the Field

What Is Public Health?

Public health's mission has been articulated as "fulfilling society's interest in assuring conditions in which people can be healthy" (Institute of Medicine, 1988, p.7). To this end, C.E.A. Winslow (as cited in Hanlon & Pickett, 1984) suggests that public health is the science and art of preventing disease, prolonging life, and promoting health and efficiency through organized community effort. Included in the definition is an understanding that those in the field are part of a collective effort to discover and intervene on factors that result in preventable and avoidable health outcomes (Turnock, 1997).

Table 18.1 Major Distinctions between Public Health and Medicine

Public Health	Medicine
Population focused	Individual focused
Public service ethic, tempered by concerns for the individual	Personal service ethic, conditioned by awareness of social responsibilities
Emphasis on prevention, health promotion for the whole community	Emphasis on diagnosis and treatment, care for the whole patient
Public health paradigm employs a spectrum of interventions aimed at the environment, human behavior and lifestyle, and medical care	Medical paradigm places predominant emphasis on medical care
Multiple professional identities with diffuse public image	Well-established profession with sharp public image
Variable certification of specialists beyond professional public health degree	Uniform system for certifying specialists beyond professional medical degree

Lines of specialization organized, for example, by:
    Analytical method (epidemiology)
    Setting and population (occupational health)
    Substantive health problem (nutrition)
    Skills in assessment, policy development, and assurance
	Lines of specialization organized, for example, by:
	    Organ system (cardiology)
	    Patient group (pediatrics)
	    Etiology, pathophysiology (oncology, infectious disease)
	    Technical skill (radiology)

Biologic sciences central, stimulated by major threats to health of populations; move between laboratory and field	Biologic sciences central, stimulated by needs of patients; move between laboratory and bedside
Numeric sciences an essential feature of analysis and training	Numeric sciences increasing in prominence, although still a relatively minor part of training
Social sciences as an integral part of public health education	Social sciences tend to be an elective part of medical education
Clinical sciences peripheral to professional training	Clinical sciences an essential part of professional training

Source: Harvey Fineberg, M.D., Ph.D., Dean, Harvard University School of Public Health, 1990. Retrieved April 6, 2004 from http://www.asph. org/document.cfm?page=724.

Public health is an interdisciplinary field that includes disciplines such as medicine, dentistry, nursing, optometry, nutrition, social work, environmental sciences, health education, health services administration, and the behavioral sciences. However, its distinction from many of these allied health professions is its focus on entire populations rather than on individual patients and its primary goal to prevent diseases or disability before they occur (Association of Schools of Public Health, n.d.; Ohio State University School of Public Health, 2002). Table 18.1 highlights the main differences between public health and medicine.

Public health strives to create healthier communities by improving the health of people and the environments in which they live (Ohio

State University School of Public Health, 2002). Public health is an organized and interdisciplinary field that addresses the physical, mental, and environmental health concerns of communities and populations at risk for disease and injury. Healthier communities are created via the application of health promotion and disease prevention technologies and interventions designed to improve and enhance quality of life. Among these technologies and interventions are three core public health functions:

1. Identify health problems and set priorities based on the assessment and monitoring of the health of at risk communities and populations.
2. Formulate public policies that seek to resolve local and national health problems and priorities via partnerships with community and government leaders.
3. Assure accessibility of appropriate and cost-effective health promotion, disease prevention, and disease treatment services to all populations, and provide ongoing evaluation of that care (Association of Schools of Public Health, n.d.).

The field of public health seeks to understand and face the health challenges of individuals and communities through research, policy, and practice (Ohio State University School of Public Health, 2002). In this vein, public health practitioners carry out this mission via 10 essential public health services:

1. Monitor health status to identify community health problems.
2. Diagnose and investigate health problems and health hazards in the community.
3. Inform, educate, and empower people about health issues.
4. Mobilize community partnerships to identify and solve health problems.
5. Develop policies and plans that support individual and community health efforts.
6. Enforce laws and regulations that protect health and ensure safety.
7. Link people to needed personal health services and assure the provision of health care when otherwise unavailable.
8. Assure a competent public health and personal health-care workforce.
9. Evaluate effectiveness, accessibility, and quality of personal and population-based health services.
10. Research for new insights and innovative solutions to health problems (Association of Schools of Public Health, n.d.).

How Do Psychologists Play a Role?

Social and behavioral sciences (e.g., anthropology, psychology, political science, sociology, health education) play a critical role in public health academics and practice. All schools of public health offer core coursework that addresses the social and behavioral issues in public health. Mental health and social research are among the many areas of concentration that are offered in schools of public health (Association of Schools of Public Health, n.d.).

Health promotion and disease control and prevention highlight the need for behavioral and social sciences in understanding the role of risk behavior and risk group characteristics for major public health concerns such as cancer, obesity, HIV/AIDS, violence, cardiovascular disease, and drug addiction (Schneiderman & Speers, 2001). Public health in the 21st century is heavily focused on the prevention of disease. Thus, there has been recognition that behavior changes may significantly reduce many risk factors associated with disease and may have a positive impact on recovery from these conditions.

Prevention strategies of late have largely concentrated on community-based interventions, which have been shown to be effective in changing the health of large populations. Behavioral and social scientists, such as psychologists, are helpful in this arena as we are trained to view individuals as belonging to complex and dynamic social systems including immediate and extended family systems, acquaintance and friendship networks, neighborhood and community systems, and cultural groups (Schneiderman & Speer, 2001). This paradigm allows for an integration of biological, psychological, social, political, economic, and cultural factors in the explanation of human behavior. Such an approach lends itself to examining individuals, their community, and the larger cultural context in which they reside, the better to understand factors that contribute to the development and maintenance of healthy or high-risk behaviors.

Psychologists in public health have been successful in applying these types of approaches to the development and evaluation of intervention for many of the nation's top public health problems (Tomes & Gentry, 2001). The benefits of this seemingly strange union of psychology and public health may be seen in both the individual and public arena. As psychologists struggle to sustain gainful employment in an ever-evolving economy, I challenge you to look at how a career in public health may best serve you and the fields of psychology and public health. The following sections of this chapter review the types of employment settings and the roles and responsibilities of psychologists in public health. In addition, I review a typical week in my current public health career and provide my take on the advantages and disadvantages of the field. Finally, the chapter concludes with some practical suggestions and recommendations for persons interested in learning more about psychologists in public health or pursuing a career in this field.

Employment Settings

Psychologists who work in the arena of public health can be found working in a number of employment settings. Among these are schools of public health, state and local departments of public health, nonprofit and for-profit public health organizations, and federal government agencies.

Psychologists employed in schools of public health are often faculty members (tenure- or nontenure-track lines) or research project directors. In addition to typical teaching responsibilities (see chapter on professions in academic settings for more details), psychologists are often sought as members of master's thesis and dissertation committees to give their expertise in social behavior and skills in designing and evaluating interventions. Psychologists are also highly recruited to direct research projects. Research project directors assist in project planning, development of instruments for data collection, data analysis, and dissemination of (via presentations and publications) research findings.

Local and state departments of public health are also settings in which public health psychologists work. These persons often hold leadership positions such as director of health education programs, coordinator of local prevention efforts (e.g., drug–alcohol prevention), manager of community relations, and consultant or advisor on local or state initiatives (e.g., commission on women's/men's/minority health). Similarly, nonprofit (e.g., American Heart Association, American Cancer Society) and for-profit (e.g., Westat, Research Triangle Institute, Abt Associates, Inc.) agencies and the federal government (e.g., Centers for Disease Control and Prevention, Health Resources and Services Administration, Substance Abuse and Mental Health Services Administration) seek to employ psychologists and other behavioral scientists as project managers and directors to oversee department projects or serve as the project officer for various funded grants.

Professional Responsibilities and Expectations

Professional responsibilities and expectations of psychologists in public health involve four main areas of focus: research, teaching/training, public health practice, and consulting. Public health research is needed to gain a better understanding of many of the nation's leading health problems. Specifically, the more we can learn about disease risk factors, the more likely we are to design effective and efficacious prevention and treatment programs. Research of late has focused more on women's health, men's health, violence, obesity, sexually transmitted diseases, HIV/AIDS, tuberculosis, and unplanned pregnancies. In addition, research-funding opportunities are expanding in the area of understanding and reducing health disparities.

Professionals in public health, like all other fields, must devote attention to the growth and development of the next generation of public health professionals. In that vein, we are charged with providing instruction and training to young professionals. This includes mentoring high school, undergraduate, and graduate students and getting them excited about careers in public health. Training new public health professionals also includes direct instruction via teaching coursework or providing opportunities for young professionals to have internships and practica on research and community projects. Other teaching and training are accomplished through guest lecturing, presentations at professional conferences, and publication of scholarly theoretical and empirical manuscripts.

Public health practice is yet another aspect that public health psychologists must negotiate. To maintain a working knowledge of population health issues, it is integral that some work be conducted "in the trenches." Public health professionals are challenged to take programs designed for research conditions (often time-limited, with incentives for participation) and see if they are efficacious (i.e., do what they are supposed to do under real-world conditions). It is this test that is often overlooked in behavioral research, but is paramount in public health work. Even the most effective intervention (i.e., one that demonstrates statistically significant behavioral change) can be essentially ineffective in the community. Public health professionals must always hold near to their hearts that the goal of public health is to improve the health and living environments of populations. In this effort, people must put into action what is articulated in the journals and textbooks.

Last, I believe that it is germane to the field of public health for psychologists to practice consultation. After all, one of the exciting aspects of this field is its interdisciplinary makeup. As such, psychologists are needed to interface with physicians, political and community leaders, public and private public health organizations, research foundations, scientists, and others to ensure that social behavior is not left out of the equation when designing and implementing public health interventions.

Typical Daily/Weekly Activities

If you choose a career in public health, your responsibilities and daily activities will vary with your employment setting, but all will include the professional responsibilities discussed previously, in varying combinations. For example, my work as Research Assistant Professor in the Department of Behavioral Sciences and Health Education of the Rollins School of Public Health at Emory University includes four main responsibilities: (1) research, (2) graduate-level teaching, (3) graduate student advisement and thesis chairing, and (4) consultation.

Research

One of the main responsibilities in my current position is providing leadership for the three federally funded projects described below.

Mental Health HIV Services Collaborative Program. In fiscal year 2001 the Substance Abuse and Mental Health Services Administration, through its Center for Mental Health Services, initiated a 5-year grant program designed to address the unmet mental health treatment needs of African Americans, Hispanic/Latino(a)s, and other communities of color living with HIV/AIDS. This initiative funded 21 community-based programs across the United States and charged them with the task of expanding their current service capacity to provide culturally competent and coordinated health, mental health, and other ancillary services to these populations. The Rollins School of Public Health of Emory University was awarded funds to serve as the coordinating center in this collaborative effort. Coordinating center staff and consultants provide technical assistance and training to sites on providing culturally competent mental health services to persons infected with HIV, as well as assist in the development and implementation of local and national program evaluation activities.

As principal investigator, I am responsible for overseeing the administration of the grant award (including personnel management and budget development/monitoring), providing clinical technical assistance, and developing a multisite evaluation design. Routine tasks associated with this role include hiring and supervising a team of more than 30 staff and consultants including psychologists, psychiatrists, public health administrators and providers, social workers, and data analyzers. To this end, I have enlisted a network of professionals with expertise in the content areas of the project (i.e., mental health, HIV, cultural competence) and make work assignments that most accurately match the staff's expertise with the needs of the site or funding agency. Additional administrative duties include maintaining and monitoring a detailed project schedule that outlines all the major tasks associated with the project, deadline dates, and responsible parties. Reports of project progress and expenditures are reviewed regularly and major changes are communicated to the funding agency on a weekly basis via conference call. More clinical responsibilities include collaboration with team members to identify training and technical assistance needs (e.g., ethical issues related to HIV mental health, Health Insurance Portability and Accountability Act [HIPAA], neuropsychiatry) and implementing interventions (e.g., workshops, meetings). I also participate in bi-annual site visits to the community-based organizations to observe services provided under this initiative and provide on-site technical assistance as needed. Finally, I participate in ongoing weekly (or more frequent) meetings with the evaluation section of the coordinating center to determine what variables are most relevant to evaluating the national initiative with respect to the program objectives (i.e., increased access to culturally competent HIV mental health care).

Prevention for HIV-Infected Persons Project. In 1999, the Centers for Disease Control and Prevention (CDC) funded this community demonstration project implemented by five health departments: the States of California, Maryland, and Wisconsin, Los Angeles County, and the city of San Francisco. In July 2000, the Health Resources and Services Administration and CDC contracted with the Rollins School of Public Health of Emory University to form the Evaluation and Program Support Center (EPSC). The EPSC is charged with designing and implementing a multisite coordinated evaluation of Prevention for HIV-Infected Persons Project (PHIPP) interventions and with providing ongoing technical assistance for grantees' quantitative and qualitative evaluation activities.

As co-principal investigator on this project, I work with the principal investigator to outline and monitor the major tasks associated with this project as described in the cooperative agreement. I provide assistance with budget development and determining which activities the EPSC will participate in for a given funding cycle. This planning effort includes communication with the funding agency and reconciling desired activities with available resources (staff and financial). In addition, I work with senior leadership in the EPSC and funding agency representatives to identify components of the multisite evaluation that would address each of the CDC program objectives for the

PHIPP initiative (including assisting in the statistical design and analysis of data). I also review requests for assistance with local evaluation design and implementation and make staff assignments that match staff expertise with the expressed needs of the site. Most often sites request assistance in capturing behavioral data overtime with targeted populations (e.g., minorities, substance users, individuals who are incarcerated). In addition, I often represent the EPSC in various regional, national, and international meetings and provide updates on the status of the national initiative based on evaluation data. Participation in the development of manuscripts for publication is also part of my routine work. Finally, I facilitate conferences and meetings involving the grantee sites and funding agency personnel on a regular basis and provide supervision to the day-to-day project manager for this project.

Go Girls! II. This research study is funded by the National Heart, Lung, and Blood Institute of the National Institutes of Health. Go Girls! II is a 5-year project designed to develop and test a culturally tailored curriculum-based intervention program for overweight 12- to 16-year-old African American adolescent girls and their parents. Go Girls! II is a multicomponent community-based intervention that is conducted in middle and upper socioeconomic African American churches in the metropolitan Atlanta area. This program is aimed at preventing obesity among teens at high risk due to their current weight. This population was selected in part because of the relatively high rates of obesity in middle- and upper-income African Americans relative to their white counterparts.

My position on this project is co-principal investigator and includes assisting with curriculum development, providing consultation on intervention design and implementation, conducting and monitoring components of the intervention, conducting focus groups, and administering assessment instruments. In addition, my duties involve writing manuscripts for publication and presentation at professional conferences and meetings.

Routine tasks include applying social cognitive theory and various behavior modification techniques to developing a written health promotion curriculum that brings about improvements in nutrition and physical activity among African-American adolescents and their families. As a behavioral scientist with expertise in multicultural counseling, I also provide guidance about what needs to be included in the intervention to best engage African-American families. I then review audio- and videotapes of intervention sessions to ensure treatment fidelity and identify potential areas of staff training. My participation in the program itself includes assisting with data collection (e.g., conducting formative focus group sessions, administering assessment instruments) and co-facilitating parent group sessions. Finally, I assist in writing manuscripts for publication and presentation at various local, national, and international venues.

My training as a psychologist has enabled me to make a significant contribution to each of the above projects. My graduate coursework in statistics and research methods (e.g., survey design), in addition to my dissertation research, prepared me to identify appropriate tools and methods to capture information on health behavior and evaluate intervention programs. For example, the two multisite evaluation projects (the Mental Health HIV Services Collaborative Program Coordinating Center and PHIPP) seek to evaluate service-delivery programs. The data collected are intended to better inform service providers of the things that the consumers most appreciate and contribute to "treatment success." A good portion of the evaluation is qualitative in nature and is very similar to the training you would receive in conducting an initial clinical interview. In addition, some of our evaluation involves the conduct of focus groups where my training as a group facilitator comes in handy. Similarly, in the Go Girls! II intervention project, the intervention is conducted in a group setting with adolescents. In addition to utilizing techniques of group therapy, my training in child psychology and multicultural counseling assists me in identifying psychosocial issues (e.g., self-esteem, self-efficacy, adjustment to puberty, racial identity) that may further exacerbate the challenges of being an overweight African-American teen. This training has also been helpful in designing a program that addresses the psychological as well as physical needs of these youth.

Teaching

In addition to research, I teach courses for our graduate-level Master of Public Health (MPH) students as part of my responsibility as a faculty member. One of the courses that I teach is one that I created soon after taking my position. I recognized that there were no courses in mental health offered within our school, and thus developed a seminar course. The "Seminar in Prevention in Mental Health" is designed to help students explore the public health impact of mental disorders and recognize effective models of prevention. Evidence is provided that underscores the importance of mental health endeavors in promoting public health. Students are provided with an overview of several mental health problems including depression, anxiety disorders, conduct disorders, learning disability, substance-related disorders, eating disorders, and psychotic disorders. Several models of prevention of mental health problems are explored, including primary, secondary, and tertiary efforts. Students also have an opportunity to critique prevention intervention research.

The second course that I teach is a core course in all schools of public health. "Social Behavior in Public Health" surveys psychological, sociological, epidemiological, and anthropological research on aspects of health and illness, particularly as it applies to public health. Using classic and contemporary references, this course explores the interaction among personality, gender, culture, race/ethnicity, spirituality, economics, and health. Students learn to analyze the relevant research articles critically.

Student Advisement and Mentoring

My academic duties further include the advisement and mentoring of graduate students. In this capacity, I have served on or chaired many master's thesis committees. Students often seek my assistance if they have interests in one of my many areas of study. I often get several requests from students who are interested in mental health as a thesis topic or would at least want to include psychosocial measures in their research design. On average, I have about three students each year that I advise or mentor. While professionally and personally rewarding, student advisement and mentoring is time-consuming and represents a major commitment by the advisor/mentor to the successful matriculation of the student.

Mentoring involves a number of activities including guidance, advising, coaching, motivating, facilitating, and role modeling. In addition, mentoring is by design relationship driven, with success, in large part, a function of whether there is a personality match between the mentor and the mentee. Some core characteristics of successful mentoring relationships include mentor expertise, a mentor who has a positive view of his or her work, positive attitude of mentee, and mutual respect between mentor and mentee. The last is critical in that both the mentor and mentee will learn from the experience.

In my role as faculty advisor/mentor I typically spend 2 hours or more each week communicating with student advisees/mentees. These communications can range from brief e-mail exchanges to more in-depth face-to-face meetings and can vary regarding frequency. In my experience, topics of discussion have included providing assistance with research activities (e.g., selection of appropriate instruments, review of data analyses), traditional academic advisement (e.g., selecting appropriate coursework, assistance with job search), mediating problems with other faculty, review of thesis proposals and drafts, and personal issues. While my involvement in multiple projects and other faculty activities severely limits my available time for students, I believe that the experience is worthwhile. To address some of the pitfalls, I have elected to limit the number of students that I advise/mentor each academic year. This ensures that I protect the time that I need to advance my career as well as allot adequate time to guiding, coaching, and motivating students. In addition, I try to ensure that the students that I work with are at different stages of their training such that I do not have all three students completing their thesis at the same time. This addresses the differential needs of students depending on where they are in their graduate training. Finally, I take significant time in the beginning of the relationship to explain my mentoring philosophy, availability, and areas of expertise to facilitate realistic expectations by the student, which may increase the likelihood of a good match.

Consultation

I participate regularly in consultation with a number of community-based organizations, nonprofit public health agencies, and private research consulting companies. In these roles I am often contracted to assist in grant writing, designing and implementing program evaluations, conducting focus groups, and conducting presentations on my areas of interest/expertise.

Psychologists in public health consult in a number of ways. The consulting services that I have provided range from providing advice or guidance on program development and implementation to writing grant applications. Often, I am enlisted to provide consultation on how to recruit and retain minorities in health education and promotion programs and how to develop culturally tailored interventions. Again, my training in multicultural counseling assists in identifying strategies for recruitment and retention as well as key elements to service delivery for racial/ethnic minorities. In addition, I have assisted programs in creating behavior modification programs for a variety of health issues. Often, community-based organizations do not have full-time staff with expertise in this area and will pay consultants to review intervention material and provide guidance on how to infuse psychological and public health theory into their programs. I have also served as a focus group facilitator for organizations that are conducting formative research prior to developing new programs. They seek to find persons with group facilitation and qualitative methods backgrounds. Finally, I have been involved with organizations that hired me to write grant applications related to health promotion programs. As a faculty member, I have experience in writing successful

Table 18.2 Common Job Responsibilities of Psychologists Working in Public Health Academic Departments

Research

Developing new research ideas (review requests for proposals, identify gaps in the literature)
Writing grant proposals
Overseeing research projects:
    Managing personnel
    Developing/monitoring budgets
    Training staff
    Monitoring project schedule
    Developing progress reports and other project documents
    Communicating with funding agency project officers and other officials
Participating in intervention research:
    Assisting in the design and implementation of the intervention
    Assisting in the recruitment and retention of participants
    Analyzing and interpreting data
Preparing manuscripts for publication
Presenting research findings at conferences and scientific meetings

Teaching and Service

Developing new courses addressing current health topics
Developing class lectures
Teaching one to two graduate courses per year
Evaluating student progress in courses taught
Advising/mentoring three to four graduate students
Attending student committee meetings (thesis, dissertation, comprehensive exam)
Attending department/college/university committee/work group meetings
Reviewing manuscripts for professional journals

Consultation

Assisting community-based organizations, local health departments/agencies, private research companies to develop health promotion programs
Assisting community-based organizations, local health departments/agencies, private research companies to write grant proposals
Evaluating health education and promotion programs
Providing staff training
Preparing presentations for community-based talks and workshops

grant applications and have access to public health resources that may assist smaller organizations (particularly community-based and non-profit groups) that seek external funding. Table 18.2 presents common job responsibilities of psychologists working the public health academic departments.

Advantages and Disadvantages of a Public Health Career

There are a number of advantages to a career in public health. Public health is a growing field with most experts agreeing that major advances in population health in the next several decades will result from the development and application of population-based prevention programs rather than advances in medical technology (Associations of Schools of Public Health, n.d.). Specifically, health services delivery systems are changing rapidly with an increased focus on health promotion and disease prevention. These strategies are believed to result in cost-effective care for our populations. As such, public health has created a broad array of new opportunities for persons with degrees in behavioral and social sciences (Associations of Schools of Public Health, n.d.). Psychologists are specifically needed in the field given that mental health is a public health problem and psychological issues are associated with all physical health conditions (e.g., efficacy, esteem, cognitive functioning, etc.). Epidemics of obesity (and related issues of body image, esteem, and eating disorders), cancer, HIV/AIDS, bioterrorism, etc. suggest the need for more behavioral researchers and practitioners.

While the prospect for psychologists in public health is quite favorable, there are some disadvantages to choosing a career in this field. Although psychology is among the disciplines considered to be part of the interdisciplinary field of public health, some seem to prefer a graduate degree in public health rather than psychology. In addition, the idea of mental health as a public health issue has been slow to reach the same appreciation as other physical conditions (e.g., HIV/AIDS, cancer), such that our natural interest in advancing the psychological health of populations may be overshadowed by these other health issues. In fact, psychologists in public health may find themselves working in areas where they find little or no connection to sustain employment in the field. Finally, psychologists who work in public health, particularly those with clinical and counseling backgrounds, must undergo a paradigm shift from individual-focused treatment interventions to population-focused preventive interventions. As such, our years of training as clinicians must be modified significantly to focus on the good of the masses rather than on an individual patient or client. Related to this issue is that many of my psychologist colleagues in public health observe that to some degree work in this field often means losing some of the professional identity of a psychologist.

Training Suggestions and Recommendations

There is not one "right" path to a career in public health. My own road to this field was quite accidental, but has been a rewarding experience. The first step is to learn more about the field and opportunities available for psychologists in your area. A number of references are available to learn more about public health and career opportunities in the field. Interested persons should review the brochures available through the Association for Schools of Public Health. (http://www.asph.org). Other resources for learning more about the field and being more marketable will come from meeting other people in the field. One of the fastest ways to accomplish this is by getting involved with local and national public health organizations such as the American Public Health Association (http://www.apha.org), the Society of Behavioral Medicine (http://www.sbm.org), and Division 38 (Health Psychology) of the American Psychological Association (http://www.apa.org/about/division/div38.html).

Becoming active (e.g., attending meetings and conferences, committee membership) in these types of organizations will allow for networking and mentoring. While some of these organizations are quite large, it is to your advantage to become involved in local chapters or choose smaller outlets (e.g., participate in a working group for one of the committees), which may be more intimate and allow you to become acquainted with the "big names" in the field. In addition, would-be psychologists in public health should search college and university Web sites and public health-related organizations in which you are interested and see what people are doing. Do not be afraid to e-mail them or call them to "pick their brains" about what it is like to work in their field and solicit advice for your own entry into the world of public health.

References

Association of Schools of Public Health. (n.d.). *What is public health?* Retrieved April 6, 2004 from http://www.asph.org/document.cfm?page=300.

Hanlon, G., & Pickett, J. (1984). *Public health administration and practice.* St. Louis, MO: Times Mirror/Mosby.

Institute of Medicine, Committee for the Study of the Future of Public Health, Division of Health Care Services. (1988). The future of public health. Washington, D.C.: National Academy Press.

Ohio State University School of Public Health (2002). *Advancing knowledge. Improving life.* ™ Columbus: Ohio State University College of Medicine and Public Health.

Schneiderman, N., & Speers, M. A. (2001). Behavioral science, social science, and public health in the 21st century. In N. Schneiderman, M. A. Speers, J. M. Silva, H. Tomes, & J. H. Gentry (Eds.), *Integrating behavioral and social science with public health* (pp. 3–28). Washington, D.C.: American Psychological Association.

Tomes, H., & Gentry, J. H. (2001). Preface: Integrating behavioral and social science with public health. In N. Schneiderman, M. A. Speers, J. M. Silva, H. Tomes, & J. H. Gentry (Eds.), *Integrating behavioral and social science with public health* (pp. xi–xiii). Washington, D.C.: American Psychological Association.

Turnock, B. J. (1997). *Public health: What it is and how it works?* Gaithersburg, MD: Aspen.

19

Trial Consulting: Moving Psychology into the Courtroom

CINDY KLUDT ANDREWS

Overview of the Trial Consulting Field

Trial consulting consists of empirical research and consulting services designed to evaluate how a judge or jury will perceive and react to case theories, themes, issues, arguments, witnesses, evidence, and exhibits. Trial consultants employ general research methodologies to design and implement jury research and rely on standard statistical methods to analyze and report data. Trial consulting services are carried out with the objectives of enhancing case effectiveness and improving attorneys' persuasive impact. The terms "trial consulting," "jury consulting," and "litigation consulting" are used interchangeably in the industry.

As the job title implies, the majority of consulting work is geared toward trial; however, trial consultants also assist attorneys in preparing for alternative dispute resolution (ADR), a form of conflict resolution that is intended to circumvent litigation and resolve conflict.

Legally binding forms of ADR include mediation, settlement conferences, advisory hearings, mini-trials, and summary jury trials. In preparation for ADR, trial consultants may conduct nonjury research such as mock arbitrations or mock bench trials, assist with witnesses, and help the attorneys develop their presentation.

Types of Cases

Trial consultants work on cases in every area of litigation; however, they may have a preference for or focus on one particular type of case (i.e., civil or criminal), area of litigation (e.g., commercial, personal injury), or side (i.e., plaintiff, prosecution, or defense). Common areas of civil litigation in which trial consultants work include antitrust, defamation, intellectual property, malpractice, fraud, premises liability, product liability, personal injury, environmental, construction, insurance coverage, commercial, contract, labor and employment, securities, toxic tort, and family.

Although trial consultants are often employed for high-profile (e.g., O.J. Simpson case) or legally significant criminal matters, they work on all types and sizes of cases. My personal experience (and our firm's focus) has primarily been in civil litigation with a handful of white-collar criminal and death penalty defense cases.

Legal and Ethical Considerations

Many trial consultants are members of the American Society of Trial Consultants (ASTC) and, thus, subscribe to and operate under a professional code of conduct. In keeping with professional standards, trial consultants work only for one side of a case; adhere to current research practices, methodologies, and statistical methods; and endeavor to provide pro bono services. Consultants work under the direction and supervision of the client who may be the attorney, the litigant, or the insurer.

Consultants work directly with the attorney to assure that all consultant–client communication is protected by attorney privileges. Although it is not impossible to gain access to certain information (e.g., consultation with an expert witness), information obtained through jury research, discussed during consulting, or provided as work product, is typically not discoverable by opposing counsel (i.e., subject to subpoena). This work is said to contain the mental impressions and trial strategy of counsel and, as such, is routinely considered privileged and confidential "attorney work product."

Reasons Attorneys Hire a Trial Consultant

Attorneys hire trial consultants for their unique expertise in jury behavior, persuasion, and decision making. Attorneys want to better understand how the trier-of-fact (judge or juror) processes and comprehends complex information and may be persuaded to render a specific verdict. Utilizing a consultant's services may maximize the likelihood that the trier-of-fact will be receptive to the attorney's arguments. As such, psychologists are considered a good professional match for trial consultation because of their training in the behavioral and social sciences.

Trial consultants are hired to educate trial counsel about how jurors' preconceptions and expectations shape their perceptions of how the world works, how social interactions operate, and how the justice system functions. Preconceptions influence jurors' information processing in several ways. For example, information consistent with one's beliefs (theory-consistent) is processed quickly and easily, and is better remembered. On the other hand, ambiguous information is filtered and interpreted as theory consistent, and information inconsistent with one's beliefs tends to be scrutinized and rejected (see, e.g., Fiske & Taylor, 1991). Regardless of their accuracy, preconceptions can affect jurors' reactions and decisions at all stages of a trial. Therefore, careful attention to jurors' beliefs and expectations can help shape effective communication strategies for the trial team. As such, trial consultants strive to improve the quality of the attorney's presentation style and persuasive impact.

Trial consultants work with counsel to determine what knowledge, biases, preconceptions, and experiences the average juror has about the subjects, issues, and parties in the case. Based on jury research findings, theory, and professional experience, consultants provide insight into how jurors are likely to have varying perceptions of the facts, which peripheral factors will influence jurors, which points would be better seen than heard, and how the attorney can emphasize certain facts and not others. Through jury research, consultants can also provide insights into case strengths and weaknesses as well as likely verdict and case value.

Trial consultants are also hired for their extensive case experience. Because some attorneys infrequently go to trial, trial consultants may actually have more trial experience or experience with jurors in a particular venue. Trial consultants approach each case with a fresh set of eyes to identify potential weaknesses from a jurors' perspective. Furthermore, they may help counsel more accurately assess the value of the case via empirical data and professional experience.

Trial consultants are also hired because some attorneys lack the experience, skill, or confidence specifically in conducting oral *voir dire* (literally, "to see–to speak," the process of questioning prospective jurors about their ability to serve) and selecting a jury. Attorneys want to maximize their ability to use jurors' preexisting attitudes to predict verdict behavior. However, because correspondence between juror attitudes and behavior is low, particularly when situational pressures (such as group deliberations) are present (see, e.g., Wicker, 1969; Davidson & Jaccard, 1979), trial consultants are relied on to improve attorneys' *voir dire* and jury selection skills. For example, the consultant educates the attorneys in the skills necessary for effective, valuable, and persuasive *voir dire* questioning. During the *voir dire* process, consultants assist in court with follow-up questions and strike strategy. They are also relied on to "profile" jurors, assess nonverbal behavior, and make judgments about jurors' motives, hidden agendas, and honesty during the *voir dire* and jury selection processes.

Trial Consulting Objectives

The trial consultant's primary goal is to help the client present the strongest case. More specifically, the overarching objectives include educating attorneys in the psychology of communication and persuasion, increasing their understanding of basic juror psychology and decision-making processes, bringing a unique and value-added perspective to case strategy, designing a research study that will address counsel's key concerns and questions, informing counsel of potential case weaknesses from a juror's point of view, providing an objective or empirical risk analysis, and enhancing the attorneys' ability to persuade and motivate the judge or jury.

Consultants strive to educate and increase attorneys' understanding of how factors such as basic psychology (e.g., defense mechanisms, locus of control), emotion (e.g., depression, anxiety), social behavior (e.g., conscientiousness), personality (e.g., neuroticism, leadership, authoritarianism), cognition (e.g., memory, attention span, cognitive dissonance), and group dynamics (e.g., attribution, majority effect) affect juror decision making. Additionally, a consultant's strategic advice takes into account jurors' life experiences and preconceptions, and applies principles of comprehension, communication, and persuasion.

These objectives are achieved by relying on both scientific methods and professional experience. For example, empirical data from community attitude and jury research studies are combined with the consultant's professional experience with juries, judges, venues, case themes, and similar case fact patterns to identify case weaknesses, conduct risk analyses, develop juror profiles, and recommend trial or settlement strategy. The science behind jury research can be based on a variety of models (e.g., social, cognitive, behavioral, communications); however, most consultants strive to evaluate jurors' cognitive processes during the presentation of arguments and evidence and, thereby, potentially identify the keys to persuasion and ultimately effect jurors' decisions.

Types of Services Provided by Trial Consultants

Trial consulting consists of empirical research and consulting services designed to evaluate how a judge or jury will perceive and react to case theories, themes, issues, arguments, witnesses, evidence, and exhibits. A number of general research methodologies are summarized below. Please note that the most common nomenclature for these services has been used; however, different firms or individual consultants may use alternative terms (e.g., label a focus group a mock trial).

Focus Group Research

In the general sense, focus group research is research that brings groups of people together to present information and assess their reaction to the information. Trial consultants design focus groups as a form of pretrial jury research. As such, these studies provide attorneys with the opportunity to test case issues, assess existing themes, discover new themes, identify case strengths and weaknesses, test exhibits, evaluate witness effectiveness, and refine case strategies.

In the prefiling stage (before the legal complaint is filed/served), focus groups are used to evaluate various claims to determine which are most likely to be effective. During the discovery phase of litigation, information from focus group research can be used to refine discovery strategy and decide what types of expert witnesses will be needed and what type of questions they should be asked during their deposition. Once discovery has been completed, focus groups are used to develop strategic themes for presentation in settlement negotiations, contested hearings, or trial (Goldberg, Goldstein, Handler, & Wentzel, 2000).

Briefly, in terms of the focus group process, trial consultants recruit demographically matched, jury-eligible surrogate jurors from the venue. Before hearing any evidence, jurors must meet strict screening criteria and complete a written questionnaire evaluating case-relevant knowledge, attitudes, and experiences. Following attorney presentations, jurors complete additional attitudinal measures to inform counsel of reactions at each phase of trial as well as the shifts or stability of those reactions or attitudes as the research exercise proceeds.

After all of the presentations have been heard, jurors are broken into smaller jury groups (balanced for demographics and verdict), are provided jury instructions, and are asked to deliberate to a unanimous decision. Attorneys watch the deliberations live from behind a one-way mirror or on a closed circuit television while trial consultants evaluate both individual and group decision-making processes.

Finally, trial consultants meet with the jury groups in a structured focusing session to gather additional information on the underlying and guiding processes in their decisions. The juries are asked questions regarding strength of arguments and themes, inconsistencies in story, rationale for verdict and damage awards, and attorney effectiveness. Additionally, new information such as a pending motion *in limine* (a pretrial request that certain inadmissible evidence not be referred to or offered before the jury) may be presented to determine its potential impact on jurors' decisions.

Data from the entire focus group exercise are analyzed and presented in a bound report. Qualitative data are analyzed for patterns and themes while quantitative analyses are used to determine the extent to which verdict and damage awards may be a function of the strength of juror opinions on particular issues and, with adequate sample size, to derive empirically based juror profiles. Additionally, a frequency distribution of likely award amounts may be calculated to estimate the probability that a damage award made by a similar jury will fall within a specified range.

Focus group research is tailored to address the clients' major concerns and objectives. For example, a study may be designed to primarily assess damages (e.g., a damage evaluation study), which is typically the case when liability has been or may be admitted. Research may also be formatted to primarily permit jurors to evaluate key fact or expert witnesses (e.g., a witness evaluation focus group). In this format, simulated direct examination and cross-examination of the witnesses is presented and jurors complete written evaluations regarding witness effectiveness and credibility and then participate in a focus session to discuss their reactions.

Most focus groups have an inherent adversarial format; however, consultants may recommend a neutral presentation format, which affords counsel interactive question and answer sessions with the jurors. Case issues are presented in a more focused seriatim fashion, which allows for a more in-depth evaluation of key case issues that could be refined and tested in a second phase of research. Additionally, this format allows consultants to test jurors' comprehension of complex scientific, technological, or patent information in greater detail than with a traditional (adversarial) focus group format.

Exploratory Focus Group

Exploratory focus groups are meant to obtain only a very general type of feedback. The format is often more informal, deliberations are optional, analyses are minimal, and the report is more akin to an executive summary. Exploratory exercises are not used for predicting verdict or damages; rather, they are useful for finding pronounced case weaknesses and for practicing opening statements. For example, short, issue-specific focus groups (i.e., case issue studies) are conducted when observing a jury's interaction on a specific issue is necessary to formulate case themes and theory. Case issue studies are often employed to generate additional research questions for subsequent or more comprehensive phases of jury research.

Experimental, Quasi-Experimental, and Comparative Studies

Experimental, quasi-experimental, and comparative studies allow counsel to assess the impact of trial strategy or type of evidence under controlled conditions using a comparative design. Experimental and control groups can be employed to compare differences between groups on certain outcome variables, for example, counsel may want to know what effect conceding liability has on jurors' damage awards.

Mock Trial

Perhaps the best-known form of jury research is the mock trial (i.e., trial simulation). A mock trial exercise is typically performed after most or all discovery has been completed and the major issues and themes of the case have been defined. The exercise involves a more comprehensive format, thereby allowing attorneys to test every step of the trial process, from opening statements to closing arguments. Live or videotaped witnesses are presented and the plaintiff is afforded a rebuttal. Akin to focus group research, surrogate jurors first complete attitudinal questionnaires, listen to plaintiff and defense case presentations, and then answer issue-specific questions. Each jury panel deliberates to a verdict and participates in a consultant-moderated focus session to further explore their thought processes, opinions, and reactions to the case.

Studies for Nonjury Settings

Trial consultants also design mock bench trials, hearings, and arbitrations, which provide counsel the opportunity to rehearse in front of surrogate judges, arbitrators, or special masters. Attorneys obtain feedback on the case's legal and factual strengths and weaknesses, and they get a description of the case from the judges' perspective and insight into their decision-making process. Consultants design and implement this type of study much like the aforementioned jury research with the exception that judges typically render a case analysis and participate in an interview rather than deliberate.

Pretrial Case Analysis

The purpose of case assessment consultation is to assist with the development of trial strategy during the early stage of a case (i.e., during the discovery period when facts and documents are disclosed and evidence is gathered). A case assessment evaluates the trial preparation requirements from communications and strategic perspectives.

Information obtained by the case assessment can include juror perceptions of the litigants, anticipated comprehension of important concepts and terms, potential heuristics, identification of evidence needed to make jurors' decisions easier, risk assessment (verdict and damages), preliminary assessment of alternative case strategies, evaluation of the venue alternatives, assessment of critical issues from visual strategy and communications perspectives, and evaluation of prospective and actual witnesses. Often, the case assessment leads to additional consulting such as opening statement analysis, or to jury research such as focus groups.

Pretrial Survey Analysis

Community attitude surveys are conducted when data from a larger sample are needed for understanding the prevailing opinions in the venue (i.e., community in which the trial is being held), or for juror-profiling purposes. Because of their large sample size, surveys provide greater statistical reliability regarding how various groups of jurors are likely to react to the litigants, key evidence, and arguments in a case. Trial consultants rely on census statistics, experience with mock trials and juries, impressions of local counsel, and unique trial factors (e.g., trial length) to develop demographic "quotas" for the surveyors as well as qualifying questions for survey participants. The result is a randomly selected, stratified sample of survey participants matching the demographic makeup of the trial venue and, more precisely, the venire (i.e., the panel of persons from which jurors are to be selected).

The most common types of community attitude surveys include venue profile surveys, juror profile surveys, and change of venue surveys. The primary purposes of a venue profile survey are to provide a demographic profile of the venue, information on jurors' case-related experiences, attitudes, and opinions, perceptions of the litigants, and, if relevant, the impact of any pretrial publicity.

A juror profile survey provides counsel with the same information as a venue profile survey but also examines respondents' reactions to specific case themes and issues, and assesses potential verdicts and damages. This survey ultimately prepares counsel for *voir dire* and jury selection by providing empirically based profiles of pro-plaintiff and pro-defense jurors or high- versus low-damage-awarding jurors.

A change of venue survey is conducted to determine if data exist to justify to the court that the level of bias/prejudice among eligible jurors would support a change of venue. The change of venue survey specifically focuses on awareness of the case, sources of the awareness, opinions about the matter, and the intensity with which opinions are held. The analysis focuses on whether a significant number of jury-eligible adults are sufficiently prejudiced or biased to prevent the defendant from receiving a fair trial. Assuming such data exist, it is used in the preparation of an affidavit in support of a motion to change the venue.

Pretrial Consulting Services

Trial consultants also provide a number of consulting services on an hourly-fee basis. These services typically serve to develop case themes and enhance witness and attorney communication skills. For example, in preparation for giving a deposition or testifying at trial, consultants evaluate witnesses and provide suggestions for enhancing credibility and improving communication style. Witnesses are assessed via mock direct and cross-examination to identify strengths and opportunities for improvement. Various exercises such as behavioral rehearsal, role play, cognitive restructuring, and anxiety management are then employed to address verbal and nonverbal communication issues.

Trial consultants are commonly relied on for theme and storyline development and to refine opening statements and closing arguments. For example, alternative versions of the opening statement may be presented to focus groups in which the consultant acts as a moderator to lead a group discussion following the presentation. Alternatively, different versions of the statement may be presented to the same focus group(s) to compare and contrast, or the trial consultant may serve as the sounding board for the statement and provide suggestions for improvement. The consultant may educate and advise the attorney on how to manage issues such as jurors' perception, information processing, psychological anchors (i.e., issues salient to jurors in deciding a case), learning and decision-making processes, comprehension and memory, cognitive dissonance, and defense mechanisms. A trial consultant guides the attorney to establish a relationship with the jury, use appropriate verbal and nonverbal language, educate jurors, develop clear and compelling story and themes, effectively use exhibits, manage witness testimony, and inoculate against damaging case facts.

Trial consultants also design supplemental juror questionnaires, which are completed by prospective jurors prior to *voir dire* and jury selection. Questionnaires can vary in length from just a few pages to the 75-page, 300-question questionnaire used in the O.J. Simpson case. Juror questionnaires are an expeditious way to collect basic information about jurors, address litigants' rights to remove biased jurors, and provide certain safeguards for jurors' rights to privacy thereby encouraging honesty (Swain & Wolfe, 1993). Trial consultants evaluate jurors' questionnaires and make recommendations for *voir dire* strategy and jury selection (see descriptions of *voir dire* and jury selection consulting services below).

In-Trial Consulting Services

There are a number of ways trial consultants can be a resource once a trial has begun. For example, during the oral *voir dire* and jury selection processes, prospective jurors are asked questions to determine their qualifications for jury service, knowledge of the parties and case, and attitudes regarding the issues and litigants in the case. During jury selection (more aptly termed jury "deselection"), the judge may disqualify a juror based on bias or prejudice (*causal challenge*) and the attorneys are given a predetermined number of *peremptory challenges*, which they may exercise without reason to dismiss a potential juror (Hans & Vidmar, 1986).

Using existing databases, case experience, theory, and, if available, the supplemental juror questionnaire or empirical data from pretrial jury research, trial consultants provide in-court assistance with the *voir dire* and jury selection processes. Research has shown that demographic variables, particularly jurors' age, race, and gender are ineffective, or only negligibly correlated in predicting how jurors would decide cases (e.g., Hepburn, 1980). Research has shown that preexisting attitudes and beliefs reliably correlate with verdict orientation (e.g., Field, 1978); therefore, trial consultants generate *voir dire* questions germane to the case and focus counsel on assessing jurors' attitudes toward the case issues.

Another form of in-trial research is the shadow jury exercise, which is akin to meeting with the actual jury each day to hear their reactions to the proceedings. A small surrogate jury matched to the demographics of the actual panel attends trial and is interviewed each day to gather feedback. The information is summarized and disseminated to counsel daily so they may track the strengths and weaknesses of the arguments and witnesses and gauge the actual jurors' reactions. Often, the shadow jury is instructed to deliberate to a verdict and participate in a focus session just prior to the actual jury retiring to deliberate. Alternatively, the trial consultant may be hired to monitor the trial and the jury and provide strategic recommendations to the team.

Posttrial Consulting Services

Posttrial interviews are conducted to ascertain each juror's reactions to case issues, witnesses, and presentation style as well as to determine how the jury arrived at its verdict and damage award. Interviewing jurors postverdict may also uncover grounds for appeal (e.g., juror misconduct). Counsel is provided with a report detailing jurors' impressions and recollections. Additionally, the consultant may conduct a postmortem trial assessment in which trial transcripts are reviewed for potential appeal.

How Trial Consultants Spend Their Time

The following description is based upon my experience working full-time in a large litigation consulting firm; thus, part-time consultants and those who are employed in-house at law firms or in academic settings may have a different experience.

Trial consultants carry out their work in a variety of settings including spending time in their office; conducting research in-house or on site at moot courtrooms, market research facilities, hotels or conference centers; preparing witnesses or attending meetings at law firms; and assisting in the courtroom during trial. In a given month, the consultant will typically design and conduct two to six focus group or mock trial exercises as well as conduct a survey, shadow jury, or post-trial interviews. Trial consultants simultaneously participate in the aforementioned hourly consulting services such as witness evaluation, theme development, opening statement consultation, or *voir dire* assistance. Consultants can also expect to travel frequently with the amount of travel dependent on the size of the firm, the type and scope of research/consulting projects, and the number of projects occurring at any given time.

A typical day might require the consultant to review case documents, focus group presentation scripts, or deliberation and focus session videotapes; prepare written proposals; organize research including developing screening questionnaires, surveys, and research questionnaires; analyze data; act as a liaison between the research staff and attorneys regarding research planning and methodology; attend case discussion meetings with the attorney; and conduct shadow jury or post trial juror interviews. Additionally, the aforementioned hourly consulting services typically comprise a portion of the consultant's time.

Depending on the size of the firm, consultants may also organize logistics of research such as selecting recruiters, researching facilities, and planning travel. In full-service litigation consulting firms (i.e., firms with graphics, technology, and trial consulting), consultants may help account managers market to attorneys to generate new business and maintain client relations. Additionally, senior-level consultants are sought after to speak within law firms and at continuing legal education (CLE) forums such as state bar associations; therefore, they may spend time preparing those presentations. Finally, many trial consultants conduct ongoing research, collect data, and write chapters, books, and articles for scientific and legal journals (see Table 19.1).

Most consultants work 40 to 50 hours a week not including travel time. The amount of travel varies from two to five times per month with most trips generally requiring one overnight stay. Consultants routinely work in a fast-paced environment juggling several projects at once, most with demanding deadlines and impending trial dates. At times, it is necessary to work at home or on the airplane, typically to review case documents, generate work products, or conduct post-trial interviews. A consultant's schedule can change on a daily and, at times, hourly basis with new projects arising and existing projects changing or abruptly ending (e.g., due to the case settling or postponing).

Typical Employment Settings for Trial Consultants

Trial consultants may work in one of several settings. I work in a large, full-service firm and such firms are typically housed in corporate office buildings in larger cities. In these firms, consultants often

Table 19.1 Common Work Duties for Trial Consultants

Research Duties

Reviewing case documents and videotapes

Developing research design and methodology (e.g., surveys, focus groups, mock trials, etc.)

Organizing research logistics (e.g., recruit, facility, travel, etc.)

Generating research protocol (e.g., screeners, surveys, interviews, questionnaires, etc.)

Monitoring and adjusting recruitment of surrogate jurors

Assisting attorneys with writing presentation scripts

Moderating jury research exercises (e.g., conducting orientation and focus session, etc.)

Conducting research debriefing with attorneys

Analyzing data

Writing research reports

Consulting Duties

Pretrial consulting (e.g., case analysis, juror profiles, *voir dire* questions, supplemental juror questionnaires, etc.)

Performing witness or attorney communications skills training

Developing case themes and storyline

In-trial consulting (e.g., assisting with jury selection, trial monitoring, interviewing shadow jurors, summarizing and presenting shadow jury feedback to trial team, etc.)

Posttrial consulting (conducting posttrial interviews, postmortem trial assessment)

Providing strategic recommendations for ADR or trial

Marketing Duties

Attending attorney marketing meetings with account managers (or making sales calls)

Attending new case discussion meetings to generate consulting recommendations

Generating written proposals

Making phone calls for client relations and proposal follow-up

Miscellaneous Duties

Collaborating/coordinating with research support staff and vendors (e.g., research facility)

Collaborating with graphics and technology consultants

Reading legal and juror psychology books and articles

Preparing presentations/articles

Presenting at law firms, seminars, and conferences

Responding to e-mail, voicemail, and phone calls

Traveling

---

collaborate with graphics and technology consultants, research support staff, account managers, and marketing and public relations personnel. A limited service trial consulting firm may focus solely on trial consulting. Solo practitioners act as independent consultants and tend to provide more limited range of services (e.g., theme development, jury selection, small-format focus groups, etc.). Some consultants are employed in academic settings where they teach, conduct research, perhaps have a clinical practice, and work as part-time, independent consultants. Finally, a few consultants are on the staff at law firms. Job availability and personal preference often dictate the setting where you will be employed.

From a personal perspective, a few advantages of working in a larger consulting firm include the opportunity to interact with other consultants and benefit from their expertise, the availability of support staff and resources, an integrated approach or interface with graphics and technology, and the ability to offer the full range of trial consulting and jury research services including very large-scale research projects.

Preparation for a Career as a Trial Consultant

Credentials/Affiliations

Currently, there is only one combined academic and certification program to be specifically trained as a litigation consultant (Towson University, Towson, Maryland). Trial consultants characteristically receive training from advanced academic programs, on-the-job training, and experience. Credentialing is currently an ongoing topic of discussion within the ASTC.

The ASTC was established in 1982 and serves to provide opportunities for networking and dialogue, encourage and assist in the professional growth and training of members, provide a forum for the exchange of ideas and experiences, encourage the development and refinement of research techniques, promote the effective and ethical use of trial consulting techniques by clients, and encourage awareness of and provide accurate information about the field. The ASTC maintains Membership, Nominating, Research, Professional Standards, Professional Visibility, and Pro Bono Committees (Gulans, 2001). Standards are being implemented yearly to define and govern the trial consulting profession. To date, the only way to assure that you are part of the trial consulting profession and governed by the current professional standards and ethics is to become a member of the ASTC (Sheldon, 2001).

Graduate Training

Because of the current lack of credentialing, anyone can call himself or herself a trial consultant. However, larger consulting firms require that trial consultants hold a doctorate degree in social or behavioral sciences or communications, and that research associates have a master's degree. Depending on the person's experience, smaller firms are more inclined to employ a professional with master's degree as a trial consultant. Some employers prefer graduates from clinical or counseling psychology programs approved by the American Psychological Association (APA) because the APA training model equips the psychologist/consultant with strong research, statistics, writing, and clinical skills.

As of this writing, there are more than 10 joint training programs that award combined law degrees and doctorates in psychology, or a Ph.D. with an emphasis in law and psychology. Students are enrolled simultaneously in an accredited J.D. program and a psychology doctoral (Ph.D. or Psy.D.) program, which contain integrative law and psychology curriculum in addition to the standard requirements toward both degrees. Research the programs well as they vary in the kinds of lawyer-psychologists they produce. For example, programs may prepare students to become litigation consultants, psychology researchers, psychologists for health and mental health policy positions, clinical psychology practitioners, or a combination thereof (Bersoff, Goodman-Delahunty, Grisso, Hans, Poythress, & Roesch, 1997). For further information about training in law and psychology, please refer to the "Suggested Readings and Web Pages" section at the end of this chapter.

Academic Courses and Experience

Students need the core knowledge of basic areas of psychology (e.g., behavioral, developmental, cognitive, abnormal, social, cultural, ethical, and professional), research design (e.g., experimental and quasi-experimental methods, survey research, case studies, program evaluation), and statistics (e.g., univariate, multivariate, and meta-analysis, parametric, and nonparametric techniques). Additionally, students should participate in developing, conducting, presenting, and publishing original research, which preferably culminates in a doctoral dissertation that is relevant to law and psychology (Bersoff et al., 1997). Trial consultants also need strong interpersonal, communication, writing, and public speaking skills.

Individuals interested in obtaining legal knowledge after establishing themselves in another profession can take interdisciplinary, law-related graduate courses or consider a yearlong Master of Legal Studies program, which teaches the basic tools of law, sources of law, and the core substance of law itself (Grisso, Sales, & Bayless, 1982).

Securing and Developing a Career in Trial Consultation

To pursue a position in the field, consider becoming actively involved in the ASTC, even as a student member or on one of its boards. Attend the ASTC conference and annual job fair and network with others in the field. Research consulting and law firms online and submit your resume as appropriate. Network through contact sources that point you in the direction of a colleague looking to hire. Additionally, find research that you consider interesting, contact the researchers, investigate the program, and apply to those that appear as though they will provide solid psychology foundation as well as more applied psychology and law opportunities.

Opportunities within the field are varied and the types of consulting and research services are broad; therefore, those interested should research these options well to determine where they may have the best "fit." For example, different backgrounds and areas of expertise may be best suited for a particular area of consulting, such as a drama background for theme and storyline development, or a strict research background for empirical jury research.

Is Trial Consulting for You?

The advantages of the trial consulting field include the ability to utilize years of scientist-practitioner training and research skills, apply cognitive, behavioral, learning, social, communications, and persuasion theories, and consult with and educate clients who are usually eager to learn. Consultants enjoy the challenge of juggling several projects simultaneously and traveling nationwide. We receive a broad experience base and engage in a variety of intellectually stimulating and challenging activities, which allows us to learn and grow professionally and personally and appeals to people who prefer variety and cognitive challenge.

Research projects are completed in a timely fashion (often within a month), which gives the consultant a great sense of accomplishment. Additionally, attorneys value our feedback and suggestions, which engenders a feeling of appreciation. Trial consulting requires the person to be self-motivated and able to attend to both the big picture and the critical details. Trial consultants do not contend with managed care, and there is no need for licensure, yet they receive all the benefits of being an active member of ASTC (as well as other professional, psychological organizations, if desired). Finally, regardless of the type of salary structure or incentive program, a trial consultant's income is almost always considered an advantage.

Some of the disadvantages to being a trial consultant include a dearth of uniform training or education and a current lack of licensure. If trained as a clinical psychologist, pursuing clinical psychology licensure after first practicing as a trial consultant could require additional postdoctoral clinical training to meet the licensure requirements. Affiliation with other psychologists may be hindered, and attendance at psychological conferences and seminars may be limited due to a lack of time or support by your employer. Consultants are often asked to sign noncompete agreements. In the most general sense, a noncompete agreement is a contract that serves to protect an employer from unfair competition by a former employee. Depending on the laws in each state and each consulting firm's practices, it could put unique constraints on a consultant's future job pursuits. Finally, consultants may at times put in long hours, travel extensively, or be required to alter their schedule with little lead time.

Summary

In summary, trial consultants act as a resource to attorneys in a variety of ways. A consultant's training and unique expertise are valuable for evaluating case strategy, educating counsel about juror psychology, and for enhancing credibility, communication effectiveness, and overall case strength. A consultant's diverse knowledge, experience, and skill base are utilized to conduct both empirical research and strategic consulting.

The field of trial consulting has gained tremendous momentum and respect over the years, and the use of trial consultants in preparation for trial and ADR has become the norm. As a result, consulting firms continue to grow and are in need of highly qualified consultants. With the appropriate education, training, and mentoring, the field of trial consulting can provide many benefits ranging from the application of learned theories to intellectual challenge and ongoing learning. Trial consulting is an exciting and dynamic field and those currently employed in it report high levels of satisfaction.

References

Bersoff, D. N., Goodman-Delahunty, J., Grisso, T. J., Hans, V. P., Poythress, N. G., & Roesch, R. G. (1997). Training in law and psychology. *American Psychologist, 52*(2), 1301–1310.
Davidson, A. R., & Jaccard, J. J. (1979). Variables that moderate the attitude-behavior relation: Results of a longitudinal survey. *Journal of Personality and Social Psychology,* 1364.
Field, H. S. (1978). Juror background characteristics and attitudes toward rape: Correlates of jurors' decisions in rape trials. *Law and Human Behavior, 2,* 73–93.
Fiske, S. T., & Taylor, S. E. (1991). *Social cognition* (2nd ed.). New York: McGraw-Hill.

Goldberg, S. I., Goldstein, L. A., Handler, S. P., & Wentzel, D. F. (2000). Use of jury consultants. In R. L. Haig (Ed.), *Successful partnering between inside & outside counsel*. St. Paul: West Group Publishing.

Grisso, T., Sales, B. D., & Bayless, S. (1982). Law-related courses and programs in graduate psychology departments. *American Psychologist, 37,* 267–278.

Gulans, R. J. (Ed.). (2001). *American Society of Trial Consultants membership directory*. Timonium, MD: American Society of Trial Consultants.

Hans, V. P., & Vidmar, N. (1986). *Judging the jury*. New York: Plenum Press.

Hepburn, J. R. (1980). The objective reality of evidence and the utility of systematic jury selection. *Law and Human Behavior, 4,* 89–102.

Sheldon, A. M. (2000, Fall). Standards make a profession. *American Society of Trial Consultants Court Call*.

Swain, B., & Wolfe, D. (1993). Strategic use of pre-trial juror questionnaires. *International Legal Strategy*, 77–80.

Wicker, A. W. (1969). Attitudes versus actions: The relationship of verbal and overt behavioral responses to attitude objects. *Journal of Social Issues*, 41.

Suggested Reading

Abbott, W. F. & Batt, J. (Eds.). (1999). *A handbook of jury research*. Philadelphia: American Law Institute–American Bar Association.

Abbott, W. F., Hall, F., & Linville, E. (1993). *Jury research: A review and bibliography*. Philadelphia: American Law Institute–American Bar Association.

Bartol, C. R. (1983). *Psychology and American law*. Belmont, CA: Wadsworth.

Green, E., & Bornstein, B. H. (2003). *Determining damages: The psychology of jury awards*. Washington, D.C.: American Psychological Association.

Hastie, R. (Ed.). (1993). *Inside the juror: The psychology of juror decision-making*. New York: Cambridge University Press.

Hastie, R., Penrod, S., & Pennington, N. (1983). *Inside the jury*. Cambridge, MA: Harvard University Press.

Kerr, N. L., & Bray, R. M. (Eds.). (1982). *The psychology of the courtroom*. San Diego, CA: Academic Press.

National Jury Project, Krauss, E., & Bonora, B. (1983). *Jurywork®: Systematic techniques* (2nd Ed.). New York: West Publishing.

Vinson, D. E., & Anthony, P. K. (1985). *Social science research methods for litigation*. Charlottesville, VA: Michie.

Waites, R. C. (2003). *Courtroom psychology and trial advocacy*. New York: ALM Publishing.

Suggested Web Sites

American Psychology-Law Society (AP-LS; Division 41 of the American Psychological Association): http://www.unl.edu/ap-ls/.

American Society of Trial Consultants: http://www.astcweb.org.

Simon Fraser University: http://www.sfu.ca.

Towson University: http://www.towson.edu.

20

Sport Psychology: Locker Room Confessions

JENNIFER E. CARTER

The room was dark and quiet as I observed 20 hockey players settling into comfortable positions on the floor. My nose tried to adjust to the pungent odor of the locker room as I began instructing, "I want you to focus simply on the sound of your breathing. Take deep breaths into the pit of your stomach ... breathing in warmth and light; breathing out tension." The athletes' eyes closed as their bodies began to relax. I continued giving verbal suggestions designed to help the athletes achieve a state of deep relaxation, so that they could vividly visualize themselves playing on the ice. I asked the athletes to feel themselves gliding on the ice, hearing the crack of the puck on the stick and the referee's whistle. Throughout the imagery exercise, I passionately repeated words like "Aggressive!" "Confident," and "Crash the net," addressing the team's past difficulty of finishing scoring efforts. Following the 10-minute relaxation/imagery exercise, I chatted with the coaches while the players left the locker room, eager for the next game. I returned to my office for a counseling appointment with an athlete, thus continuing the typical day of a sport psychologist.

Sport psychology is a stimulating field that is full of variety, including performance enhancement consultation, individual and group therapy, teaching, and research. Sport psychologists often work in universities (academic departments, athletic departments, or university counseling centers) and in private practice. Sport psychologists also work in unique settings such as sports medicine centers, Olympic training centers, or anywhere that psychologists can meet with athletes, including the locker room.

Although many consider sport psychology a young field, the psychological study of athletics began in the 19th century (McCullagh, 1995). Early researchers Norman Triplett and Coleman Griffith contributed valuable information in areas such as motor learning and the philosophy of coaching (Davis, Huss, & Becker, 1995; Gould & Pick, 1995). Sport psychology became more organized and recognized beginning in the 1960s, when scientists applied their research findings to consulting with athletes, to assist athletes in achieving high motivation and focus (Williams & Straub, 1993). In the past 20 years, the concept of mental training has gained acceptance as sport psychology continues to grow.

Because I am a counseling sport psychologist working in a university athletic department and sports medicine center, I focus more on applied work with a college population than on sport psychology in academia. I describe the typical activities and responsibilities of a sport psychologist, training recommendations, and advantages/disadvantages of the career. My goal is to provide information and insight into this fun and rewarding profession.

Activities of a Sport Psychologist

The Typical Day of a Sport Psychologist

The typical day of a sport psychologist working in a university athletic department includes a variety of consulting and therapy activities. For example, the day might begin at 6:00 A.M. when I visit a team practice, followed by a "journal club" meeting in which sports medicine and psychology fellows discuss recent research. I then attend an "injury report meeting" with physicians and athletic trainers, to consult about injured athletes' treatment and rehabilitation. I drive to my office at the sports medicine center to return phone calls to coaches and then to meet with a former postdoctoral fellow whom I supervise. I then travel to an academic building to teach the "Mental Toughness Academy," a performance enhancement workshop open to all varsity athletes at the university. I stop by another team practice before returning to the office for three counseling appointments before the day ends. The first is a female athlete struggling with a relationship

Table 20.1 Common Work Duties for Counseling/Clinical Psychologists
in University Athletic Departments

Clinical/Counseling Duties

Individual therapy with varsity college student-athletes
Group therapy with teams for clinical issues (trauma, eating disorders, etc.)
Crisis management
Creating and delivering wellness programs
Consulting with medical staff (physicians, athletic trainers, dietitians)
Assessment
Individual therapy with high school, professional, and recreational athletes
Supervising the clinical work of graduate students and postdoctoral fellows
Participating on athletic department alcohol/drug committee
Consulting with athletic department administrators
Participating in case conference (colleague supervision)
Applying research findings to clinical work

Performance-Enhancement Duties

Meeting with sport teams to enhance mental skills
Facilitating teambuilding exercises
Attending practices and competitions
Meeting with individual athletes or small groups for mental skills training
Consulting with coaches
Delivering educational workshops to coaches
Delivering presentations to college, high school, and professional teams/camps

Research/Teaching Duties

Preparing grant proposals
Collaborating with athletic and academic departments on research projects
Reviewing the research literature in areas of interest
Collecting and analyzing data
Writing manuscripts and presentations
Presenting at professional conferences
Teaching sport psychology and/or counseling classes

Service Duties

Participating on university wellness task forces
Mentoring students
Responding to e-mail, phone calls

---

problem, the second is a male athlete referred for counseling after testing positive for marijuana, and the third is a male athlete suffering from depression. On another day, I might consult with an administrator about a coach–athlete conflict. Or I may deliver a presentation on mental skills to a youth sports camp or a high school team. See Table 20.1 for a list of typical duties.

What exactly is performance enhancement? What clinical issues predominate for athletes? What roles do teaching and research activities play? The following section describes typical sport psychology responsibilities in greater detail.

Performance Enhancement

When I ask athletes what percentage of their performance is mental, they respond that about 90% of the game is mental. When I subsequently ask them what percentage of their practice time is devoted to mental training, they sheepishly reply somewhere between 0 and 5%. Pointing out this discrepancy helps athletes to understand the importance of training their minds as well as their bodies. Performance enhancement, or mental skills training, is a core activity of the sport psychologist. Unmotivated or unfocused athletes can learn effective goal-setting and focusing strategies. Athletes who become too nervous at the big game can learn relaxation skills. And athletes who fail to recover from mistakes can learn to use positive self-talk. Goal-setting, energy management, relaxation, imagery, focus, confidence, self-talk, precompetition routines, and teambuilding are all mental skills that athletes can develop to gain an edge on their competition.

Sometimes there is a perception that sport psychology is a quick fix for slumping athletes. Although I have seen athletes respond well to brief, straightforward interventions, it is more likely that athletes will have to devote time and energy to mental training to improve their performance significantly. It is most effective to address mental training throughout the year so that athletes can learn and apply mental skills. Sport psychologists enjoy having close relationships with coaches who know the pulse of the team and who devote practice time to mental training. However, the reality is that some coaches do not believe in sport psychology, or will seek mental training only at crisis points during the season. It is beneficial to offer individual appointments or small group mental skills training for those athletes without frequent team mental training.

Athletes seem to learn the most when mental training is active, creative, and engaging. Sport psychologists usually have an array of stories, quotes, and activities to assist the development of mental skills. For example, I met with one team to address self-talk, or athletes' ongoing inner dialogue during a performance. We illustrated the importance of positive self-talk by having one athlete shoot simulated basketball free throws, once while teammates shouted encouraging statements and once while teammates shouted negative, discouraging statements. These statements represented the positive or negative self-talk inside the athlete's head. It wasn't surprising that the athlete made more baskets in the positive self-talk environment, but he also learned how to block out some negative statements. The athlete later informed me that he felt amused and unaffected when spectators yelled abusive comments to him at a subsequent away game, because he had already prepared for that situation in our team activity. It is very gratifying when athletes can apply mental skills training to improve their performance in competitive situations.

When sport psychologists attend practices and competitions, one of their roles is to help athletes apply mental skills to their sport activity. Sport psychologists observe team dynamics, coach–athlete interactions, and individual athlete behavior (e.g., how an athlete competes at an away game vs. a home game) (Andersen, 2002). They use these observations to provide feedback to coaches and athletes about their strengths and weaknesses. A wonderful aspect of team or individual mental skills training is the power to assist basically healthy people in achieving greater heights. The sense of capitalizing on an individual's strengths, instead of trying to fix some problem or pathology, is quite appealing. A strength-based model is compatible with the philosophy of counseling psychology and positive psychology.

Individual Counseling

The world of sports is an insider culture, and it can be challenging to break into the inner sanctum. Performance enhancement consultation is one way to gain trust and credibility with athletes. Once athletes see that sport psychologists understand their sport culture and genuinely care about them as people, those athletes become more likely to explore performance or personal issues individually with a sport psychologist. It is common for athletes to schedule individual appointments with the sport psychologist in the training room or following a team meeting. Athletes tend to underutilize counseling services (Pinkerton, Hinz, & Barrow, 1989) for various reasons, including time constraints and the need to portray a tough exterior. When the sport psychologist fulfills the dual role of team performance consultant and individual therapist, one advantage is that more athletes can utilize counseling resources.

The dual role of performance consultant and individual therapist has its disadvantages, including numerous ethical dilemmas regarding confidentiality and boundaries. For example, sport psychologists often travel with teams to competitions or training trips. While it is relatively rare for psychologists to self-disclose about their personal lives when conducting individual therapy, it is difficult to maintain a strict professional role in the midst of spending all day together with athletes on the road. I recall one situation that occurred when I accompanied a team on a trip to Florida. I was sunbathing near the pool when a female athlete (who was an individual client) approached me and asked if she could borrow my nail polish. Embedded in her question seemed to be an astute awareness that borrowing cosmetics from the psychologist might represent a boundary crossing. Sport psychologists have to monitor continually their professional boundaries while in essence living with athletes.

Athletes present with a continuum of concerns in counseling, ranging from strictly performance issues to severe psychopathology. College student-athletes face difficulties similar to any college student, such as relationship problems, identity development, anxiety, depression, substance abuse, and grief. Their athletic participation also creates unique pressures that bring athletes to counseling, including injuries, eating disorders, and delayed career development.

Sport psychologists utilize various theoretical approaches to counseling, including cognitive-behavioral and interpersonal/psychodynamic approaches. Mental training involves cognitive restructuring activities, and a cognitive-behavioral approach also works well when counseling athletes (Petrie & Sherman, 2000). Active and determined athletes enjoy developing power over their moods and performance, through learning how to modify maladaptive thinking patterns. Interpersonal approaches also translate well into working with athletes (Cogan, 2000), and I have often explored the connection between family experiences and current relationships with athletes. For example, a common presenting concern of athletes is a conflict with their coach, and we might explore how the coach is similar to or different from athletes' parents or caregivers. When athletes learn that their coach may be triggering their own issues, they tend to deal with the conflict better. A short-term therapy model appears to fit well with counseling athletes, as their busy schedules make long-term counseling unlikely.

Consultation

Another responsibility of sport psychologists is consultation. Mental skills training represents a form of consultation with athletes, but sport psychologists also consult with coaches, medical staff, businesses, and others. Coaching athletes is itself a challenging performance, and sport psychologists often work with coaches to enhance their performance through learning relaxation, communication, goal-setting, and anger management skills. Each coach has an impact on a

SPORT PSYCHOLOGY

large number of athletes, and improving the coach's performance can trickle down to improved athlete performance and greater enjoyment of the sport.

Physicians, athletic trainers, and dietitians are important resources for athletes. In a university athletic department, athletic trainers spend a great deal of time with athletes and tend to know the most about athletes' personal lives. Sport psychologists often consult with members of the medical team, including athletic trainers, regarding injury and medication questions. Sport psychology colleagues have begun referring to the field as "Performance Psychology," since the principles of mental training are quite applicable to all sorts of performances, including business, music, and the military. Although industrial/organizational psychologists specialize in performance consultation with businesses, some employees respond very well to the teambuilding and sports metaphors that sport psychology can offer.

Teaching and Research

Sport psychologists with a sport science background often choose to teach and conduct research in university departments, such as sport psychology or kinesiology. There are many sport psychology programs located in sport science departments, and there are also programs that offer combined training in sport psychology and counseling (see Sachs, Burke, & Schrader, 2002). Typical classes that are offered in sport science programs include Performance Psychology, Sport Behavior, Psychological Aspects of Sport Injury, Exercise Psychology, Athletic Counseling, Research Methods, and Statistics.

What is the current status of research in sport psychology? Sport psychologists are not at the point where they can claim that mental training increases athletic performance by a certain percentage, but the field is gaining knowledge about what mental skill works for which athlete in a particular setting. Greenspan and Feltz (1989) conducted a meta-analysis of psychological interventions with athletes, finding that educational relaxation exercises and cognitive restructuring interventions are generally effective. Major journals in the field include the *Journal of Sport & Exercise Psychology*, the *Journal of Applied Sport Psychology*, and *The Sport Psychologist*.

While applied settings offer less time for writing and research, postdoctoral fellows and I have engaged in research exploring prevalence rates of body image/eating problems in athletes. Currently we are identifying the most common presenting concerns of athletes in counseling, as well as exploring the link between coaches' attitudes toward sport psychology and their team's utilization of counseling.

Training to Be a Sport Psychologist

There are two main pathways for training: clinical/counseling psychology and sport science. The clinical/counseling path involves earning an advanced degree in counseling or clinical psychology and specializing in sport psychology, whereas the sport science path consists of earning an advanced degree in sport psychology or a similar field.

Clinical/Counseling Pathway

For students who are fascinated by helping many types of people overcome personal difficulties, the clinical/counseling path is a good fit. The American Psychological Association (APA) has clear guidelines for graduate training in clinical or counseling psychology, and students must clear each successive hurdle before achieving licensure. To pursue master's-level licensure (such as Licensed Professional Clinical Counselor or Clinical Social Worker), students need to complete graduate coursework, clinical practica, and oral exams or a research thesis. Students often ask me if there are many opportunities for employment in sport psychology with a master's degree. I believe that the competition is so fierce for the few applied positions that the professionals with doctorate degrees are at a distinct advantage. However, as I explore later, many different professionals can slowly build a sport psychology practice if they are creative and effective.

In nearly all states, provinces, and territories, licensure as a psychologist requires a Ph.D. or Psy.D. in Clinical, Counseling, or School Psychology. I earned a Ph.D. in Counseling Psychology and I believe that training in an APA-approved program gave me a solid foundation for a position in sport psychology. After gaining admission to a competitive doctoral program, students usually progress through the following training elements: coursework in therapy, psychopathology, assessment, ethics, and supervision, more than 1,000 hours of clinical practica, a research thesis and dissertation, doctoral exams, and a 2,000-hour clinical internship. After students earn a doctorate degree, they usually need at least 1,500 to 2,000 supervised postdoctoral hours before taking their licensing exams. Keep in mind that training requirements for licensure can vary by state or province.

Although the clinical/counseling path provides a good foundation, it is clearly not sufficient for gaining competency as a sport psychologist. One of my colleagues jokes that a licensed psychologist who reads *Sports Illustrated* is not automatically a sport psychologist! Some clinical/counseling students are fortunate to attend schools with formal sport psychology programs, where they can find sport science classes as well as applied sport psychology experiences. Other clinical/counseling students have to create training opportunities in sport psychology, which can be a disadvantage of choosing this path. I was a collegiate swimmer, and I began working as a graduate assistant swim coach at the university where I did my graduate training. The head swim coach knew about my research in sport psychology and he invited me to do some teambuilding workshops. I gradually switched from graduate assistant coach to mental training consultant, under the supervision of the university's sport psychologist. I also sought a counseling internship and postdoctoral fellowship providing specialty training in sport psychology. (A list of schools that offer APA-accredited predoctoral internships with opportunities for working with athletes is available at: http://www.psyc.unt.edu/apadiv47/studentinfo.html.) Each exposure to sport psychology left me with an excited feeling that I had found my niche within counseling psychology.

One reason I recommend the clinical/counseling training route is the paucity of full-time applied sport psychology positions. Licensed psychologists are trained as generalists, and they should be able to find employment working with various populations until they can build a sport psychology practice. The most important advantage of the clinical/counseling path is that sport psychologists can cover a broad range of athletic concerns. Some athletes are strictly interested in mental training, and individuals from the sport science path are well suited to help those athletes. However, my experience indicates that most athletes also want to deal with personal concerns, such as depression or family problems. The clinical/counseling sport psychologist is trained to address a continuum of issues for athletes, and this breadth of service is attractive to financially strapped athletic organizations.

Sport Science Pathway

For students who love teaching and exploring ideas in research, the sport science path is a good fit. Students in sport psychology, kinesiology, or physical education programs have coursework in performance enhancement, motor learning, social bases of sport, and counseling. Graduate programs frequently offer internships in applied sport psychology and solid research training through the completion of master's theses and dissertations. Many prominent researchers and mental training consultants in sport psychology have sport science degrees. The advantages of this path are the formal training in performance enhancement, the better understanding of physiological processes connected to performance enhancement, and the availability of faculty positions in universities. Disadvantages include the inability to label themselves as psychologists and the need to refer athletes for assistance with clinical issues.

Experience as a Former Athlete

Experience as a former athlete can provide a greater understanding of the unique athletic culture. While it is obvious that my experiences are likely quite different from those of the athletes with whom I work, my participation in sports has helped my connection and credibility with athletes at times. I am familiar with the frustration and uncertainty of athletic injury, the importance of the coach in athletes' lives, the extreme time demands of elite sports, handling successes and failures publicly with class, and treating elite athletes as people first without fawning over them like sports fans might. It is also helpful to feel comfortable in the locker room, listening to coaches' pep talks or to athletes' joys and fears.

Professional Organizations and Certifications

Sport psychologists often belong to the Association for the Advancement of Applied Sport Psychology (AAASP) and the Sport and Exercise Psychology division of the APA (Division 47), organizations that promote sport psychology research, training, and applied work. AAASP (www.aaasponline.org) has criteria for certification as a sport psychology consultant as well as ethical principles for consultants. Qualification as an AAASP Certified Consultant is necessary for inclusion in the U.S. Olympic Committee registry of sport psychology consultants. APA Division 47 (http://www.psyc.unt.edu/apadiv47/) is developing certification criteria, although it is difficult to reach consensus for certification criteria with two disparate pathways to the field.

Landing a Position, Keeping It, and Moving Up

When I began my graduate training, I often heard predictions that the field of sport psychology would explode in 5 years. While this explosion has not quite occurred, more sport psychology "fires" are starting around the world. Some high school athletes are familiar with sport psychology and seek out mental training. Many university athletic departments utilize the services of a sport psychologist, whether that be a sport science professor, counseling center psychologist, or community consultant. It is also becoming more common for professional sports teams to have a sport psychologist on staff. Landing a position with a professional sports team usually requires many years of experience.

Although full-time sport psychology positions are scarce, individuals can find success through serving their time and networking. New consultants might volunteer as mental training consultants for youth teams or organizations. Ravizza (2003) advised consulting with sports like golf, tennis, and equestrian for the most lucrative potential. Lesyk (1998) suggested building a sport psychology practice by using techniques such as goal-setting and relaxation training with current nonathlete clients, and creating a marketing package. Offering to write a sport psychology newsletter for a high school athletic department and shadowing a sport psychologist are other ways to gain experience. It is very important to find a sport psychology mentor who can supervise these training experiences. Complicated situations arise when dealing with the system of a sports team, and it is helpful to review strategies with a more experienced professional. Beginners should ask themselves which career path feeds their passion, then seek out training experiences with professionals engaging in that career.

Solid interpersonal skills are essential for succeeding as a sport psychologist. Leaving the security of the office necessitates extroversion and the ability to maintain professional boundaries while also appearing approachable. Sport psychologists often portray a confident, hopeful attitude even in the face of adversity, and they need to juggle multiple relationships in a competent and ethical manner. In his description of core competencies for sport psychologists, Ward (2002) noted, "Sport psychologists know how and when to intervene with institutions and organizations on behalf of their athlete clients while appreciating the complexity of confidentiality issues in a sport environment" (p. 19). Sport psychologists may work long, odd hours, and they must be willing to travel often. Because athletics is an insider culture, positive word-of-mouth from coaches and athletes is necessary for success.

There are several opportunities for moving up the career ladder in sport psychology. Sport psychologists can build positive reputations through quality service and research, allowing them to move from part-time, informal consultations to full-time, formal relationships with athletic organizations. In addition to appropriate training and personal qualities, sport psychologists need to assess the needs of athletes accurately and obtain sport-specific knowledge to move up through the ranks (Baillie & Ogilvie, 2002). Often there is increasing prestige in the process of advancing through youth sports, small colleges, NCAA Division I universities, Olympic teams, and professional sports.

Sport Psychology: The Good and the Bad

I often unabashedly proclaim that I love my job. The advantages of this career are many. I find it fun and energizing to spend time with student-athletes, who are generally healthy, inspiring people. I had a wonderful experience as an athlete, and I enjoy the opportunity to stay involved in sports and to try to contribute to young athletes' enjoyment of sport. Another advantage is that working involves being a spectator at a sporting event, something people usually pay money to do. I delight in the daily variety of working with different sports in different settings. Also, counseling athletes can provide a sense of closure not found when counseling non-athletes. It is rare for a psychologist to observe the effects of counseling, but a sport psychologist can watch an athlete apply new coping strategies at a practice or competition.

One disadvantage of sport psychology is the dearth of applied positions available. The field is not well established, necessitating marketing skills, patience, and creativity. Often, students are not prepared for business aspects of consultation, such as marketing yourself and writing contracts. I have also struggled to negotiate being a woman in the masculine culture of sports. I feel uncomfortable entering a men's locker room or listening to male athlete chatter with sexist or homophobic overtones. I have wrestled with simple issues such as what to wear — the polo shirt and khaki pants uniform worn by my male mentors doesn't quite fit my style; yet skirts and heels are impractical for the playing field.

Sport psychology is a fun and interesting career for new psychologists. The variety of consulting, counseling, teaching, and research activities makes the field appealing and challenging. Whether students choose the clinical/counseling path or the sport science path, they will ultimately enjoy the opportunity to have a positive influence on the lives of athletes.

References

Andersen, M. B. (2002). Comprehensive sport psychology services. In J. L. Van Raalte & B. W. Brewer (Eds.), *Exploring sport and exercise psychology* (pp. 13–24). Washington, D.C.: American Psychological Association.

Baillie, P. H., & Ogilvie, B. C. (2002). Working with elite athletes. In J. L. Van Raalte & B. W. Brewer (Eds.), *Exploring sport and exercise psychology* (pp. 395–415). Washington, D.C.: American Psychological Association.

Cogan, K. D. (2000). The sadness in sport: Working with a depressed and suicidal athlete. In M. B. Andersen (Ed.), *Doing sport psychology* (pp. 107–119). Champaign, IL: Human Kinetics.

Davis, S. F., Huss, M. T., & Becker, A. H. (1995). Norman Triplett and the dawning of sport psychology. *The Sport Psychologist, 9,* 366–375.

Gould, D., & Pick, S. (1995). Sport psychology: The Griffith era, 1920–1940. *The Sport Psychologist, 9,* 391–405.

Greenspan, M. J., & Feltz, D. L. (1989). Psychological interventions with athletes in competitive situations: A review. *The Sport Psychologist, 3,* 219–236.

Lesyk, J. (1998). *Developing sport psychology within your clinical practice.* San Francisco: Jossey-Bass.

McCullagh, P. (1995). Sport psychology: A historical perspective. *The Sport Psychologist, 9,* 363–365.

Petrie, T. A., & Sherman, R. T. (2000). Counseling athletes with eating disorders: A case example. In M. B. Anderson (Ed.), *Doing sport psychology* (pp. 121–137). Champaign, IL: Human Kinetics.

Pinkerton, R. S., Hinz, L. D., & Barrow, J. C. (1989). The college student-athlete: Psychological considerations and interventions. *Journal of American College Health, 37,* 218–226.

Ravizza, K. (2003). Lessons learned working in applied sport psychology. Invited address at the annual meeting of the American Psychological Association, Toronto, ON.

Sachs, M. L, Burke, K. L., & Schrader, D. C. (2002). *Directory of graduate programs in applied sport psychology* (6th ed.). Morgantown, WV: Fitness Information Technology.

Ward, D. G. (2002, Fall). Identifying athlete-counseling competencies for sport psychologists. *Exercise & Sport Psychology News — APA Division, 47,* 18–19.

Williams, J., & Straub, W. (1993). Sport psychology: Past, present, and future. In J. Williams (Ed.), *Applied sport psychology: Personal growth to peak performance* (pp. 1–10). Mayfield, CA: Mayfield Publishing.

Suggested Reading

Goldberg, A. S. (1998). *Sports slump busting: 10 steps to mental toughness and peak performance.* Champaign, IL: Human Kinetics.

Huang, A. C., & Lynch, J. (1994). *Thinking body, dancing mind: Taosports for extraordinary performance in athletics, business, and life.* New York: Bantam.

Jackson, S. A., & Csikszentmihalyi, M. (1999). *Flow in sports.* Champaign, IL: Human Kinetics.

Janssen, J. (2002). *Championship team building: What every coach needs to know to build a motivated, committed, and cohesive team.* Tucson, AZ: Winning the Mental Game.

Orlick, T. (2000). *In pursuit of excellence: How to win in sport and life through mental training* (3rd ed.). Champaign, IL: Human Kinetics.

Suggested Web Sites

American Psychological Association, Division of Sport & Exercise Psychology: www.psyc.unt.edu/apadiv47/.

Association for the Advancement of Applied Sport Psychology: www.aaasponline.org.

Career Paths in Sport Psychology: www.wcupa.edu/_ACADEMICS/sch_cas.psy/Career_Paths/Sports/Career07.htm.

The Field of Sport Psychology: www.sportpsychology.com/index.html.

Youth Sports Parenting Information: www.momsteam.com/.

Ohio State Sport Psychology Services: www.ohiostatebuckeyes.collegesports.com/general/sport-psych.html.

21

Disaster Psychology: Keep Clients out of Your Office — Get into the Field!

TERI L. ELLIOTT

Introduction

Each day, natural and human-made disasters devastate our communities and significantly influence the lives of our families, friends, and neighbors. In addition, large-scale disasters such as armed conflict, famine, and poverty significantly affect us all by demonstrating the fragility of life, as well as the devastating costs to our economy and social structures. Although we may not be able to prevent these catastrophes from occurring, as disaster psychologists we can assist in the preparatory, response, and recovery processes. This chapter defines disaster mental health and outlines what it means to be a disaster psychologist. Examples of situations in which disaster psychologists might find themselves are provided throughout. The chapter also discusses the unique struggles and opportunities that go hand-in-hand with being pioneers in this burgeoning field.

What Is Disaster Mental Health?

As a relatively new area of professional psychology, a definition of what is meant by disaster mental health is necessary. In contrast to clinical therapy, the presumption in the field of disaster mental health is that the majority of people affected by a disaster or critical event (throughout this chapter, the terms *critical event* and *disaster* are used interchangeably) will *not* become traumatized. In disaster mental health, the focus is on preventative support rather than long-term treatment. To make sense of this presumption, clear definitions of what constitutes trauma or traumatization as well as what is meant by a disaster or critical event are necessary.

People tend to use the words "trauma" and "traumatized" fairly loosely. You may have heard people comment that they were traumatized because they missed an important deadline or adolescents say they were traumatized because they were not allowed to attend an all-night party. However, the question is whether or not these circumstances truly constitute a traumatic event. To answer this question we must first define and differentiate between the terms traumatic event and trauma. Although numerous definitions exist in the literature, this chapter considers an event traumatic if it fulfills three conditions: (1) overwhelms an individual's perceived ability to cope, (2) violates an individual's central belief systems, and (3) is sudden, unexpected, or non-normative (McCann & Pearlman, 1990).

The first condition an event must meet to be considered traumatic is that it overwhelm the individual's perceived ability to cope with it. The two key words here are "overwhelm" and "perceived." A traumatic event overwhelms an individual's normally effective coping skills (American Psychiatric Association, 1994; Mitchell & Everly, 1997). For example, whereas an individual may have talked to friends or exercised when stressed, these coping skills are no longer effective. If individuals are not overwhelmed, they are not considered traumatized. When individuals feel or perceive that they are able to cope with an event, even a horrific event like the murder of a loved one, they will likely manage. That is not to say that the event will have no impact on their lives or that the healing process will be immediate; rather, it suggests that the individuals trust that they have the strength to cope with the horrible situation and hence it is not defined as traumatizing.

The second condition that must be met for an event to be considered traumatic is that the affected individual's central psychological needs, beliefs, and frame of reference are violated. Adults' central convictions or belief systems are deeply ingrained and are rarely thought of on a conscious level. Children react to and process disasters differently from adults (for a discussion of children's reactions refer to Elliott, 2002). Although these beliefs may differ from culture to culture, some principles appear to be globally accepted. For example, across cultures, it is believed that bad things will not happen to good people. Even though these beliefs may be illusionary, they provide a sense of safety and comfort. Traumatic events shatter this feeling of safety (Herman, 1992; Janoff-Bulman & Frieze, 1983; McCann & Pearlman, 1990). In addition, traumatic events force individuals to consciously or unconsciously revise their frame of reference (Herman, 1992). For example, when asked to describe themselves, individuals may refer to the roles they hold such as psychologist, student, mother, etc. A woman in her early 20s may describe herself as a manager, sister, and athlete. If she is paralyzed in a car accident, will she still consider herself an athlete? If her only sibling is killed, will she still consider herself a sister? Turmoil in individuals core belief systems can disrupt their sense of self and the stability they feel in their environment. Consequently, after a traumatic event people are often forced to reevaluate the world around them and their role in it. They may question their faith, their ability to care for themselves, and even their desire to live in a world that appears to be unjust.

Finally, a traumatic event must be sudden, unexpected, or non-normative. Unexpected events such as flash floods and automobile accidents are quite easy to identify, but non-normative events can be more difficult to isolate. A non-normative event is something that society as a whole feels is unacceptable (e.g., child molestation). By including non-normative situations in this definition, destructive experiences or situations that are not sudden or unexpected are included.

So, traumatic events overwhelm individuals perceived ability to cope, violate their central belief systems, cause them to reevaluate their role in the world, and are sudden, unexpected, or non-normative (for a complete explanation of these definitions, see Elliott, 2002). However, it is important to clarify that disaster psychologists do not specialize in *all* traumatic events. Disaster psychologists work with individuals or groups of individuals affected by natural or human-made disasters such as floods, terrorism, or large-scale transportation accidents. Although non-normative events can be traumatic, it is unlikely that a disaster psychologist would become involved in these situations. This eliminates situations such as spousal abuse, from the disaster psychologist's field of specialization.

Now that we have a definition of what makes an event traumatic, it is necessary to define what it means to have experienced a "trauma" or to have been "traumatized." The word trauma has both medical and psychological definitions. In medical terms, trauma refers to a physical injury or wound (Taber, 1993). In psychological terms, and for the purposes of this chapter, trauma is defined as a response to a traumatic event (McCann & Pearlman, 1990) that is experienced through an individual's thoughts, feelings, and senses. Trauma is associated with significant distress and a sense of helplessness and can initiate a shift in individuals' view of the world and themselves. This distress is revealed by emotional and behavioral reactions, which abate with time in most individuals. Disaster psychology postulates that disaster reactions, although a natural response to an extreme event, have the potential to cause long-term negative effects if not appropriately addressed. These can include (but are not limited to) relationship difficulties, post-traumatic stress disorder and depression.

Consequently, it is the disaster psychologist's role to utilize crisis intervention processes with the goal of preventing natural distress due to the critical event from developing into a more harmful, long-term psychological condition. This author believes that a primary goal of disaster psychology is to help individuals see themselves not as victims of or even survivors of an event, but rather as individuals who have experienced the event. Although the event will certainly remain memorable and perhaps even life-changing, the hope is that it will come to be merely one part of the individual's history and not an all-encompassing part of the individual's life.

What Does a Disaster Psychologist Do?

There is a wealth of opportunities in this field ranging from working in academia to consulting or becoming part of a first-response team. Disaster psychologists are often distinguished from other psychologists by their tendency to carry out their clinical interventions in the field and to focus specifically on the impact of the critical event rather than on emotions and feelings surrounding the person's overall identity or development.

The three main stages of interventions that a disaster psychologist creates or maintains are (1) preparedness, (2) response, and (3) follow-up. In these stages, the disaster psychologist's level of guidance (i.e., assisting, directing, or actually implementing) will depend on the training and level of disaster response expertise of the individual, group, or organization participating in the response. The disaster psychologist's participation will also vary from event to event. In some circumstances you will be involved from the beginning while in others you may be sent out only to assist in the follow-up phase of service delivery. Finally, even though the disaster psychologist will make proposals, it is ultimately the funding or enacting parties' decision whether or not to implement the recommendations. Refer to Table 21.1 for an overview of the three main stages of intervention.

Table 21.1 Common Tasks during the Three Stages of Intervention

Stage	Description
Preparedness	Develop response plans
	Develop or maintain cooperative arrangements
	Maintain group and community familiarity with the response plan — practice
	Ensure necessary training
Response	Ensure psychological support procedures and crisis intervention processes are implemented
	Provide direct support to first responders and those directly affected
	Provide indirect support to the affected community
	Ascertain and promote referral options
Follow-up	Evaluation of programs and interventions
	Ascertain and publicize available follow-up care

During the preparedness stage of intervention, the disaster psychologist's focus is on assisting individuals, groups, organizations, and communities to develop response plans to be used when a critical event occurs. This includes developing and maintaining cooperative arrangements with all involved internal and external organizations or groups prior to a critical event. Some of these organizations may include first responders, humanitarian aid organizations, and city or county agencies. The different groups are often composed of concerned parents or retired service workers who are not affiliated with a larger organization yet want to assist their community. Additionally, relationships with the media are particularly important. A disaster psychologist should ensure that the communities' media are properly educated about the potential mental health consequences of particular critical events and can provide appropriate corresponding media presentations. This might include providing predeveloped public service announcements or offering educational interviews.

The development of the response plan is highly detailed, and should take into consideration as many variables as possible, to cover both physical and psychological safety components. In the development of this plan (for example, what to do in case of a flood or school shooting), the disaster psychologist will ensure that the necessarily wide range of variables is taken into consideration. These variables include, but are not limited to, organizing shelters, food services, emergency first aid stations, animal care, financial assistance programs, clean-up options, tracking services (to locate or relay information about the whereabouts of affected individuals and their families), child care services, and crisis intervention possibilities. Although psychologists will not run or even participate in many of these programs, it is their responsibility to recommend that the programs are all adequately researched, developed, and placed into readiness prior to a critical event.

Once the cooperative agreements are arranged and the plan is developed, the involved individuals and groups need to practice the plan periodically (e.g., biannually), acquire any necessary items (tangible or not), continually ensure that all developed options are still viable, and maintain the appropriate training level for all involved individuals in their respective roles. The disaster psychologist will usually continue to be involved every step of the way as a consultant or guide to the process. In particular, personnel from all of the responding groups or agencies must be trained in, or at least made aware of, the concept of psychological first aid and the procedures for referral of mental health issues. In addition, all potential mental health responders will need to be trained in psychological first aid methods, crisis intervention techniques, triage assessment techniques, and referral options. Finally, the disaster psychologist will ensure that the mental health needs of the responders as well as those directly affected by the critical event are incorporated throughout the plan.

The second stage of intervention is the response. This stage is set in motion during and immediately following the occurrence of a disaster. During this time, the disaster psychologist will work to ensure that the carefully developed response plan is activated (or if there is no plan, to create one on the fly) and, if necessary, to troubleshoot any and all problems with the plan's implementation. An ongoing reassessment of all procedures will be undertaken throughout the period of response to ensure that all goals are met. Any necessary contingencies not previously addressed are attended to now. The disaster psychologist will provide training, supervision, and support. This can occur either in the field or by being in electronic contact with the affected groups or organizations and guiding them through the necessary response steps.

During the response stage, the disaster psychologist will implement, or assist others in implementing, psychological support procedures and crisis intervention processes. It is important for the disaster psychologist to convey, or ensure methods are in place to convey, that struggling with difficult, confusing, and painful emotions is a natural part of the recovery process. Individuals affected by a critical event can be helped by learning about typical responses to such events, as sometimes just knowing what to expect can bring relief.

The disaster psychologist will provide direct support through crisis intervention processes to responders (for example, fire and police personnel, as well as other disaster mental health staff) and those directly affected. Indirect support is provided to the community as a whole through presentations and group discussions about the event and possible emotional reactions. During this stage of the disaster response, referral options for further mental health evaluation and support would be determined and made clear to all relief workers as well as those directly affected by the event.

The third stage of intervention in which disaster psychologists are involved is follow-up. In this stage the disaster psychologist's expertise in program or intervention evaluation is critical. It will need to be ascertained whether the procedures set in place are working and which measures will be taken to correct any problems, if necessary. All groups or agencies involved will be recontacted to ensure that they are aware of the continued assistance available.

One area that is not typically part of a disaster psychologist's follow-up is the care of individuals directly affected by the critical event. It is not the disaster psychologist's role to provide therapy. Consequently, once an intervention (or series of interventions; e.g., psychological first aid or debriefings) has been made, there is little or no further communication. Although this may sound as if individuals are being abandoned, such is not the case. A good disaster psychologist will ensure that the crisis intervention processes cover the length of the recovery period. For example, appropriate support services will be developed for the 1-year anniversary of the event. In addition, the disaster psychologist will ensure that appropriate follow-up care is available for those who need it and that this availability is widely known. The ultimate goal of the disaster psychologist is to support groups or communities in assisting themselves. The community should be left more empowered and competent than before.

No Really, What Does a Disaster Psychologist Do?

It is difficult to describe the career of a disaster psychologist because the job is always changing. Unlike the traditional clinical psychologist who has regularly scheduled clients, a disaster psychologist has little or no schedule. Consequently, the best way to describe the role of the disaster psychologist may be to discuss the professional and personal requirements necessary to succeed in this field.

Professional and Personal Requirements for a Successful Career in Disaster Psychology

The pursuit of a career in this growing area is difficult at times. If you are interested in becoming a competent disaster psychologist, it is important to have training in both the professional and personal arenas.

Table 21.2 Requirements for a Successful Career in Disaster Psychology

Professional Requirements

Competency or expertise in trauma psychology, organizational psychology, crisis intervention, and assessment processes and techniques

Competency or expertise in program development and evaluative procedures

Communication skills

Organizational skills

Problem-solving skills

Negotiation skills

Willingness to advocate for affected individuals

Willingness to advocate for disaster psychology and support services

Personal Requirements

Flexibility

Physically and emotionally able to work in chaotic environments

Ability to respond on a moment's notice

Ability to balance fieldwork with family and personal relationships

Cultural sensitivity

A thick skin

Strong boundaries, yet an ability to empathize

Thorough understanding of your personal trauma triggers

Ability to remain engaged and productive in spite of potentially insurmountable challenges

Ability to transition out of the operation before "everything" is complete

Ability to understand and respect the limits of your role and abilities

Strong support system

Ability to implement effective self-care

Unfortunately, the number of appropriate graduate and postgraduate training programs is quite limited. You may find that you have to develop your own program of study and find original ways to obtain the proper training, experience, and supervision. Refer to Table 21.2 for an overview of the professional and personal requirements for a successful career in disaster psychology.

Professional Training Requirements

It is necessary to have a thorough understanding of trauma psychology, organizational psychology, crisis intervention, and assessment processes and techniques, as well as program development and evaluation procedures. Because you will be guiding and interacting with a wide array of individuals from varying backgrounds and cultures (those directly affected and those there to assist in the recovery process) who are all under a great deal of stress, it is essential to have strong communication, problem-solving, and negotiating skills. Although these areas may not be covered in many graduate programs, they are fairly easy to obtain through workshops or postgraduate training.

When preparing to enter the field of disaster psychology, an important concept to understand is that skills taught in the classroom, particularly in didactic courses, often do not translate well in the field. Techniques need to be adapted to a situation that is constantly changing. For example, if you have been trained to facilitate a debriefing in a quiet room with snacks readily available, what do you do when there is no room, let alone snacks? Flexibility, decisiveness, and ability to work with whatever resources are available no matter how limited are essential.

In addition to the modified and expanded academic and clinical skills necessary for this career, disaster psychologists' also must be willing to advocate for affected individuals and for the importance of disaster psychology in general. Again, this is where political savvy and negotiating skills are necessary. It is not enough to be "right"; you have to be able to convince others that you are right.

Personal Training Requirements

The ability to adapt and work in chaotic conditions is essential. Providing services in the field often requires working in physically and emotionally difficult situations such as flood zones, refugee camps, terrorist attacks, or with organizations where psychologists are neither desired nor respected. As a result, the personal requirements (both physical and mental) are perhaps even more difficult to master than the professional.

Physical Challenges

Unlike traditional psychological therapy that is conducted in an office, disaster psychologists usually do their clinical work in the field under very stressful conditions. Long hours, poor environmental conditions, and health risks are common. For example, if you are helping a community recover from a flood or terrorist attack, it is likely that you will be working 12- to 16-hour days in unsanitary or contaminated conditions. The disaster may have destroyed the water supply or limited the available electricity. If you are out walking among the affected people (which is where you will do most of your "clinical" interventions), you will likely be walking through mud, water, and debris, such as tree branches and the remains of destroyed buildings. If you are working in a small or rural community, the limited housing may have been destroyed or is being used to accommodate local people who have lost their homes. Consequently, you may have to sleep in a tent, a temporary shelter, or travel a considerable distance to find lodging. In addition, it is often necessary to share hotel rooms or tents with other responders who are strangers to you. You may or may not have running water and electricity, not to mention hot water and clean towels. It is incumbent on the disaster psychologist to be physically and emotionally up to the challenge of enduring these physical hardships, all the while helping others deal with the crisis.

Working in disaster psychology also affects your personal and professional time. Because you are often called into the field with little or no warning, it is important to arrange your other work and family affairs in a manner that allows you to travel on a moment's notice. If you are in academia, procedures need to be in place for someone to cover your classes for weeks or months at a time, depending on the assignment. If you are consulting or working as a clinician, arrangements need to be made for your clients and other professional responsibilities. Family life also has to be seriously considered. You may be asked to work at a disaster site for several weeks and many overseas positions require yearlong obligations. You will need to ask yourself several questions: "Is it possible to leave my loved ones for weeks or months at a time?" "Can I take them with me and would I want to?" Maintaining your responsibilities while working with the real-time considerations of disasters can be a challenging balancing act that needs constant care and consideration.

Emotional Challenges

The emotional challenges of working as a disaster psychologist are many and varied. For those used to a predictable routine, the chaotic and ever-changing work environment can be quite stressful. It is often difficult to impose organization on this environment, and yet that is what is required of you. Disaster psychologists need to make the chaotic manageable for themselves, the affected individuals, and the relief workers. This is why flexibility, quick problem solving, and strong organizational skills are essential.

Disaster psychologists work best as part of an interdisciplinary team. This team can consist of health professionals, religious leaders, military personnel, humanitarian aid agency representatives, and members from the local community. All of these individuals will have their own agenda, biases, and styles of communication. This may be less of an issue if the disaster psychologist has worked with the community in the preparatory stage, when these issues should have been addressed. However, if the disaster psychologist is sent into an unfamiliar community, or if some of the involved groups or organizations have altered their agendas, differences of opinion may need to be addressed quickly to avoid or minimize any organizational pressure from negatively affecting the disaster response.

There may also be cases in which the people "in charge" of a disaster response, or even those sending you out on assignment, do not respect the disaster psychologist's role. They may consider it more of a token position created to pacify a current inclination of including emotional concerns into the disaster response plan. Therefore, working effectively within this complex environment requires cultural sensitivity, political savvy, and flexibility, not to mention a thick skin.

When it comes to cultural sensitivity, it is essential that all disaster psychologists thoroughly examine their own cultural beliefs and prejudices. To be effective, any concerns or biases need to be understood *prior* to arriving on the scene. Consequently, an experiential course or seminar series in understanding prejudice and ethnocentrism from a personal perspective is strongly recommended.

The work environment itself is often taxing. Because disaster psychologists are out in the field experiencing pieces of the event, they may be exposed to grisly scenes or physically dangerous situations. For example, in the aftermath of an armed conflict or terrorist attack there are often military tanks and armed soldiers patrolling the streets, wounded and confused individuals looking for loved ones, and the associated noises and visual images can be very unnerving. Additionally, disaster psychologists will hear, repeatedly, stories of fear and horror, as told to them by affected individuals and relief workers. All this will likely cause disaster psychologists' emotions to be running hot, and therefore their own "issues" will be closer to the surface. As a result, secondary or vicarious traumatization is possible.

Secondary or Vicarious Traumatization

A number of terms have been used in the literature to describe the vulnerability of trauma helpers to the unique stresses of working in the area of trauma. You may have heard of secondary victimization, secondary traumatic stress, vicarious traumatization, compassion fatigue, emotional contagion, or even burnout (Miller, 1998). Although there are differences among these terms, the relevant concept is that helpers may undergo a transformation as a result of the empathetic act of trying to understand an affected person's traumatic experience and hence risks becoming traumatized themselves. Secondary trauma or vicarious traumatization is more likely to occur when the therapist is unable to adequately process the "trauma material" presented by the affected individual; this appears to be more severe in helpers with their own trauma history (Figley, 1995, and Pearlman & Mac Ian, 1995, as cited in Miller, 1998). Consequently, it is essential that disaster psychologists process their own trauma histories and have a thorough understanding of their own trauma triggers before entering a scene. In this manner, they can more adequately protect their own boundaries and ensure that their personal concerns will not overwhelm their professional objectivity. For example, if a disaster psychologist experienced a severe car accident as a college student and never worked through the surrounding feelings, it may be inappropriate for that individual to work a large transportation accident. In this vein, personal experience with therapy can benefit the disaster psychologist both personally and in their professional role as a disaster psychologist. By experiencing what it is like to be "on the other side of the couch," so to speak, disaster psychologists are able to enhance their ability to empathize with affected individuals and help ensure that their own histories of trauma do not interfere with their clinical skills.

Another particularly difficult challenge for the disaster psychologist is the ability to remain in the field when it is clear that there is no "solution." For example, if you are working in an inner city ghetto or a large refugee camp, with the typically limited resources, the feeling that there is no "cure" for the pain and suffering you are witnessing can be difficult to handle. Even if you are able to assess correctly that many individuals are experiencing post-traumatic stress disorder or depression, with a proven therapeutic treatment, the resources to provide these services are often unavailable. It is also commonly apparent that the affected population is struggling not only with the current crisis, but also with a host of preexisting problems such as poverty, community violence, sexism, prejudice, punishing regimes, and so on. The ability to remain engaged and productive in these circumstances is paramount for a good disaster psychologist.

Finally, a disaster psychologist is often not able to stay until the "end" of a disaster response. For example, you may arrive immediately following a hurricane (at the beginning of the response) or you may be brought in months after the hurricane, as the disaster response continues. Your tasks will likely differ depending on the stage of the disaster response in which you are working. Therefore, you may have to "hand off" your work to someone else or you may have to pick up where another disaster psychologist left off. The disconcerting feeling of not being able to know how things work out or how to "fix" the situation can be particularly difficult to handle. While there is a follow-up stage of intervention, in many situations the options are very limited. For example, in some countries there are no mental health personnel to provide the necessary care. In some cases, illnesses like schizophrenia or epilepsy are not considered mental or physical health problems per se and are subsequently treated in a manner completely different from one with which you may be comfortable. The ability to understand and respect the limits of your role and abilities are essential for a disaster psychologist.

The capacity to endure these mental, physical, and emotional hardships is often made more difficult by a lack of privacy or quiet space to process the experience. Disaster psychologists often feel that they can or should be able to handle all situations and hence do not always adequately prepare for their own emotional reactions to critical events. As part of preparing for work in disaster psychology, you must be able to establish a support system and implement good self-care techniques (e.g., exercise, healthy eating, and sleeping patterns). You have to take care of yourself first. If you are not emotionally and physically fit, you will be of limited use to the disaster response.

With All This Hardship, Why in the World Would Anyone Want to Become a Disaster Psychologist?

Even given the many hardships in the field, many professionals find that disaster psychology is a wonderful profession. The rewards are numerous and varied. However, although the hardships of being in the field are easy to enumerate, the benefits are much harder to describe.

A clear benefit of working in the field of disaster psychology is that the job is constantly evolving and changing. With an endless variety, as well as a seemingly endless amount of work to be done, boredom is not an issue. In addition, because there is a never-ending supply of natural and human-made disasters, there will always be a job opportunity.

An adrenaline rush comes with being a disaster psychologist. You may be one of only a few people heading into a disaster zone and the thrill of the upcoming challenge can be intense and is often quite exhilarating. You will find yourself working with motivated, interesting people from all walks of life. You are also able to travel to some of the most spectacular and isolated places in the world. Frequent flyer miles can really add up.

The opportunity to continually challenge yourself both intellectually, by trying to rapidly adapt your training and experiences to the current field situation; and emotionally, by trying to understand and help people in a tremendous amount of pain and confusion, is a wonderful benefit. This self-development can lead you to learn a great deal about yourself as a person, as well as a professional.

Although it is true that you may not be able to "fix everything," you do make significant and noticeable changes in people's lives. This is endlessly rewarding. You will never forget the times you reunite parents with their lost child, or worked with a stoic, private farmer who opened his heart to you.

Taking part in a large-scale humanitarian effort can also be an antidote to the often violent and demoralizing nature of our world. With ethnic and prejudicial conflicts, child abuse, poverty, and famine epidemic around the globe, taking part in a disaster recovery response is a unique experience. The often-overwhelming outpouring of goodness from stranger to stranger without regard for color, age, sexual orientation, or wealth that occurs during a disaster response is a wonder to observe. During those times the feeling of belonging and altruism is payment and reward in and of itself.

In summary, disaster psychologists work with individuals, groups, and organizations affected by natural or human-made disasters to lessen the often devastating impact of critical events on people's lives. When you have the opportunity to create workable disaster response plans that save lives, you may vow to stay in the field forever in spite of the many challenges.

How Do You Get a Job as a Disaster Psychologist?

In recent years, the response of mental health personnel to critical events has increased dramatically in terms of both the speed and overall organization of response. As part of this restructuring, humanitarian aid agencies and public service agencies are starting to include psychological support in their relief efforts. Consequently, disaster psychologists have a wealth of new opportunities. The stage for disaster preparedness consultation as well as intervention and regrowth assistance is also open and rife with opportunity. Private corporations, states, school districts, and national/international humanitarian organizations are but a few examples of the far-reaching range for consultation and collaboration for disaster psychology. These opportunities present in a variety of forms. It is possible to have an academic position as a disaster psychologist and combine the distinct yet complementary roles of clinical fieldwork, teaching, and research. It is also possible to become a consultant, researcher, or field responder, or even to combine all of these roles. It is also important to note that you don't have to spend all of your time in the field or travel extensively. It is possible to work as a disaster psychologist in your own community or to provide disaster-related services only a couple of times a year. There is a tremendous amount of variability in the proportion of professional time disaster psychologists spend on disaster services.

While the opportunities available to disaster psychologists are expanding, describing how to obtain a job in this field is extremely difficult because traditional approaches to securing employment do not apply. Commonly, the impetus is on psychologists to create their own position. Most psychologists working in the field of disaster started out in other specialties and slowly gravitated toward disaster work. Perhaps the easiest way to obtain experience in disaster psychology is to volunteer with a humanitarian aid organization. Once you have the appropriate experience, you can attempt to secure a job with whatever humanitarian agency you are comfortable with or branch out on your own.

These innovative opportunities allow you to chart your own course. Because disaster psychologists work best as part of an interdisciplinary team, the goal is to promote yourself as a critical component of a disaster response team. It appears that there is often a window of opportunity when organizations are more inclined to include mental health issues in their planning. Unfortunately, this is typically right after a critical event has occurred. In the immediate aftermath of a disaster, organizations tend to be eager to have the assistance of disaster psychologists and they are often willing to pay for that assistance. Networking can be a very useful way to acquire contacts; although it is best to develop relationships prior to an event, if that has not been possible, once an event has occurred is a perfect time to offer your services. In this vein, it is very important to get your name out there. You can conduct research, publish articles, do presentations and lectures, and simply arrange to meet the people with whom you want to work. Once you become known as an experienced and competent disaster responder, when a critical event occurs someone may just call you up and ask you to get on a plane.

In terms of monetary reimbursement for your services, it might be difficult in the heat of a crisis, but to make this a paying profession it must be done. Many organizations would like you to volunteer your time and services, and this is a great way to get started in the field. But at some point, you need to decide what your services are worth, set a price, and start asking to be paid. Disaster psychology is not usually the field to enter if you are looking for a high financial standard of living. Reimbursement levels can range from poor (if you are working solely as a disaster responder) to adequate (for an academic position) to quite high (if you are working full-time as a consultant).

In sum, people who gravitate toward the field of disaster psychology include those who enjoy a challenge, welcome the possibility of helping individuals and entire communities, and desire to be part of a growing and ever-changing field. While the endeavor of entering this exciting profession may appear daunting, I can testify that the end result is well worth the effort.

Summary

Throughout this chapter, I have attempted to describe the complex field of disaster psychology. Many of the challenges and rewards of being a disaster psychologist have been enumerated, and yet conveying the full experience is difficult if not impossible. A description of the career of a disaster psychologist often makes the career sound as if it is full of hardship and sacrifice, and yet it is a wonderful opportunity to expand your physical and emotional limits. Like many possibilities in life, the challenging aspects of the experience are often easier to describe than the rewards. For a comparison, imagine a journey where your feet and back ache. Your mouth longs for water as your body sweats and labors with the strain of carrying all your belongings. As you move forward, you cannot see past the next bend or ridge and yet you know the path leads on much farther. You and your companion are completely alone. The sounds all around you are ominous yet vaguely familiar. Never quite sure if you are on the right track, you walk on and on. Despite or perhaps because of all this, you are determined to finish this journey you started: this backpacking trip up over the timberline and into the beautiful clouds above. Like backpacking, the career of a disaster psychologist is not for everyone; yet this rapidly growing field offers a wealth of opportunities for those brave enough to take them and run.

Acknowledgment

I thank Jessie T. Kaster, M.F., for her insightful and detailed assistance.

References

American Psychiatric Association. (1994). *Diagnostic and statistical manual of mental disorders* (4th ed.). Washington, D.C.: Author.

Elliott, T. L. (2002). Children and trauma: An overview of reactions, mediating factors, and practical interventions that can be implemented. In C. E. Stout (Ed.), *The psychology of terrorism: Clinical aspects and responses* (Vol. 2, pp. 49–73). Westport, CT: Praeger.

Herman, J. L. (1992). *Trauma and recovery.* New York: Basic Books.

Janoff-Bulman, R., & Frieze, I. H. (1983). A theoretical perspective for understanding reactions to victimization. *Journal of Social Issues, 39*(2), 1–17.

McCann, I. L., & Pearlman, L. A. (1990). *Psychological trauma and the adult survivor: Theory, therapy and transformation* (Vol. 21). New York: Brunner/Mazel.

Miller, L. (1998). *Shocks to the system: Psychotherapy of traumatic disability syndromes.* New York: W. W. Norton.

Mitchell, J. T., & Everly, G. S. (1997). *Critical incident stress debriefing: An operations manual for the prevention of traumatic stress among emergency services and disaster workers* (2nd rev. ed.). Ellicott City, MD: Chevron.

Taber, C. W. (1993). *Taber's cyclopedic medical dictionary* (17 ed.). Philadelphia: F. A. Davis.

Suggested Reading

American Psychological Association. (2001, February). New careers for psychologists. *The Monitor*.

Danieli, Y., Rodley, N. S., & Weisaeth, L. (Eds.). (1996). *International responses to traumatic stress: humanitarian, human rights, justice, peace and development contributions, collaborative actions and future initiatives*. Amityville, NY: Baywood.

Elliott, T. L. (2000). *Helping children and families cope with the aftermath of armed conflict and displacement*: Reykjavik: Icelandic Red Cross.

Elliott, T. L. (2002). Children and trauma: An overview of reactions, mediating factors, and practical interventions that can be implemented. In C. E. Stout (Ed.), *The psychology of terrorism: Clinical aspects and responses* (Vol. 2, pp. 49–73). Westport, CT: Praeger.

Gibbs, M. S., Drummond, J., & Lachenmeyer, J. R. (1993). Effects of disasters on emergency workers: A review, with implications for training and postdisaster interventions. In *Handbook of post-disaster interventions,* Allen, R. D. (Ed.). (pp. 189–212). Corte Madera, CA: Select Press.

Hanlon, P. (2000). Psychologists find valuable niche in disaster response. Available online at the official Web site of *Massachusetts Psychologist*. Retrieved November 2003 from www. masspsy.com/leading/0011_coverdisaster.html.

Harriman, P. (1999, April 4). USD professor chronicles Balkans' trauma. *Argus Leader,* p. 12A.

Morrison, J. (1999). *When disaster strikes: Where are the psychologists?* Retrieved July 22, 2003, from http://siop.org/tip/backissues/TipJuly99/9Morrison.htm.

Weaver, J. D. (1995). *Disasters: Mental health interventions*. Sarasota, FL: Professional Resource Press.

Suggested Web Sites

American Red Cross. (2002). Disaster services. Retrieved July 20, 2003, from http://www. redcross.org/services/disaster/.

APA Online. Disaster Response Network: A pro-bono service of the American Psychological Association and its members. Retrieved July 22, 2003, from http://www.apa.org/practice/ drn.html.

Association of Psychology Postdoctoral and Internship Centers. Retrieved July 20, 2003, from http://appic.org/.

International Federation of Red Cross and Red Crescent Societies. Health and community care: psychological support. Retrieved July 20, 2003, from http://www.ifrc.org/what/health/ psycholog/.

National Center on Disaster Psychology and Terrorism. Retrieved July 22, 2003, from http:// www.ncdpt.org/index.htm.

World Health Organization. (2003). Mental health in emergencies: mental and social aspects of health of populations exposed to extreme stressors. Retrieved July 20, 2003, from http:// www.who.int/disasters/tg.cfm?doctypeID=21.

22

Research Consultation: Psychologists as Research Consultants

ERIKA D. TAYLOR, DIONNE R. DOBBINS, AND
DARREN W. WOODRUFF

So you're about to complete your Ph.D. in psychology. You've passed your qualifying exams, you've defended your proposal, and you are ready for your dissertation defense. Before you're finished, here's one more pop quiz:

- Do you prefer to focus on affecting
  a. individual behavior or
  b. infrastructure and policy?
- Do you prefer to focus on
  a. a particular program of research or
  b. a wide range of research topics?
- Do you prefer
  a. basic research or
  b. applied research?

If you chose more "b"s than "a"s, you may want to consider a career as a research consultant.

In this chapter, we discuss our experiences as research consultants at a nationally known social policy research firm. This organization provides consultation to a wide variety of federal, state, and private educational agencies, as well as other corporate clients. We take the reader through the personal and professional journeys that led us to social policy research.

We understand that many graduate students have little access to information about career options outside of academia. Our goal is to present the work we do as a viable option to new Ph.D.s who are developing their career paths. This chapter is organized across the following topics: How We Got Here, What a Research Consultant Does, Working at a Social Policy Research Firm: Things to Consider, Additional Opportunities for Research Consultants, and Lessons Learned and Advice for New Professionals.

How We Got Here

This section is a discussion of our personal entry points into the field of psychology and how these choices led us to our work as consultants in social policy research. A common thread across our stories is how our experiences provided a strong impetus to investigate and learn more about psychological processes on both an individual and group level. In addition, we all have the desire to examine systems and social structures and their impact on life opportunities, behavior, and other outcomes. Also evident in each of our stories is the commitment to engaging in research designed to influence social change. Through our stories, we also hope to convey that there is no "conventional" way to become involved with this type of work, and provide information that will make others' paths to consulting more direct. We describe our stories below.

Erika's Story

I must begin by fully admitting that my journey consisted of a series of uninformed decisions. However, I strongly believe that without many of these decisions, I would not have accomplished nearly as much as I have to date. I decided that I wanted to be a psychologist in the eighth grade. I do not recall any major life experience or encounter that led to my decision — it just came to me and I stuck with that resolution. I took *Introduction to Psychology* during my first semester of college and hated it. I began to wonder if I had made the right (uninformed) decision 5 years before. Nevertheless, I continued to take more courses in psychology, as I wanted to be absolutely certain that I hated it before exploring other career options. Ultimately, I realized that I could not have made a better choice.

Although my first love was psychology, I developed a number of interests within and related to the discipline. I love children, and was interested in how they develop, which led me to developmental psychology. I was raised by parents who (although neither of them have college degrees) held education in very high esteem. In addition, my experiences as the only African American participating in the honors track at a predominately white public high school led to my interest in issues of equity in education. I also have an interest in how the educational experiences of African Americans affect perceptions of themselves and others and how these perceptions are related to educational outcomes. I still hold fast to these interests and have examined them in my own research.

My decision to go to graduate school was based on the unspoken rule that you cannot do anything with a bachelor's degree in psychology, or any social science for that matter. I decided that I would go on to get my master's degree during my sophomore year, a short time after I officially declared psychology as my major. However, during my junior year, I decided that I should just "go ahead and get my Ph.D., as it was only two more years of school." Oh, the workings of the young mind! I obviously had no idea of the amount of commitment, perseverance, and patience that getting a Ph.D. would require. In retrospect, it was probably better that way.

While I was in graduate school, I realized that I did not want to conduct research "for research's sake." I wanted my work to have a more direct impact on the populations that interested me. It was then that I developed an interest in educational policy and policy research. I began to research my options in terms of doing policy-related research. I searched the Internet for the names and descriptions of research organizations, university research centers, and foundations that were doing work that interested me. I also took a summer internship at a local research foundation to get an idea of what it might be like to work in this environment. I decided that this was the way I wanted to begin my career after completing my doctoral degree.

I continued to conduct Internet searches of research organizations in the geographical areas where I planned to move when I finished graduate school. I also narrowed my choices by the type of work in which I was interested. Then, somewhat serendipitously, the psychology and sociology departments at my graduate institution sponsored a 2-day seminar on alternative careers in social sciences during my final year in graduate school. The seminar included invited guests from a variety of nonacademic work environments, including social policy research firms and schools. We had the opportunity to hear about the types of work done in these environments, and the skills and experiences required to carry out the work. In addition, we were able to speak individually with the seminar guests, in an informal interview format, to determine whether or not to seriously pursue our interest in that organization. It was at this seminar that I decided to pursue a position at this research firm.

Dionne's Story

My journey to the field of psychology was a circuitous one. My mother was a kindergarten teacher and I felt her work was thankless. Ignoring my natural calling to work with children and issues of mental health and education, I chose a major that kept me as far from children as possible — business management. I was miserable, and left college after my freshman year.

As "punishment," my mother made me volunteer in her classroom for a semester. I worked in an inner-city school with children labeled "at risk." I worked with people who believed that all children could learn, even those from poor environments. I saw so many success stories during the semester and I loved it! To my mother's delight, I decided to return to college and focus on an undergraduate degree in psychology that would allow me to work with minority children, mental health issues, and early childhood education. Later, I continued my education by attending a graduate program in applied developmental psychology. This field that allowed me to study in applied settings (i.e., schools, intervention centers, hospitals) and work with at-risk populations.

After earning my doctorate, I was not sure if the academic environment fit my professional needs. However, I knew of no other option (in graduate school, anything less than academia was seen as a failure). I did something that I highly recommend to anyone unsure of the academic option — I took a postdoctoral fellowship. This turned out to be a great way to test the waters of academia without having the pressure of publishing for tenure. I taught, wrote, ran research projects, and learned a lot from my colleagues in faculty positions.

At the end of my postdoctoral fellowship, I knew that I did not want to work in an academic environment at this point in my life. I wanted to work in an applied setting where I could work directly with those in the field. I looked for a position that would provide me the opportunity to have an impact on educational and social policy.

I found out about the social policy research world as I began to search for my first job. I had a friend who was working at large research firm. She mentioned that the resources were plentiful, that she worked on a variety of interesting projects, that she worked directly with agencies that affected policy, and that the pay and benefits were generous. This sounded like the change that I was ready to make and I was early enough in my career to take the chance on something different. Coincidently, I saw an ad on the Internet for such a position. On a whim, I applied. Just 2 months later, I had a position at a large educational research firm.

Darren's Story

My decision to pursue and complete a master's degree in education and a doctorate in educational psychology is a direct extension of personal life experiences from a very young age — experiences that to this date continue to validate and inform my work. As an African American male who was labeled "academically inclined" from a very young age, I have lived much of my life as both a curious observer and direct beneficiary of this designation. In relation to my choice of career, I have also had the opportunity to observe the differential treatment and eventual negative outcomes, both academic and otherwise, of many of my peers, friends, relatives, and neighbors who were labeled "academically challenged," "behaviorally challenged," or more simply "at risk." The results of these school-determined labels were in stark contrast to my own academic success. The stratified school environment of my boyhood years also put me somewhat at odds with my less positively reinforced peers, particularly African American boys. The dichotomy that I observed in treatment, support, school, and life outcomes for peers who were *at least* as capable as myself continues to drive my interest in the social, psychological, and environmental factors underlying the educational process. The focus of my work is the development of learning environments that will allow all children to thrive and develop to the full extent of their potential.

In college I majored in psychology and after gaining real-world experience as both a teacher and a counselor made the decision to pursue graduate study. My decision to work in a nonprofit research setting, as opposed to academia or other options, was largely the result of opportunity and location. After completing a postdoctoral faculty appointment, my desire to return to the city where I went to graduate school led me to investigate available opportunities in the area. The first opportunity emerging from my job search was the firm where I currently work. The challenges and benefits of this occurrence are discussed in detail below. Although my own arrival to this field was largely a matter of chance, I strongly encourage our readers to think carefully about their personal and professional needs and make an informed decision regarding their employment options.

What a Research Consultant Does

In general, research consultants engage in a wide array of research-oriented activities primarily at the request of others. Our collective project work has included quantitative data analyses (e.g., survey development, statistical analysis), qualitative data analyses (e.g., observations, focus groups), report preparation, writing for publications, presenting at meetings and conferences, and technical assistance delivery. It is entirely possible to be involved in more than one area of work, as consultants are often staffed on more than one project at any given time.

Project work is generally obtained by responding to requests for consultation work. Requests for consultation (advertised in the form of Request for Proposals, or RFPs) most commonly come from government agencies at the federal, state, or local level. However, they can also come from private agencies, foundations, or businesses (usually referred to as a prospectus). The types of research requested and the places in which the research is conducted vary as well.

The funding process for consulting work is similar to obtaining grant funding for academic research, such that much of the work is based on the quality of the proposal submitted by the research firm. However, one major distinction between writing grant proposals and writing proposals for consulting work is that consultants compete for funding to carry out work specified by the client. For example, a government agency may issue an RFP to conduct an evaluation of a program it has been funding to test its effectiveness on the target population. Consultants interested in conducting the evaluation then submit proposals to carry out the work. The proposals are submitted to the agency requesting them, and are then reviewed.

The foundation prospectus may follow a similar process as the RFP, although most of the time the funder is familiar with the work done at your firm and requests a written description to do work that fits its mission statement. Typically, the scope of work for a foundation is more likely to be investigator driven, yet it is based on the general interests of the foundation.

The funding process for consulting work also differs in terms of the structure of the proposal, and the amount of time it takes to put the proposal together. Generally, proposals for consulting work usually do not require an extensive literature review; rather, the conceptual framework is often established by the client. In addition, grant proposals may take months to write. Proposals for consulting work are generally completed in 2 to 4 weeks. Consulting projects can be funded in as little as 1 to 2 months, depending on how the funds are appropriated.

Our work has been done on behalf of large federal agencies and programs, state and local school systems, community organizations, private foundations, and international corporations. Consequently, research consultants may work with an array of clients: inner-city school teachers, parents, corporate executives, foundations, policy-makers, advocates, and government project officers. A critical element to success in this work is being comfortable across each of these settings. An important part of having a certain level of comfort across settings is the ability to write for varied audiences. These audiences reflect the diversity of the clients with whom consultants work. For example, writing products (commonly referred to as deliverables) must be written in a manner that is useful to the client. Therefore, a consultant must be able to convey information using different writing styles and formats.

Given the many demands of this profession, it is difficult to say what a "typical" day as a consultant might entail. As an employee at a social policy research firm, you are expected to manage subordinates, prepare budgets, and have a customer service orientation when working with clients. Additionally, a research consultant's day may be altered by staffing patterns, deadlines, and the demands of the client. For this reason, flexibility is key — this position is not for the "creature of habit." See Table 22.1 for a list of typical duties.

Working at a Social Policy Research Firm: Things to Consider

Because our experiences speak directly to working in a social policy research firm, we are able to write specifically about that environment. However, it is important to bear in mind that social policy research environments vary as well. For example, firms vary in size, and some specialize in a particular research area, whereas others are known for specific methodology. Your area of focus within psychology or sociology, coupled with your research interests, is probably the best guide to determining where you would be most comfortable working.

Depending on the structure of the firm, you may be staffed on more than one project, and those projects may be very different in scope. For the individual research consultant, this arrangement can be both a

Table 22.1 Duties Typical of a Ph.D.-Level Research Consultant Working at a Midsize Social Policy Research Firm[a]

Research Duties

Participating in team meetings
Collecting data
Analyzing data
Writing research proposals
Designing research instruments
Preparing presentations for conferences and clients
Managing duties of research assistants
Designing studies
Writing research reports, strategy briefs, or other products as specified by the client
Preparing journal manuscripts
Presenting at conferences

Training and Technical Assistance Duties

Conducting site visits/meeting with project staff
Interpreting research literature for practitioner audiences
Providing training (electronic, written, face-to-face) for differing audiences depending on project objectives
Facilitating meetings (e.g., coalition building and planning for sustainability)
Evaluating client progress and program outcomes

Other Project Duties

Communicating regularly with client
Evaluating research assistants
Meeting with colleagues and supervisors
Maintaining budgets
Planning meetings and conferences

General Duties

Attending staff meetings
Responding to e-mails and phone calls
Participating in company social events
Attending staff workshops and brown bags
Participating in recruitment and/or business development efforts

[a] Duties may vary according to type of firm and project involvement.

blessing and a curse. Although most firms may be known for one specific area, many firms are contracted to perform an array of duties on a variety of projects. The type of work a firm does depends on the contracts it wins and, as a result, the skill sets required for the various projects are constantly evolving. For example, our work experiences across projects has ranged from program evaluation, secondary data analysis, training and technical assistance, information dissemination for different audiences, survey development, literature searches, meeting planning, and product development. Application and, if necessary, development of new skill sets to meet the demands of these projects are challenging. If you are interested in this type of work, make sure that you find out the type of research that the firm does and if it fits with your training and skills.

If you are interested in eventually entering academia, another issue to consider (depending on the firm) is the widely held conception that the research conducted in social policy research firms is not as rigorous or relevant as research conducted at universities. This is not entirely true. Many of the projects that we have collectively worked on have allowed us to engage in very practical and useful research activities — involving school improvement, early childhood education, and parent training. In fact, many universities bid for the very same work conducted at social policy research firms and sometimes end up as collaborative partners with research firms.

People of color have an additional challenge in this environment, as there are very few senior-level people of color after whom to model your career. Professional socialization is a key issue in terms of success. You must learn to navigate the workplace culture, which is much easier when there are colleagues of color who have been successful and who understand the challenges people of color may face. Unfortunately, because so few people of color have Ph.D.s, most firms lack a critical mass of people on staff who can help you through this process. Therefore, you have to be open-minded and creative in developing your support network.

Advantages to a Career in a Social Policy Research Firm

There are many advantages to a career in social policy research. A key advantage to our work is the ability to contribute to work designed to effect change. Working in this setting allows us to apply our newly acquired research skills to current social problems. By focusing on current issues, our work is always relevant to those in the field. The work we do is dynamic and our fingers are always on the pulse of the government initiatives.

A second advantage is the ability to work in applied settings on multiple levels. For example, one of your projects may have you providing local-level technical assistance to teachers, school boards, and government officials. At the same time, this information may be aggregated across local settings and viewed from a national perspective. In sum, our work provides the opportunity to influence policy on local, state, and national levels.

If financial considerations are a priority, realize that there is a range of salaries available to the new Ph.D. Working at a social policy research firm provides you the opportunity to earn a higher salary than you would in the academic world. Based on the 2001 *Salaries in Psychology* report by the American Psychological Association, a recent Ph.D. at a private research organization earns on average about $13,000 more than an assistant professor.

Disadvantages to a Career in a Social Policy Research Firm

It is important to note that we have experienced issues that may be considered disadvantages to working as a research consultant. One such issue is the lack of control you may have over the projects on which you are staffed. Many firms make a concerted effort to staff researchers to projects on which they are interested. However, that is not always possible, and you may find yourself on a project that has nothing to do with your interests. As a result, you will need to be flexible and patient.

A challenge for each of us is to make sure that the work that we do is as closely aligned as possible with our interests as scholars, researchers, and agents for positive social change. Generally, the longer you are with a firm, the more attentive it will become to your interests, and the more familiar senior staff will become with your skills. In addition, as your skills and seniority within the firm expand you will increasingly gain the ability to seek funding that is specific to your interests and skills.

Among consulting firms, support for publishing in scholarly journals varies. Carving out the time to engage in writing may be a challenge, because any time used to present or publish may be your personal time. This is important to consider when choosing the firms in which you are interested. At many research firms, work done during the workday is billable to the client; any work that is not contract related is done after hours or weekends. On the other hand, some firms have writing time built into their employees' staffing, such that you are expected to spend a certain percentage of your workday writing. This is immensely helpful for developing and maintaining a writing routine.

Additional Opportunities for Research Consultants

Working at a large social policy research firm is not the only option for research consultants. For those interested in consulting, we describe a few additional options below:

Small Research Policy Organizations

In large settings new Ph.D.s may find it difficult to find their niche or become leaders. For example, a new Ph.D. entering a large organization with many layers of management and multimillion-dollar projects would need to realize that it might take a long time to reach upper management. In this case, it may be more fruitful to work in a smaller setting, such as a university research center or small social policy research firm, where you can begin leading projects earlier in your career.

In addition, smaller firms tend to be more mission oriented, focusing on a narrower field of research. For example, if you are committed to working on issues surrounding welfare reform, you may want to look for small research firms that concentrate on that area of work. Also look at the Web sites of funding agencies that support your research interests. Find out the projects that they fund and to which firms they have awarded contracts. Then look for positions within those firms.

Government or Nonprofit Advocacy Organizations

Government and nonprofit advocacy organizations often look for research consultants to explain research findings to practitioners and policymakers. It is important for you to understand the current political environment and the political leanings of the organization in order to translate research in a way that is heard by decision makers. Writing for such organizations requires that you describe the problem and findings in simple, declarative terms and explore implications for practice. If you are interested in this type of work, we suggest you take classes in government and politics, or work in a government setting.

Independent Consultant/Setting Up Own Business

Working as a researcher in a social policy research firm is certainly a great way to learn the business aspects of research. However, there are many consulting options available that do not require the infrastructure of a social policy research firm. For example, independent consultants procure small contracts or subcontracts with larger organizations. There are several appealing aspects of this arrangement including the ability to have a flexible schedule, work only on issues that match their interests, and continue their own research agenda and publish. In addition, several independent consultants can pool together to compensate for the lack of resources afforded by the social policy research firm environment. Each consultant should ideally bring a different skill to the table to make for a more complete package for clients.

Lessons Learned and Advice for New Professionals

As is true with any other work environment, the quality of your experience is enhanced by learning from the wisdom of others. Some of the lessons we have learned from our experiences follow.

Be Very Clear about Your Research Interests

Many social policy research firms select new Ph.D.s to serve as "generalists" in their companies. Generalists have a breadth of knowledge and a group of useful research skills, which can be used on any given project at any given time. This is good for the firm, because it allows for great flexibility in meeting the staffing needs of a wide array of projects. As an employee, you will need to be flexible. However, if you are wedded to a specific stream of research, or a specific population of study, it is important to ensure that your needs will be satisfied. Conduct a thorough review of the projects that are underway at the firms in which you are interested, and also try to get a feel for the direction in which the firm plans to go. If you are interested in survey development, and the firm in which you are interested is moving toward providing more technical assistance, you may eventually become dissatisfied with the type of work you are asked to do. For example, if the firm hired you because you are an excellent writer and a dynamic trainer, the fact that most of your writing and training has been focused on family involvement is irrelevant. As you move forward in your career you can advocate for work that is related to your interests and respond, in an entrepreneurial fashion, to available grants and contracts in your area of interest.

Develop as Many Alliances as Possible

Your allies should include people across as many staffing levels of the firm as possible. While it is vital to communicate with members of senior management, it is also important to develop the support of colleagues on your own level as well. Positive relationships and alliances can make transitioning to new projects easier, and you can share information with colleagues that may be helpful to everyone's professional development. As opportunities develop to take on leadership roles or to join interesting projects, the alliances you have established can make the difference in successful advancement or remaining at your current level.

Know Your Worth

After spending several years living the impoverished lifestyle of the average graduate student, many of us are conditioned to believe that we will not be able to earn a significant salary with careers in the social sciences. For that reason, many of us come into the world of consulting with a false sense of what a decent salary is, and we often "lowball" ourselves in salary negotiations. This view is a mistake to be avoided.

Do your homework. Talk to others who have worked at social policy research firms, or try to get an idea of salary ranges from the human resources office (if you can do so politely). When the time comes to discuss salary with your prospective employer, you should present the higher end of your compensation goals but also be prepared to demonstrate flexibility. Keep in mind the possibility of negotiating things like signing bonuses, health benefits, retirement packages, leave options, moving expenses, and any other extras. Do what you can to make sure that you are treated fairly upon accepting the position. At the same time, you must not appear arrogant or overly demanding in your interactions with human resources staff or other staff. You may cost yourself the position. Remember, you're not the only person there with an advanced degree.

Sample the Real World

The skills required for this job are not necessarily congruent with those received from a social science graduate program. We advise new and aspiring Ph.D.s to pursue activities that provide experiences relevant to working as a research consultant such as taking business courses, interning at a government agency or research firm, doing a postdoctoral stint or a policy fellowship.

Taking business courses such as accounting, marketing, and management is useful in the consulting world. These courses can help prepare you for such duties as budget preparation and projection, staff management, and client relationships. Although these courses may not be directly connected to your discipline, by taking them you will acquire skills essential to your role as a project manager.

It may also be helpful to work as an intern at a research firm to gain a feel for the expectations of the environment. Some firms do not have an official internship program but do not be afraid to approach human resources if you are interested in their line of work. Some firms have dissertation funding that will allow you to gain experience and complete your dissertation at the same time. Companies may also have postdoctoral opportunities that allow you to "get your feet wet" in the social policy arena.

You may want to consider a policy fellowship. One of the authors took a year off from social policy research to work in a federal office as a Head Start Fellow. This opportunity allowed her to experience the federal system and become better versed in policy development. Other policy postdoctoral opportunities you may want to consider include the American Psychological Association Policy Fellowship and the Society for Research in Child Development Policy Fellowship, both of which place participants in policy positions that are related to their research interests.

In sum, research consulting can be an exciting, intellectually challenging, and rewarding experience. As you embark on your own professional journey, we encourage you to use our experiences as a guide. We hope that we have equipped you to make an informed decision about your career path.

23

New Psychologists Online: Changing the Face of Psychology through Technology

RICHARD VAN HAVEREN, COREY J. HABBEN,
AND TARA L. KUTHER

Much of the content of this chapter is being written and revised each day. The application of psychology using the Internet and technology is affected by two powerful and interwoven forces; the rapid flux of technology's evolution and our profession's ever steady uncertainty about what to do with applying our craft in this domain. If you finish this chapter today and reread it a year from now, technology already will be markedly different. When Gordon Moore (cofounder of Intel) predicted in 1965 that computing power would double once every 18 months, he made a bold prediction about technology and circuitry that had then only recently been discovered. His prediction (now commonly referred to as "Moore's law") has not only held true and steady over several decades, but it is also expected to hold for at least the next decade and probably more. Because of this, we experience the common frustration of seeing our new computers and gadgets become antiquated within a year or two of purchase. We also experience the breathtaking exponential growth of technology and all of the possibilities it provides.

Our profession is not used to this sort of rapid pace. If you were able to transport back in time to the 1950s, the actions of a lecturing academic psychologist or a practicing clinical psychologist would look very similar. There have been few advances in the evolution of the office, pencil, clipboard, couch, classroom, or lab desk. Granted our empirical knowledge does evolve, but even that takes place as part of a relatively and painstakingly slow process. The very idea that something we do or something we use can become virtually obsolete within a span of 10 years can be foreign to any psychologist, regardless of age. What we do relies primarily on our minds, and the "things" we use are only vehicles to enhancing the application of our expertise. Anyone who has taught at an old university or practiced in an old federal building knows that you can do what you do, even if your chair is 30 years old and your office is much older.

What will technology look like in 5 years? What will we be able to do with the Internet and technology in 5 years? It is both exciting and discomforting to be uncertain of answers to these questions. What we do know is that innovations with the Internet, computers, and telecommunications have produced technologies that have created new possibilities for psychologists, regardless of how you apply your expertise. A profession that has relied so heavily on face-to-face or written communication can now do things that were impossible only decades ago. For example, interconnected networks of computers (or the Internet), fast and compact processors, and telecommunication bandwidth, which now provides for the transfer of large amounts of data instantaneously, have all converged and evolved to make possible videoconferencing. One person can communicate live with another person at any other part of the globe, all the while seeing, hearing, and interacting with the person in real time. Cellular networks, wireless broadband technology, and the availability of affordable and compact mobile phones and computers have since made possible the ability to communicate with another person, whether by phone or by e-mail, nearly anywhere at any time in real time. The awe inspired by these realities will become more and more quaint as this book ages. Nevertheless, there are many more advances that have become a part of our daily lives, and many more to come.

These changes in technology have required that we adapt the way in which we communicate; to a great extent as a culture, and to a lesser extent as a profession. Just as we adapt to these technologies, new ones come and further rattle our equilibrium. There is no end point at which technology's advance is "finished." Because of this, we often find ourselves adapting to yesterday's technology while today's is being sold and tomorrow's is months away from changing everything. Because of this, books on technology are often outdated by the time they are published. And because of this, coupled with our profession's slower adaptation to technology, this is a chapter that has yet to be written. In fact, new psychologists (yourself included) will spend the next several decades evolving the profession of psychology in step with the evolution of technology. At the end of your career, should you choose to spend several decades as a psychologist, you will most certainly reflect on the decades of the 1990s and early decades of the 21st century as a truly amazing time of rapid growth. Until then, we can only say this with true certainty: we have a lot to learn about how technology can and should be used in the profession of psychology.

There are some applications of technology that have already become common and accepted in psychology because of their over-whelming advantages and relatively limited risks, costs, or disadvantages. The use of statistical analysis software and computers for the analysis of scientific data is one clear example. Senior psychologists can still tell you about the days when all statistical analysis was done entirely by hand; not-so-senior psychologists can tell you about the days when "punch cards" were used. Today, it is common practice to make very complex analyses as fast as the data can be entered while storing and comparing enormous databases with little space required and employing a variety of protective measures. Overwhelming benefits, minimal disadvantages. Peer communication through e-mail and online journal databases are two more examples that even the more technophobic psychologists will use on a regular basis with little problem or dilemma.

Our primary mode of action as psychologists occurs through communication. We tend to focus most of our communication with four types of parties: students, patients, the public en masse, and other psychologists. When technology is used to enhance the communication among psychologists, whether directly via e-mail or indirectly through statistical analysis software, the ethical and practical complications are limited. Things become more problematic as we aim to apply our expertise as psychologists with other nonpsychologists, be it students, patients, or the public. Evolving technologies create new ethical dilemmas that have yet to be fully understood. Because any attempts to describe the current state of the art of technology in various modes of psychology will be quickly and increasingly outdated, we will instead briefly address two key recipients of our communication: patients (online therapy) and students (online teaching). [*Editors note:* Although psychologists are developing strategies using technology and the Internet to communicate with the public, particularly using web marketing, its use and the corresponding ethical issues involved are not reviewed in this chapter. The revised APA ethical code (American Psychological Association, 2002) addresses many of these issues and should be your first resource.]

Online Therapy and Telehealth

Historically, most therapeutic interactions have occurred with both patient and psychologist occupying the same room. Technology has evolved to the point at which virtual communication can occur. Perhaps the two most common current applications are telehealth/telemedicine (utilizing videoconferencing technology to perform therapy with someone at a remote location) and online therapy (utilizing e-mail, instant messaging, or other forms of real-time typed communication via the Internet to perform therapy with someone at a remote location) since these applications come with more ethical and practical issues, that most of today's psychologists still practice the old-fashioned way; live and in person. How, for example, is therapy affected when the patient is on a video monitor and not in the room? Are you able to practice as a psychologist if your license is in one state and your patient is communicating with you "virtually" from another state? Can you truly understand your patient accurately and develop a therapeutic relationship when your main mode of communication is text? Is your communication secure, or can someone hack into your therapy session, read through your communications, or pretend to be you while online? Are you technically competent to use this medium of communication? Will third-party payers reimburse you for virtual services? These are merely a few of the ethical issues that result.

These issues are currently being reviewed by psychologists and no definitive answers seem to have emerged as yet. Perhaps the best recent review of these issues is provided by Holland, Kulynich, and Stromberg (2004). We advise you to obtain and read this, as it reviews the current understanding of these issues with a level of detail that cannot be explored for the purposes of this book. Perhaps, in the next edition of this book we will have more answers to the issue of online therapy and telehealth; currently, there are too many questions. This generation of new psychologists will play a major role in defining and shaping the profession and its use of technology in the domain of psychotherapy and practice.

Online Teaching

For decades, graduate students and new psychologists have supplemented their income by teaching as adjunct instructors at nearby colleges and universities. The Internet permits new opportunities for adjunct instructors. With online teaching, teaching via the Internet, you are not tied by geography and can teach at a college across the country — or around the world. Most traditional universities offer at least some of their courses online; some traditional institutions offer entire degrees online.

A newer form of educational institution, the nontraditional for-profit institution, offers all degrees entirely online. For example, the University of Phoenix (http://www.phoenix.edu), Fielding Institute (http://www.fielding.edu), Walden University (http://www.waldendegrees.com), and the Pacific Graduate School of Psychology (http://www. pgsp.edu) all offer graduate degrees in psychology online (as well as degrees in several other areas such as management, information technology, education, and criminal justice. Currently, one of us (R.V.H.) is an adjunct professor in the Harold Abel School of Psychology at Capella University (http://www.capella.edu), another Web-based institution.

Like most online psychology programs, Capella University offers a variety of courses. Professors typically post a discussion question a few times per week. Students then respond to the discussion question and the responses of other students; this creates an online discussion. Students then periodically attend an in-person residency with faculty and other students throughout their academic program.

Teaching at an online university offers many advantages to faculty. First, faculty have great flexibility because courses are asynchronous; they do not meet at a specified time during the week, permitting outside projects such as consulting and private practice. Second, many of the students in online universities are adult learners, including individuals from other disciplines such as nursing or business administration. Many adult learners bring a wealth of life experience to enhance the learning environment. Finally, students come from a variety of geographic locations, with some living abroad. This unique aspect allows the opportunity for students living in urban, suburban, and rural areas (and even in other countries!) to share in the same learning environment.

Of course, online teaching also entails challenges — mainly because there are opportunities for miscommunication. Instructor expectations and deadlines must be clear and easy for students to understand. The absence of face-to-face communication means that e-mail and discussion postings must be carefully composed to reduce potentials for miscommunication. The substantial amount of reading can become tiresome for the mind as well as the eyes. Moreover, students can present challenges if they enter online courses believing that they are easier than traditional classes. Students quickly learn that online learning requires a higher level of independence and motivation, as it is a more active form of learning than that which occurs in most traditional classrooms. Online learning is not for everyone. Neither is online teaching. It requires an awareness and ability to use computer technology as well as patience in responding to students' often-frantic questions (i.e., many students fear that they will "miss" something and ask lots and lots of questions!).

As we have mentioned, many colleges and universities offer courses online and there are several online universities. If you are interested in online teaching, consult college and university Web sites. Often the pages that include online offerings also have links for faculty who wish to teach online. Academic search Web sites such as http://www.academic360.com, http://www.higheredjobs.com, and http://www.chronicle.com/jobs may also be helpful. Before accepting an offer to teach online, be sure that the college or university is accredited by the relevant accrediting bodies (see the resources at the end of this chapter). Why is accreditation important? Accreditation signifies that the university has met the standards of the accrediting agency and is not a diploma mill. If you are considering a career in academia, be sure to limit your online teaching to accredited institutions, as many faculty who sit on search committees for academic positions may look unfavorably at any experiences obtained at unaccredited institutions.

Colleges and universities rely on several course management programs for online teaching. The most widely used are Blackboard, WebCT, and eCollege. Knowledge of these programs may be helpful in securing Web-based teaching opportunities; however, many universities offer training opportunities in online technology and pedagogy, sometimes requiring new faculty to complete training. For an overview of each online learning platform, visit http://www.edutools.info.

Conclusion

Overall, there are many opportunities for graduate students and new psychologists to utilize the Internet. These can be unique practice opportunities, ways to develop your practice, or teach. In 1998, I (R.V.H.) completed my comprehensive examinations. One of the questions attempted to assess what I saw for the future of career counseling. Ironically, discussion of the Internet was not mentioned in my response. Training in and the practice of psychology have been significantly changed by the Internet. The Web will continue to be a part of our daily lives and will likely become a more integral part. Therefore, judicious psychologists will envision the Internet as a part of their practice. However, you must maintain an opportunistic and open-minded mind-set. This is paramount. Opportunities are available, but they are not going to come to you; you must be active and entrepreneurial.

References

American Psychological Association. (2002). Ethical principles of psychologists and code of conduct. *American Psychologist, 57*, 1060–1073.

Holland, C., Kulynich, J. J., & Stromberg, C. (2004). *The psychologists legal update 14: Psychology in the electronic age.* The National Register of Health Service Providers in Psychology. Reprinted in *The Register Report, 30,* 32–45.

Suggested Reading

Ko, S. & Rossen, S. (2001). *Teaching online: A practical guide.* Boston: Houghton Mifflin.

Stadtlander, L. M. (1998). Virtual instruction: Teaching an online graduate seminar. *Teaching of Psychology, 25*(2), 146–148.

Accrediting Bodies of Higher Education

Middle States Association of Colleges and Schools (MSA) Middle States Commission on Higher Education: http://www.msache.org.

New England Association of Schools and Colleges (NEASC-CIHE) Commission on Institutions of Higher Education: http://www.neasc.org.

New England Association of Schools and Colleges (NEASC-CTCI) Commission on Technical and Career Institutions: http://www.neasc.org.

North Central Association of Colleges and Schools (NCA-HLC) The Higher Learning Commission: http://www.ncahigherlearningcommission.org.

Northwest Commission on Colleges and Universities (NWCCU): http://www.nwccu.org.

Southern Association of Colleges and Schools (SACS) Commission on Colleges: http://www.sacscoc.org.

Western Association of Schools and Colleges (WASC-ACCJC) Accrediting Commission for Community and Junior Colleges: http://www.accjc.org.

Western Association of Schools and Colleges (WASC-ACSCU) Accrediting Commission for Senior Colleges and Universities: http://www.wascweb.org.

24

Our Future Is Up to Us: The New Psychologist's Role in Shaping the Profession

ROBERT D. MORGAN, COREY J. HABBEN, AND TARA L. KUTHER

At some point early on in every new psychologist's career, the realization sets in that some of the most important things you need to know to develop as a professional are not taught in graduate school. When you think back to your days as a student, you certainly received a great deal of training that fostered your development as a practitioner, scientist, or academic. At the same time, it is also a safe bet that you did not receive the same level of preparation to develop as a new professional in the early part of the 21st century. This is not a criticism of today's training in psychology, but unfortunately it is an unavoidable by-product of the academy of psychology.

As we stated at the beginning of this book, senior psychologists pass on valuable knowledge to students and future psychologists. At the same time, there is a wealth of information and insight about the experience of a new psychologist that only a new psychologist can provide. We hope that we achieved our goal of providing you with insight, advice, and information from today's new psychologists as they talk about their various roles as a 21st-century psychologist. If you have gained that priceless commodity of information as a result of reading this book, then we have achieved our main goal.

Developing Your Career, Defining the Profession

We have presented to you that your doctoral degree in psychology has provided you with skills and knowledge that are valuable in a variety of careers. As psychologists, we are essentially experts in human thought, behavior, and emotion. We bring to the world an expertise that touches the lives of all individuals, groups, systems, organizations. Although psychology has primarily settled into the comfortable roles of practitioner, scientist, and academic, there are a virtual endless number of new roles we have yet to fill or thrive in. Just as we only use a small fraction of our brain's capacity, so do we as psychologists only utilize our expertise in a limited number of roles. As delineated in this book, you are most certainly trained for the traditional careers that frequently come to mind for graduate students and new psychologists, careers such as professional practice, teaching, or research positions. However, as noted in these pages, your doctoral degree affords you much more flexibility than these traditional careers. In fact, you are limited only by your imagination. The contributors for this book for example have given you a blueprint for developing the foundation (albeit a flexible foundation) for your career. Although this blueprint is not overly sophisticated, it does require effort on your part.

To create a career that fits your needs, you must first complete an accurate self-assessment. You must be cognizant of your professional interests, strengths and limitations. For example, if you trained in clinical psychology because you like to help people, yet are determined that you really do not enjoy face-to-face therapy as you would rather work with technology or the Internet, you might consider a career that allows you to work on treatment interventions via electronic means. In other words, are there treatment protocols that could be developed and published on the Internet for clients (and possibly therapists) to use? Or, maybe you prefer to develop other technological uses for your practice. This is just one example of where you might start in your self-assessment to integrate your interests into your career.

Contributors have also consistently encouraged readers to seek learning experiences that transcend traditional educational classes.

Many of our contributors have encouraged you to take classes that are out of your area of study. You may seek relevant coursework online to supplement your traditional education. You should seek mentorship from others in the field and network with professionals engaged in activities that are of similar interest. In other words, your career is contingent on you adopting a consumer approach and actively seeking training and experiences in your particular area of interest. Astute professionals are doing exactly this, and they are developing their careers in the manner that they want.

Today's New Psychologist, Tomorrow's Future Profession of Psychology

As you set out to develop your career, do not forget your role in fostering and shaping the future of the profession. Although you are a new psychologist now, your designation as a new psychologist will essentially end within a matter of a few years. You will be looked to for mentorship of tomorrow's new psychologist. We urge you to remember that as the profession has evolved, new roles have emerged. This can continue only as long as we continue to innovate. Of course, the profession will continue to need someone to provide therapy, or contribute to the empirical literature, or mentor the future psychologists. But we will also need new psychologists applying their expertise in areas that have yet to be explored by psychology. If this sounds idealistic or grandiose, stop for a moment and ask yourself: "Can I think of any one place where an expert in human behavior, thought, and emotion could not be of use?" What human endeavor does not require analysis or change in the domain of thought, behavior, or emotion? Several decades ago, when psychologists were forging roles in practice and academia, it may have seemed bizarre to consider a psychologist serving a valuable purpose with athletes, or software companies, or in the courtroom. As you have read in previous chapters, psychologists have since proved their worth in these fields. What remains? Next time you walk down the business district of your city or town, stop and look at each door and ask yourself: "Could a psychologist walk through this door and help whoever is behind it?" If you consider what we can provide, it is very difficult to find someone who could not benefit from our expertise. There are many frontiers for psychology yet to explore, and it is our turn as new psychologists to continue the exploration.

Keep in mind that we owe a good part of our future to those who came before us. Psychologists were not originally the providers of therapy. Practitioners were not originally recognized by a license. You did not see many, if any, psychologists in business or medicine. Many of the disciplines we currently accept as part of our domain are our domain only because previous generations of psychologists took chances and forged new ground. Our current generation of psychologists is perhaps better poised than any other to change the face of psychology and take the profession into new frontiers. This underscores a point that cannot be overstated: *our future is up to us*. What we, as new professionals, do now will determine how we thrive as senior psychologists and what tomorrow's new professionals will build upon.

How will the profession of psychology look in the next several decades? It is primarily limited by our creativity and our willingness to assume risk, take on challenges, and innovate. Do not be afraid to step outside of old roles and create new ones.

Remember the future of the profession is up to you; *it is up to us*.

Index

A

Academia: teaching experience and, 35–36; undergraduate, 15–28; (*See* university counseling centers)

Academics: interviews, 40–41; job talks for, 39–40; jobs for, 37–40; psychologists (*See also* doctoral and graduate psychology instructors; psychology instructors), 15–28; tenure and, 3–4, 27, 30, 53; women in, 3–4

Aeromedical psychology (*See also* psychologists in the military), 144–147

American Academy of Forensic Psychology (AAFP), 135

American Association of Correctional Psychologists, 163

American Board of Professional Psychology (ABPP), 51

American Psychological Association (APA): Division 13 (Consulting Psychology), 193, 195; Division 14 (Industrial and Organizational Psychology), 195; Division 16 (School Psychology), 180; Division 18 (Criminal Justice Psychology), 163; Division 38 (Health Psychology), 50–51, 255 (*See also* Division 38); Division 41 (APLS), 128, 129, 135, 274; Division 42 Web site, 112; Division 47 (Sport and Exercise Psychology), 284; helpful career publications of, 52, 98; New

Psychologists listserv, 52; Policy Fellowship, 320; Web sites, 38, 85, 112, 121, 180, 195, 255, 274

American Psychology–Law Society (APLS): Web site, 126

American Public Health Association, 255

American Society of Trial Consultants (ASTC), 258, 270

Anti-Drug Abuse Act of 1986, 160

APA Monitor, 52, 121

Applied developmental psychology, 59–60

Association for Applied Psychophysiology and Biofeedback, 51

Association for the Advancement of Applied Sport Psychology (AAASP), 284

Association of Psychology Postdoctoral and Internship Centers (APPIC): membership in, 141; Web site, 51

Association of Psychology Postdoctoral and Internship Centers (APPIC) Directory, 127

B

Benton, S. A., J. M. Robertson, W. C. Tseng, F. B. Newton, and S. L. Benton, 28

Budman, S. H., and B. N. Steenbarger, 98

Building a Group Practice: Creating a Shared Vision for Success, 98

number of, 2–3; role in shaping the profession, 329–332; telehealth and, 155–156

Psychologists as management consultants (*See also* psychologists in executive management), 183–184; career as, 187–189, 190–192; coaching and, 185–186; consulting firms and, 188–189, 194; interventions by, 185–187, 193; networking and, 194–195; preparation as, 192–195; role of, 184, 187, 189–190, 192; Web sites, 195

Psychologists as research consultants, 307–313; advice for, 318–320; career as, 315–320; duties of, 312–314; pros and cons of, 315–316; social policy research firms and, 313–315

Psychologists in community mental health centers, 113–115; developing validated treatment programs and, 115–117; duties of, 119, 121; pros and cons of, 117–119, 122–124; securing a job as, 121–122, 123; supervising treatment protocols and, 113–115, 120; teaching and, 118, 120; training of, 119–120; treatment teams and, 114, 115–117, 120; Web sites, 121, 124

Psychologists in correctional institutions: career as, 157–164; crisis managment and, 153, 161; diversity issues and, 159–160; drug abuse treatment and, 160, 162; duties of, 151–152, 156–159, 161; internships for, 162–163; nontraditioinal services and, 155–156; preparation for, 161–163; role of, 157–158, 160; security issues and, 158–159; three-level system and, 153–154, 161; traditional services and, 153–155

Psychologists in executive management (*See also* psychologists as management consultants): benchmarking data and, 226, 230; career in, 230–232; consultation and, 228–230, 231; definition of,

225–226; duties of, 235–236, 237; employment law firms and, 230–231; industry research and, 226–227, 228; market research and, 227–228, 231; nonprofit organizations and, 231, 232; pros and cons of, 236–237; role of, 228–230; training and professional development for, 232–235; workplace and, 227–228

Psychologists in forensics, 125–126; APA Division 41 and, 128, 129; careers in, 135–138; developing a career as, 135–136; duties of, 130–135; expert witness testimony and, 134–135; internships and training for, 126–127, 135; postdoctoral training in, 128; pros and cons of, 136–138; securing a job as, 128–130; Web sites, 126, 127, 138

Psychologists in group practice: advantages of, 99–102, 103; business aspects of, 105–110, 111; career as, 97–99, 103–105; disadvantages of, 102–103; duties of, 110–111; referrals and, 99–100, 104; salary and, 100–101, 102, 105–108; *versus* private practice, 101, 103–105; Web sites, 112

Psychologists in private practice: business side of, 89–91, 178; changing nature of, 88, 95–96; duties of, 89, 93–94; fees for, 90, 92; HIPAA and, 91, 95; how to start as, 88–90; insurance plans and, 87, 88, 89, 91, 92; preparing for career as, 95–96; pros and cons of, 92–95; school psychologists as (*See* school psychologists in nontraditional settings)

Psychologists in public health (*See also* public health), 241–244; community-based organizations and, 252; consultation and, 252–253; duties of, 245–253; health-delivery programs and, 250, 254; HIV/AIDS and, 247–249; multicultural counseling and, 249, 252; preparation for,